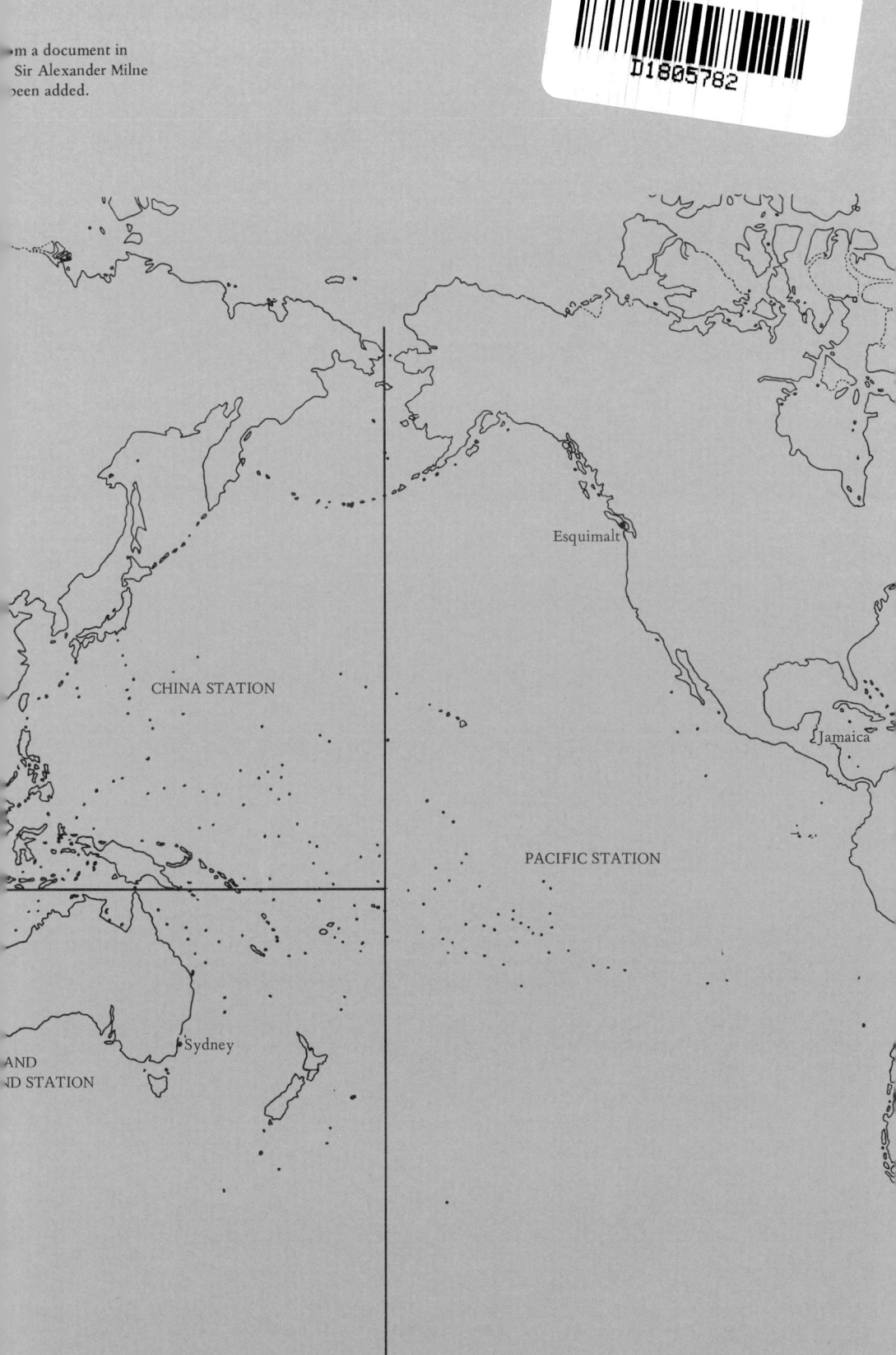

m a document in
Sir Alexander Milne
been added.

Esquimalt

CHINA STATION

Jamaica

PACIFIC STATION

Sydney

AND
D STATION

Guide to the Manuscripts in the National Maritime Museum

June 22 nd 1798

The Vessel spoke with this morning is from Malta one day, he says the two frigates in sight are french, that the French Colors and Garrison are in Malta, that the Fleet & Transport left it Six days to day, but they did not know when they were going, some said to Sicily—

with this Information what is your Opinion, Do you believe under all Circumstances which we know that Sicily is their destination,

Do you think We had better stand for Malta, or Steer for Sicily

Should the armament be gone to Alexandria and get safe there our Possessions in India are probably lost do you think we had better push for that place

Draft memorandum of 22 June 1798
Nelson consults his captains before the Battle of the Nile. Their opinion was to set a course for Egypt (Croker Collection, CRK/14).

Guide to the Manuscripts in the National Maritime Museum

VOLUME

I

The Personal Collections

EDITED BY

R. J. B. KNIGHT

MANSELL 1977

© 1977 National Maritime Museum
Mansell Information/Publishing Limited
3 Bloomsbury Place, London WC1A 2QA

International Standard Book Number: 0 7201 0714 8

Printed and bound in Great Britain at
The Scolar Press Limited, Ilkley, Yorkshire

British Library Cataloguing in Publications Data
National Maritime Museum
Guide to the manuscripts in the National
Maritime Museum.
Vol. 1: The personal collections.
1. National Maritime Museum   2. Great Britain –
History, Naval – Manuscripts – Catalogs
I. Title   II. Knight, R J B
   016.359'00941   Z6611.N/
ISBN 0-7201-0714-8

Contents

Foreword

The first volume of the *Guide to the Manuscripts in the National Maritime Museum* opens the door to the personal papers of some three hundred people connected with the Royal Navy and the Merchant Shipping Industry. These papers have been acquired through the generosity of donors since the inception of the Museum and continue year by year steadily to increase by gift, loan, or purchase. It is hoped that those scholars and researchers who have already worked in the Museum will welcome this full statement of the holdings and that others as yet unacquainted with Greenwich, will find it of value.

Various individuals have been responsible for the preparation of this work, which has been compiled over a number of years by the archivists of the Department of Printed Books and Manuscripts of which Mr David Proctor is now Head. Dr R. J. B. Knight, as Editor, has undertaken the main task, working under Mrs Ann Shirley, the Custodian of Manuscripts, but Miss Margaret Deacon, Mrs Jacqueline Skidmore, and Mrs Gervaise Vaz have contributed a great deal. Very valuable assistance has come from Mr Alan Pearsall, the Museum's Historian, and from Miss Dorothy Osbon, whose checking of provenance records has been much appreciated. Particular thanks are due to Rear-Admiral P. W. Brock, C.B., D.S.O., for many years a Trustee of the Museum, Mr William Kellaway and Mr J. M. Collinge of the Institute of Historical Research, Mr Mark Hamilton of the London School of Economics and Captain A. B. Sainsbury, V.R.D., M.A., R.N.R.

BASIL GREENHILL
Director

National Maritime Museum
London

Introduction

The National Maritime Museum was formally established by Act of Parliament in 1934 for the illustration and study of the maritime history of Great Britain. Preparatory work had, however, been going on for many years beforehand. The Society for Nautical Research, from its foundation in 1910, advocated the formation of such a museum, but only in 1927 did the opportunity arise to bring the institution into existence. A Board of Trustees was then set up under the chairmanship of the 7th Earl Stanhope (1880–1967) to proceed with the purchase of the Macpherson Collection of paintings, prints, and drawings of maritime subjects which had come on to the market. The generosity of Sir James Caird (1864–1954) 1st Bt. of Glenfarquhar, Co. Kincardine, enabled the Board to do this and it subsequently made further purchases as well as receiving material on permanent loan. Many of the Board's acquisitions were due to the contributions of Sir James Caird and other benefactors. Their names, in the case of manuscripts, will be found in this book.

At about the same time a gift of land and money from Gifford Sherman Reade (1845–1929) enabled the Royal Hospital School, Greenwich, to build and move into a new range of buildings at Holbrook in Suffolk. It was decided by the Board of Admiralty that the vacated buildings would be the home of the new maritime museum. The Board also transferred to the Museum the Greenwich Hospital Collection of pictures from the Painted Hall and the contents of the Royal Naval Museum, Royal Naval College, which included seventeenth century models and collections of naval records. Thus, by the time of the National Maritime Act (24 and 25 Geo. V. c.43) important collections had already been assembled. The Museum was opened by H.M. King George VI on 27 April 1937.

Additions to the collections from institutions, firms, individuals, and the saleroom have proceeded steadily ever since. During the Second World War many of the contents of the Museum were moved to Somerset. In 1962 the Museum was recognized by the Lord Chancellor as an official repository under the Public Records Act of 1958, confirming the holding of some 9,000 official volumes of Admiralty records transferred before the war. Today the collections occupy over 9,000 feet of shelving.

The scope and subjects of the manuscript collections can be simply stated: they may include any papers which relate to the sea, seamen, or maritime affairs. No limitation of date, type, or nationality was stipulated and this policy continues. The oldest document in the Museum is a charter party of 1322, while there are many twentieth-century papers.

In the early days, the first Director of the Museum, Professor Sir Geoffrey Callender (1875–1946), built up and arranged the collections. Unfortunately, at this time, owing to wartime evacuation, there are some gaps in acquisition records. After the war, Miss Katherine Lindsay-MacDougall, then Custodian of Manuscripts, rearranged the manuscripts into two basic divisions commonly used in archive administration in this country: the Natural Collections, groups of papers brought together in the course of the transaction of daily affairs by an organization or by an individual; and the Artificial Collections which were deliberately brought together by the interest of a collector, to whom they owe their unity. The two categories of papers are subdivided as follows:

Natural Collections

SECTION 1. Public Records: Records of the Central Administration of the Royal Navy and of the Merchant Navy

SECTION 2. Public Records: Local Records of the Royal Navy and of the Merchant Navy

SECTION 3. Records of semi-governmental and non-governmental organizations

SECTION 4. Personal Papers

Artificial Collections

SECTION 5. Artificial Collections previously assembled

SECTION 6. Manuscript volumes acquired singly by the Museum

SECTION 7. Manuscript documents acquired singly by the Museum

SECTION 8. Copies of manuscripts not in the Museum

This volume covers Section 4, the Personal Papers. A small number of groups of personal papers within artificial collections in Section 5 have also been included. The second volume of this *Guide* will describe all the other manuscript holdings in the Museum. This is the first time that a comprehensive guide to the Collections has appeared, although in 1954 Miss Lindsay-MacDougall briefly summarized the holdings in 'Manuscripts at the National Maritime Museum', *The Mariner's Mirror*, vol. 40, 1954, pp. 223–8, and in 1960 she produced a pamphlet *Guide* for students as a first step towards a complete guide.

DIRECTIONS FOR USERS

The text of the *Guide* consists of 300 short biographies of individuals together with a brief description of their papers. The length and emphasis of each biography are governed by the extent of the relevant material; therefore the entries only give an indication of the contents of the collection of papers rather than a balanced summary of the individual's career. Thus, if there are no early papers, the biography will contain few, if any, details of the early part of the individual's life. This approach was adopted because of the extremely diverse nature of the collections. A more detailed listing, omitting biographies, but concentrating on the papers themselves, item by item, could have been attempted but such a method would have failed to underline the interest and perhaps even the importance of the papers of personalities who, though obscure, were present at great events.

1. Brief details of provenance are included in the descriptive section of each entry.

2. The length of shelving required to house an individual's papers is given in feet and then in centimetres. If this amounts to less than one foot, the items are described individually.

3. References to selected printed sources have been included but when a number of biographies have been written on an individual, in general only the more recent have been listed. Care has been taken to cite works based on papers in the Museum.

4. Papers known to the Museum directly relating to the individual but held in other repositories are mentioned.

5. Access to some of the modern papers is restricted and this is indicated.

6. Details of the decorations of nineteenth- and twentieth-century naval officers have been omitted because of their length and complexity.

7. Dates have generally been indicated by the year only. Prior to 1752, 1 January, not 25 March, has been taken as the beginning of the year.

8. Chronological, general, and ship indexes are given and the references are to the biographical serial numbers rather than to pages.

It is hoped that this arrangement will demonstrate adequately to researchers the scope and content of the Museum's manuscript collections. While every effort has been made to ensure that the biographical entries are accurate, it is realized that errors may well have occurred. Corrections will be gratefully received.

GLOSSARY OF TERMS

Official Service Documents

This term should be taken to mean commissions, training and discharge certificates, 'flimsies' (certificates of service in each ship), or other papers containing no more than lists or summaries of careers. Where there are only service documents for a period of a man's life, the biographical entry will not give details of that period.

Logs, Journals, and Diaries

For purposes of simplicity, this work uses the word 'log' as meaning primarily a record in tabular form, of weather, navigation and handling the ship. The term 'diary' has been used to describe day-to-day entries which form a continuous personal record. The word 'journal' has been largely avoided, except in the officially titled 'Admiral's Journal'.

Watch, Station, and Quarter Bills

These are lists, made by the First Lieutenant, allotting posts to the crew. Watch Bills were for posts at sea, Station Bills for entry into harbour and Quarter Bills for the ship while in action.

Home and Overseas Stations

Care has been taken to indicate not only the ships in which individuals served but also where those ships served, using for this purpose the distinct geographical entities defined by the Navy and known as 'stations'. Although there were changes in name and organization, these areas remained essentially the same from 1700 to 1950. The following brief account traces their growth and development. References to each station are given in the General Index, while further details can be gained from the map on the end-papers.

Ships of the Royal Navy were normally commissioned in peacetime to be employed on one specific task or in one area until they were paid off three or four years later, although in wartime arrangements were less orderly. The term 'station' was originally applied to an area in which a ship was ordered to cruise. Many small stations existed up to the middle of the eighteenth century, frequently consisting of a single ship 'attending on' one of the American colonies; but in more important areas there was a squadron under a senior officer or commander-in-chief and a shore base. With the extension of British power and interests, the word 'station', by the nineteenth century, came to mean a large area covered by a considerable force supported by a dockyard and other establishments.

Home Waters is a difficult definition because of the frequent changes in name and organization of the fleet or fleets operating in the seas around the British Isles. The main force was variously known as the 'Channel Squadron' or 'Fleet', the 'Western Squadron', the 'First Fleet' or the 'Home' or 'Atlantic Fleets'. During the First World War it was the 'Grand Fleet' and then the 'Battle Cruiser Force'. At times a 'North Sea Fleet' and 'Baltic Fleet' also existed. In addition, there were ships in full or partial commission such as port guardships, training ships, fishery protection and surveying vessels. There were also yachts, ships in various reserves and the 'ordinary', later known as the 'Reserve Fleet' or 'Second' or 'Third Fleets'. These variations have not been specifically indexed other than under 'Home Waters' unless there is particularly good reason for doing so.

The *Mediterranean Station* was instituted in the 1670s although it was not in continuous existence until the eighteenth century. Apart from the Mediterranean itself, it included the approaches from Cape St. Vincent and Lisbon, and, after the opening of the Suez Canal, the Red Sea was added to it. In the eighteenth century the force was based on Minorca and Gibraltar, but later Malta became the principal base.

The arrangement of stations on the North American and West Indies seaboard were initially very fragmented. Before 1756 there was a ship for each colony and until 1830 there were never less than three stations. In the West Indies, because of the prevailing winds, the *Leeward Islands Station* and *Jamaica Station* were separate, based respectively upon Antigua and Port Royal. To the north, after 1763, there was the *Halifax* or *North American Station*. *Newfoundland* was an unusual station of its own; the naval Commander-in-Chief was also the civil Governor, proceeding from the United Kingdom every season to supervise the fisheries. In 1830 all these stations were combined to form the *North American and West Indies Station*.

The *East Indies Station*, founded in 1744, was an extensive area which included all the seas east of the Cape of Good Hope; its base was at Bombay. However, by the middle of the nineteenth century, the number of vessels had increased and communications were so difficult that subdivision was inevitable. This was particularly the case after the First China War (1840–3) had shifted the centre of power to the China Seas. After some years of virtual independence under its own permanent senior officer, the *Australian Station* became a separate entity in 1859 and the *China Station* was separated from the *East Indies* in 1864.

The *Cape of Good Hope Station*, founded during the Napoleonic Wars, was continued to guard Napoleon during his captivity at St. Helena and was maintained after his death. The west coast of Africa was frequently visited by warships in the eighteenth century, but there was no *West African Station* until the decision was made to suppress the slave trade. Between 1831 and 1839 the two stations were combined to form the *Cape and West African Station*, while finally in 1869, with the slave trade eliminated, the West African Squadron was merged with the *Cape Station*, with its base at Simonstown.

In the 1820s South America, having thrown off Spanish rule, remained politically unstable and a squadron was stationed off its coasts, with its base at Rio de Janeiro. In 1837 this station was split into the *Pacific Station* running along the west coast of the Americas and out as far as 170° west, while the *Brazil* or *South East Coast of America Station* covered the eastern coast of South America.

At various times short-lived attempts were made by the Admiralty to reduce the numbers of overseas squadrons. From 1839 to 1841 and again from 1860 to 1862 the *Cape and Brazil Stations* were under one command, while from 1864 to 1866 the *East Indies and the Cape Stations* were combined. This arrangement of stations continued until after the First World War, although numbers of ships overseas had been reduced in 1905 by the Fisher reforms. The *Pacific Station* almost disappeared in 1905 and was later handed over to the Royal Canadian Navy, while Australian and New Zealand waters became the responsibility of the Royal Australian Navy and the Royal New Zealand Navy. The *North American and West Indies Station* became the *America and West Indies Station* in 1926, taking the remaining commitments on both shores of both Americas, while the *Cape Station* was renamed the *South Atlantic Station* in the same year. With these changes, the stations survived until the 1950s.

Bombay Marine and Indian Navy

The Bombay Marine was the fleet of armed ships maintained by the East India Company. Formed in the seventeenth century, it was the only representative of British seapower in the Indian Ocean until the mid-eighteenth century. In 1830 it was renamed the Indian Navy. At the time of its disbandment in 1863 its responsibility stretched from the Cape of Good Hope eastwards to New Zealand and China. The Royal Indian Marine provided the transport and survey service for the Government of India until 1928, when it formed the nucleus of the Royal Indian Navy.

'Particular Service'

In the nineteenth century, ships, except for the permanent squadrons serving on the various stations, could be given special orders and were described in the Navy List as being on 'particular service'. This could apply to anything from an Arctic expedition or a search for a wreck to a training cruise.

Flying Squadrons

There were also several special-purpose squadrons formed during the nineteenth century. In the 1830s and 1840s there were a number of Evolutionary or Experimental Squadrons operating in home waters, usually for one summer only. Their object was partly to gain experience of new designs and partly to keep officers and men exercised in squadron evolutions together. In the mid-Victorian era, the same theory produced the idea that the police work, which then formed so much of the Navy's function, could be done better by squadrons of large ships cruising than by numerous small vessels on a permanent station. The result was three successive squadrons which circumnavigated the globe. They were the *Flying Squadron* of 1869 to 1871, the *Detached Squadron* of 1876 to 1877 and that of 1880 to 1882.

Shore Establishments

Apart from dockyards, victualling yards and hospitals, the Navy had few establishments on shore until the end of the nineteenth century. The one exception was the Naval Academy at Portsmouth, founded in 1729, which became the Royal Naval Academy in 1773 and then the Royal Naval College in 1806. It was closed between 1837 and 1841 and its functions were transferred to the College at Greenwich in 1873. Old ships were generally used for accommodation or training, but by 1900 they were considered too small and unhealthy. A large programme of building ashore therefore took place and most of these establishments took over the name of the old receiving or training ship. HMS *Excellent*, gunnery school, was the first of these establishments to come ashore in 1890, at Whale Island in Portsmouth Harbour. The other principal ones were:

Dryad Navigation School
Ganges Boys Training
Mercury Signal School
Pembroke Barracks, Chatham

Vernon Torpedo School
Victory (now *Nelson*) Barracks, Portsmouth
Vivid (later *Drake*) Barracks, Plymouth

The Royal Naval College, Greenwich was founded in 1873 to provide a higher education for junior officers, while the College for officer cadets at Dartmouth came ashore from *Britannia* in 1905. The Royal Naval College, Osborne, was founded in the same year and merged with Dartmouth in 1921.

Coastguards

The coastguard service underwent many changes during the nineteenth century. In the 1820s a large naval force was concerned in the protection of the revenue, particularly along the south coast. This function was transferred to the Customs and Excise in 1822. With the coming of free trade, these precautions became less necessary and in 1856 the Coastguard once again became a naval force whose duties were especially concerned with lifesaving, but was regarded more particularly as a naval reserve. In 1857 a modern warship was allotted to each of the coastguard districts, only partly manned, it being intended that in wartime the coastguards would complete the crew as well as for the summer manoeuvres each year. These ships were called 'First Reserve' ships and are the coastguard ships referred to in some biographies.

The Packet Service

The Packet Service was transferred to the Navy from the Post Office in 1837, its commanders usually becoming masters. The service had ceased to exist by 1860 with the increasing use of contract mail packets.

Name List of Entries

1. ABDY, *Sir* William, 6th Bt., *Captain*, 1733–1803
2. ALDRICH, Pelham, *Admiral*, 1844–1930
3. ALTHAM, Edward, *Captain*, 1882–1950
4. AUSTEN, Charles John, *Rear-Admiral*, 1779–1852
5. AUSTEN, *Sir* Francis William, *Admiral of the Fleet*, 1774–1865

BAILLIE GROHMAN *see* GROHMAN
6. BAIRD, *Doctor* Andrew (Physician of the Fleet), *ca.* 1757–1843
BARHAM *see* MIDDLETON
7. BARLOW, Charles James, *Vice-Admiral*, 1848–1912
8. BAX, Bonham Ward, *Captain*, 1837–1877
9. BAX, Henry Bonham, *Commander* (H.E.I.C.), 1798–1869
10. BAX, Robert Nesham, *Admiral*, 1875–1969
11. BAYNES, Henry Compton Anderson, *Rear-Admiral*, 1852–1922
12. BAYNES, *Sir* Robert Lambert, *Admiral*, 1796–1869
13. BAYNTUN, *Sir* Henry William, *Admiral*, 1766–1840
14. BEAVER, Philip, *Captain*, 1766–1813
15. BEDFORD, *Sir* Frederick George Denham, *Admiral*, 1838–1913
16. BELCHER, *Sir* Edward, *Admiral*, 1799–1877
BELLASIS *see* OLIVER-BELLASIS
17. BERRY, *Sir* Edward, *Rear-Admiral*, 1768–1831

18. BETHUNE, Charles Ramsay Drinkwater, *Admiral*, 1802–1884
19. BETHUNE, Henry, *Captain*, 1858–1939
20. BLAKE, *Sir* Geoffrey, *Admiral*, 1882–1968
21. BLAKE, William Hans, *Captain*, 1832–1874
22. BLANE, Arthur Rodney, *Captain*, 1834–1891
23. BLANE, *Sir* Gilbert, 1st Bt. (Physician of the Fleet), 1749–1834
24. BOND, Francis Godolphin, *Rear-Admiral*, 1765–1839
25. BOSANQUET, Henry Theodore Augustus, *Captain*, 1870–1959
26. BOUGAINVILLE, Louis Antoine de (Admiral, French Navy), 1729–1811
27. BOYLES, *Sir* Charles, *Vice-Admiral*, 1756–1816
28. BRACKENBURY, John William, *Admiral*, 1842–1918
29. BRENT, Harry Woodfall, *Vice-Admiral*, 1834–1911
30. BRIDGE, *Sir* Cyprian Arthur George, *Admiral*, 1839–1924
BRIDPORT *see* HOOD
31. BROUGHTON, William Robert, *Captain*, 1762–1821
32. BROWN, Francis Clifton, *Vice-Admiral*, 1874–1963
33. BROWN, *Sir* Harold Arthur, *Vice-Admiral*, 1878–1968
BURET *see* PURCELL-BURET
34. BURT, Turner Warner (Mate, Indian Navy), 1839–*ca.* 1920
35. BURTON, Alfred, *Captain* (Royal Marines), 1787–1840

36. BURTON, Cuthbert Ward, *Major-General* (Royal Marines), 1832–1890

BYROM *see* JONES-BYROM

37. CALDWELL, *Sir* Benjamin, *Admiral*, 1737–1830
38. CALDWELL, Henry, *Captain*, 1815–1868
39. CAREW, *Sir* Benjamin Hallowell, *Admiral*, 1760–1834
40. CARTERET, Philip, *Rear-Admiral*, *ca.* 1733–1796

CARTERET *see* SILVESTER

41. CHAMBERS, William Wylly, *Captain*, *ca.* 1810–1860
42. CHATFIELD, Alfred Ernle Montacute, *Admiral. of the Fleet, 1st Baron Chatfield*, 1873–1967
43. CHATFIELD, Henry (Master Shipwright), *fl.* 1820–1860
44. CHILDERS, William Henry, *Lieutenant*, 1837–1869
45. CLARKE, *Reverend* Thomas Brooke (Auditor, Naval Asylum), *fl.* 1800–1821
46. CLEMENTS, Michael, *Rear-Admiral*, *ca.* 1735–*ca.* 1796
47. COCHRANE, Archibald, *Rear-Admiral*, 1874–1952
48. COCKBURN, *Sir* George, 10th Bt., *Admiral of the Fleet*, 1772–1853
49. CODRINGTON, *Sir* Edward, *Admiral*, 1770–1851
50. CODRINGTON, *Sir* Henry John, *Admiral of the Fleet*, 1808–1877
51. COLES, Cowper Phipps, *Captain*, 1819–1870
52. COLLINGWOOD, Cuthbert, *Vice-Admiral, 1st Baron Collingwood*, 1750–1810
53. COLLINSON, *Sir* Richard, *Admiral*, 1811–1883
54. COPE-CORNFORD, Leslie (journalist), 1867–1927
55. CORNWALLIS, *the Hon. Sir* William, *Admiral*, 1744–1819
56. COWAN, *Sir* Walter Henry, 1st Bt., *Admiral*, 1871–1956

CUMBY *see* PRYCE-CUMBY

57. CUNNINGHAM, Andrew Browne, *Admiral of the Fleet, 1st Viscount Cunningham*, 1883–1963
58. CUNNINGHAM, *Sir* Charles, *Rear-Admiral*, 1755–1834
59. CURZON-HOWE, *the Hon. Sir* Assheton Gore, *Admiral*, 1850–1911

60. DANNREUTHER, Tristan, *Captain*, *ca.* 1872–1963
61. DARE, Joseph Stafford (First Mate), 1863–1951

DARTMOUTH *see* LEGGE

62. DAVISON, Alexander (naval agent), 1750–1829
63. DAWKINS, Richard, *Rear-Admiral*, 1828–1896
64. D'EYNCOURT, *Sir* Eustace Tennyson, 1st Bt. (Director of Naval Construction), 1868–1951
65. DE VITRE, *Reverend* John Durham Denis (Chaplain, Royal Navy), *ca.* 1870–*ca.* 1949
66. DEWAR, Kenneth Gilbert Balmain, *Vice-Admiral*, 1879–1964
67. DIXIE, *Sir* Alexander, 9th Bt., *Captain*, 1780–1857
68. DOMVILE, *Sir* Barry Edward, *Admiral*, 1878–1971

DORRIEN *see* SMITH-DORRIEN

69. DOUGHTY, Frederick Proby, *Rear-Admiral*, 1834–1892
70. DOUGLAS, *Sir* James, 1st Bt., *Admiral*, 1703–1787

DRINKWATER *see* BETHUNE

71. DUCKWORTH, *Sir* John Thomas, 1st Bt., *Admiral*, 1748–1817
72. DUDMAN, Joseph, *Commander* (H.E.I.C.), *ca.* 1790–1865
73. DUFF, *Sir* Alexander, *Admiral*, 1862–1933
74. DUFF, Robert, *Vice-Admiral*, *ca.* 1720–1787
75. DUNCAN, Adam, *Admiral, 1st Viscount Duncan*, 1731–1804
76. DUNDAS, Henry, *1st Viscount Melville* (First Lord of the Admiralty), 1742–1811

119. HAMILTON, *Sir* Frederick Tower, *Admiral*, 1856–1917
120. HAMILTON, Henry George, *Captain*, 1808–1879
121. HAMILTON, John, *Commander* (H.E.I.C.), 1763–1837
122. HAMILTON, *Sir* Louis Henry Keppel, *Admiral*, 1892–1957
123. HAMILTON, *Sir* Richard Vesey, *Admiral*, 1829–1912
124. HAMILTON, *Sir* William (diplomat), 1730–1803
125. HAMMILL, Tynte Ford, *Captain*, 1851–1894
126. HAMOND, *Sir* Graham Eden, 2nd Bt., *Admiral of the Fleet*, 1779–1862
127. HAMPSHIRE, Cyril Beaumont, *Commander, ca.* 1875–1963
128. HARVEY, *Sir* Thomas, *Vice-Admiral*, 1775–1841
129. HAWKE, Edward, *Admiral of the Fleet, 1st Baron Hawke*, 1705–1781
130. HAWKER, Edward, *Admiral*, 1782–1860
131. HEALD, *Doctor* Charles Brehmer (Temporary Surgeon), 1882–1974
   HEATHFIELD *see* ELIOTT
132. HENDERSON, *Sir* William Hannam, *Vice-Admiral*, 1845–1931
133. HENSLOW, *Sir* John (Surveyor of the Navy), 1730–1815
134. HERSCHEL, *Sir* John Frederick William, 1st Bt. (astronomer), 1792–1871
135. HERSCHEL, *Sir* William Frederick (astronomer), 1738–1822
136. HOLBURNE, Francis, *Admiral*, 1704–1771
137. HOOD, Alexander, *Admiral, 1st Viscount Bridport*, 1726–1814
138. HOOD, Alexander, *Captain*, 1758–1798
139. HOOD, Samuel, *Admiral, 1st Viscount Hood*, 1724–1816
140. HOOD, *Sir* Samuel, 1st Bt., *Vice-Admiral*, 1762–1814
141. HORNBY, *Sir* Geoffrey Thomas Phipps, *Admiral of the Fleet*, 1825–1895
142. HORNBY, *Sir* Phipps, *Admiral*, 1785–1867
143. HORNBY, Robert Stewart Phipps, *Admiral*, 1866–1956
144. HORNBY, Windham Mark Phipps, *Commander*, 1896–
145. HORTON-SMITH, Lionel Graham Horton (naval propagandist), 1871–1953
146. HOWE, Richard, *Admiral of the Fleet, 1st Earl Howe*, 1726–1799
   HOWE *see* CURZON-HOWE
147. HULBERT, George Redmond (naval agent), 1774–1825

148. INVERNAIRN, *Lady* Elspeth, *fl.* 1902–1952
149. ISMAY, Margaret, *fl.* 1859–1907

150. JENKINSON, Henry, *Rear-Admiral*, 1790–1865
151. JERRAM, *Sir* Thomas Henry Martyn, *Admiral*, 1858–1933
152. JERVIS, John, *Admiral of the Fleet, 1st Earl St. Vincent*, 1735–1823
153. JOHNSTONE, Charles, *Vice-Admiral*, 1843–1927
154. JONES, Jenkin, *Captain, ca.* 1793–1843
155. JONES-BYROM, William Henry, *Commander*, 1829–1867

156. KEATS, *Sir* Richard Goodwin, *Admiral*, 1757–1834
   KEITH *see* ELPHINSTONE
157. KELLY, *Sir* John Donald, *Admiral of the Fleet*, 1871–1936
158. KELLY, *Sir* William Archibald Howard, *Admiral*, 1873–1952
159. KENNEDY, James Branch (Master Mariner), 1816–*ca.* 1891
160. KEPPEL, Augustus, *Admiral, 1st Viscount Keppel*, 1725–1786
161. KEPPEL, *the Hon. Sir* Henry, *Admiral of the Fleet*, 1809–1904
162. KINGSMILL, *Sir* Robert Brice, *Admiral*, 1730–1805

208. NEPEAN, *Sir* Evan, 1st Bt. (Secretary to the Admiralty), 1751–1822
209. NIAS, *Sir* Joseph, *Admiral*, 1793–1879
210. NOEL, *Sir* Gerald Henry Uctred, *Admiral of the Fleet*, 1845–1918
211. NORRIS, David Thomas, *Admiral*, 1875–1937
212. NORTH, Frederick, *Paymaster-in-Chief*, 1839–1927

213. OLIVER, Algernon Hardy, *Commander, ca.* 1855–1934
214. OLIVER, *Sir* Henry Francis, *Admiral of the Fleet*, 1865–1965
215. OLIVER, Richard Aldworth, *Admiral*, 1811–1889
216. OLIVER, Robert Dudley, *Admiral*, 1766–1850
217. OLIVER, Thomas William, *Commander, fl.* 1848–1872
218. OLIVER-BELLASIS, Richard, *Captain*, 1900–1964
219. OMMANEY, Erasmus Dennison St. Andrew, *Rear-Admiral, ca.* 1853–1936
220. ORDE, *Sir* John, 1st Bt., *Admiral*, 1751–1824
221. OSBORN, Henry, *Admiral*, 1694–1771
222. OWEN, *Sir* Edward William Campbell Rich, *Admiral*, 1771–1849
223. OWEN, William, *Commander*, d. 1778
224. OWEN, William Fitzwilliam, *Vice-Admiral*, 1774–1857

225. PAKENHAM, Edward Michael, *Captain, 2nd Baron Longford*, 1743–1792
226. PARKER, *Sir* William, 1st Bt., *Admiral of the Fleet*, 1781–1866
PARRY *see* WEBLEY-PARRY
227. PEACHEY, Allan Thomas George Cumberland, *Captain*, 1896–1967

228. PELL, *Sir* Watkin Owen, *Admiral*, 1788–1869
229. PELLEW, Edward, *Admiral, 1st Viscount Exmouth*, 1757–1833
230. PENN, *Sir* William, *Admiral*, 1621–1670
231. PHILLIMORE, *Sir* Augustus, *Admiral*, 1822–1897
PHIPPS HORNBY *see* HORNBY
232. POCOCK, *Sir* George, *Admiral*, 1706–1792
233. POLE, *Sir* Charles Morice, 1st Bt., *Admiral of the Fleet*, 1757–1830
234. POLLARD, Edwin John, *Rear-Admiral*, 1833–1909
235. PORTER, *Sir* James, *Surgeon Vice-Admiral*, 1851–1935
236. PRIDHAM-WIPPELL, *Sir* Henry Daniel, *Admiral*, 1885–1952
237. PRYCE-CUMBY, William, *Captain*, 1771–1837
238. PURCELL-BURET, Theobald John Claud (Master Mariner), 1879–1974
239. PURVIS, John Child, *Admiral*, 1746–1825

240 RAINIER, John Harvey, *Admiral*, 1847–1915
241. RAINIER, John Sprat, *Rear-Admiral*, 1777–1822
242. RAINIER, Peter, *Admiral, ca.* 1741–1808
243. RAINIER, Peter, *Captain*, 1784–1836
244. REES, William Stokes, *Admiral*, 1853–1929
245. RICE, William McPherson (Master Shipwright), *ca.* 1799–1853
246. RICHMOND, *Sir* Herbert William, *Admiral*, 1871–1946
247. RIOU, Edward, *Captain*, 1762–1801
248. ROBERTS, John Charles Gawen, *Admiral*, 1787–1874
249. RODDAM, Robert, *Admiral*, 1719–1808
250. ROWLEY, *Sir* Charles, 1st Bt., *Admiral*, 1770–1845

St. Vincent *see* Jervis
Sandwich *see* Montagu
Saunders dundas *see* Dundas

251. Saxton, *Sir* Charles, 1st Bt., *Captain*, 1732–1808

252. Scott, *Reverend Doctor* Alexander John (Chaplain, Royal Navy), 1768–1840

253. Scott, *Sir* James, *Admiral, ca.* 1790–1872

254. Scott, William Dundas (shipbuilder), 1846–1924

255. Sergison, Charles (Clerk of the Acts), 1654–1732

256. Sharpe, Phillip Ruffle, *Vice-Admiral*, 1831–1892

257. Shirreff, William Henry, *Rear-Admiral*, 1785–1847

258. Silvester, *Sir* Philip Carteret, 1st Bt., *Captain*, 1777–1828

259. Sisson, James Joseph Lawson, *Commander*, 1846–1883

260. Smith, *Sir* William Sidney, *Admiral*, 1764–1840

Smith *see* Horton-Smith

261. Smith-Dorrien, Arthur Hale, *Rear-Admiral*, 1856–1933

262. Smithett, *Sir* Luke (Master, Packet Service), *ca.* 1800–1871

263. Spratt, Thomas Abel Brimage, *Vice-Admiral*, 1811–1888

264. Steevens, Charles, *Rear-Admiral*, 1705–1761

265. Stephenson, *Sir* Henry Frederick, *Admiral*, 1842–1919

266. Stephenson, Thomas, *Captain*, 1741–1809

267. Stewart, Archibald Thomas, *Commander*, 1876–1968

268. Stewart, *Sir* William Houston, *Admiral*, 1822–1901

269. Stokes, John Lort, *Admiral*, 1812–1885

270. Stopford, *Sir* Montagu, *Vice-Admiral*, 1798–1864

271. Stopford, *the Hon. Sir* Robert, *Admiral*, 1768–1847

272. Stopford, Robert Fanshaw, *Admiral*, 1811–1891

273. Stuart, *Lord* William, *Captain*, 1778–1814

274. Tait, *Sir* William Eric Campbell, *Admiral*, 1886–1946

275. Tennant, *Sir* William George, *Admiral*, 1890–1963

Tennyson D'Eyncourt *see* D'Eyncourt

276. Thesiger, *Sir* Bertram Sackville, *Admiral*, 1875–1966

277. Thompson, *Sir* Charles, 1st Bt., *Vice-Admiral, ca.* 1740–1799

278. Thursfield, Henry George, *Rear-Admiral*, 1882–1963

279. Thursfield, *Sir* James Richard (journalist), 1840–1923

280. Tiddeman, Richard, *Captain, ca.* 1702–1762

281. Tizard, Thomas Henry, *Captain*, 1839–1924

282. Tupper, Charles George de Beauvoir, *Lieutenant*, 1872–1893

283. Tyler, *Sir* Charles, *Admiral*, 1760–1835

284. Upton, Henry, *Commander* (H.E.I.C.), b. 1769

285. Vernon, Edward, *Admiral*, 1684–1757

286. Vernon, *Sir* Edward, *Admiral*, 1723–1794

287. Vivian, Gerald William, *Captain*, 1869–1921

288. Walker, *Sir* Baldwin Wake, 1st Bt., *Admiral*, 1802–1876

289. Waters, George Alexander, *Captain*, 1820–1903

290. Webley-Parry, William Henry, *Rear-Admiral*, 1764–1837

291. Wemyss, Edward William Elphinstone, *Vice-Admiral*, 1866–1938

292. White, Arnold (journalist), 1848–1925

293. Whitshed, *Sir* James Hawkins, *Admiral of the Fleet*, 1762–1849

Guide to the Manuscripts in the National Maritime Museum

1   ABDY, *Sir* William, 6th Bt., *Captain*, 1733-1803

Abdy began his career by serving in the East India Company's
ships *True Briton*, 1750 to 1752, on a voyage to China and
Stafford, 1753, to India. He then entered the Navy and was
commissioned as lieutenant in 1758. He was promoted to
commander in 1761 and served in the *Beaver*, 1761 to 1766, in
home waters and then in the West Indies. In 1766 he was promoted to Captain of the *Actaeon* in the West Indies, but he
returned home before the end of the year and did not serve
again because of ill-health.

The papers are part of the Caldwell collection presented by
Mrs C.B.H. Caldwell in 1938. They consist of logs, 1750 to
1753, and two combined letter and order books, 1761 to 1766.
There are also copies, made by Abdy in his retirement, of
despatches describing actions, 1778 to 1782 and 1793 to 1797,
and of the *Agamemnon*'s log, 1782 to 1783. (5 vols)

2   ALDRICH, Pelham, *Admiral*, 1844-1930

Aldrich entered the Navy in 1859 in the *Marlborough*,
Mediterranean Station, later serving in the *Scout*, 1865 to
1867, on the South American Station. He was promoted to
lieutenant in 1866 and was First Lieutenant in the *Challenger*
between 1872 and 1874. He then joined the *Alert*, 1875 to
1876, as senior lieutenant during the British Arctic expedition led by Sir G.S. Nares (*q.v.*). In the spring of
1876 he explored the northern coast of Ellesmere Island with
the sledge *Challenger*. For service in this expedition he
was promoted to commander. He was employed in the surveying
vessels *Sylvia* and *Fawn* in the Far East and off Africa
between 1879 and 1884, being promoted to captain in 1883.
He continued to serve until 1908 when he retired with the
rank of admiral.

The papers, which were presented in 1955 by Aldrich's niece,
Miss B. Champion, cover only a short period of his career.
There are extracts from journals, 1860 to 1867, returns from
the sledge *Challenger* and notes and journals concerning
surveying 1879 to 1884. There are no papers for the
Challenger expedition in this collection: the main Arctic
papers are with the Scott Polar Research Institute at
Cambridge. (4 vols; 1 file)

3   ALTHAM, Edward, *Captain*, 1882-1950

Altham entered the Navy in 1896 and from 1898 served in the
Prince George, *Crescent*, *Royal Sovereign*, Channel Station,
and *Hood* and *Hussar*, in the Mediterranean. He was promoted
to lieutenant in 1902, qualified as a gunnery specialist and
was promoted to commander in 1913. For the first few months
of the First World War he commanded the *Wildfire* in operations
off the Belgian coast. He later continued in these operations
in the monitor *General Craufurd*. In 1918, during the North
Russian operations, he was acting captain of the *Attentive*
and was promoted to captain at the end of the year. Then,
in 1919, he was appointed to the *Fox* and was senior officer
of the Archangel River Expeditionary Force. Altham was
retired in 1922 and was appointed naval correspondent to the
Morning Post. In 1924 he became editor of the *Journal of the
Royal United Service Institution* and in 1927 also Secretary
of the Institution, which posts he filled until his death.
He was recalled to the Navy in 1939 and was employed throughout the Second World War as head of the Postal and Telegraph
Censorship Section of the Naval Staff.

The papers form part of the collection of naval manuscripts
transferred from the Royal United Service Institution in 1968.
They consist of logs, 1898 to 1904 and 1919. There are order
books, 1915 to 1919, and a number of technical notebooks as
well as printed material. In addition, there are a number
of miscellaneous loose papers and photographs collected by
Altham. (3ft; 91cm)

4   AUSTEN, Charles John, *Rear-Admiral*, 1779-1852

Austen, younger brother of Francis William Austen (*q.v.*) and
of Jane Austen, the novelist, entered the Navy in 1794, was
promoted to lieutenant in 1797 and to captain in 1810. After
service on the North American and Mediterranean Stations, he
was from 1815 engaged in the suppression of piracy in the
Aegean until his ship, the *Phoenix*, was lost in a heavy gale
off Smyrna in February 1816. He served as second-in-command
of the Jamaica Station from 1826 to 1828 and his success in
the suppression of the slave trade led to his nomination as
Flag-Captain of the *Winchester*, North American and West Indies
Station, 1830. He was invalided after an accident in 1830
and was not re-employed until appointed to the *Bellerophon*
in 1838. He served in her in the Mediterranean, where he was
present at the bombardment of Acre in November 1840, until
she was paid off in 1841. He was made rear-admiral in 1846

but saw no further employment until 1850 when he was appointed Commander-in-Chief, East Indies, flying his flag in the *Hastings*. He died in Burma while still in this command.

The papers have been on loan from Commander D.P. Willan, R.N., since 1962. They are a complete series of sixty-three diaries kept between 1815 and 1852. (2½ft; 76cm)

5   AUSTEN, *Sir* Francis William, *Admiral of the Fleet*, 1774-1865

Austen, brother of Charles John Austen (*q.v.*) and of Jane Austen, the novelist, entered the Royal Naval Academy in 1786 and in 1788 joined the *Perseverance* in the East Indies. He was made lieutenant in 1792, commander in 1799 and captain in 1800, while in the *Peterel*. In 1805 he was Flag-Captain to Rear-Admiral Sir Thomas Louis (*q.v.*) in the *Canopus* and was at the battle of San Domingo in 1806. Whilst on convoy to the East Indies in 1809 he successfully settled a dispute with the Chinese, which earned the approval of the Admiralty and the award of a thousand pounds by the East India Company. He was Flag-Captain to Admiral Lord Gambier (1756-1833), then commanding the Home Fleet, in 1810 and, from 1811 to 1814, was in the *Elephant* in the North Sea and the Baltic. In 1830 Austen was promoted to rear-admiral and to vice-admiral in 1838. He was Commander-in-Chief, West Indies, 1844 to 1848, and was made Admiral of the Fleet in 1863.

The papers were presented by Captain Ernest Leigh Austen in 1930. They cover almost all Austen's active service from his entrance into the Royal Naval Academy, 1786, until the end of his commission as Commander-in-Chief in the West Indies, 1848, and include offical log books, 1795 to 1814; letter-books, 1801 to 1814, 1845 to 1848; order books, 1807 to 1813, 1829 to 1848, and loose papers, which are mainly general remarks and notes. (2ft; 61cm)

6   BAIRD, *Dr* Andrew (Physician of the Fleet), *ca*.1757-1843

Baird, a naval surgeon, served with Earl St Vincent (*q.v.*) in the 1790s. He was Commissioner for Sick and Wounded, 1803 to 1804, and appointed Inspector-General of Naval Hospitals in 1804. Baird's association with St Vincent continued after the latter's retirement and he attended him in his last illness in 1823.

The papers were presented by Lieutenant-Commander P.K. Kemp in 1964. They consist of fifty-three letters written by St. Vincent to Baird between 1812 and 1823. (1 file)

7   BARLOW, Charles James, *Vice-Admiral*, 1848-1912

Barlow entered the Navy in 1862, serving first in the *Scylla*, China Station, 1863 to 1867, and then in the Pacific. He was promoted to lieutenant in 1872 and joined the *Immortalité*, Detached Squadron, 1874 to 1877, followed by service in the *Flamingo* in the East Indies, 1877 to 1880. Promoted to commander in 1884, he was appointed to the *Bacchante*, flagship of the East Indies Station, 1885 to 1888, and was involved in the Burma War, 1885 to 1886. After his promotion to captain in 1889, he commanded the *Orlando* on the Australian Station and then the *Empress of India* and the *Jupiter*, both in the Channel, until 1899. He became Admiral Superintendent of Pembroke Dockyard, 1899 to 1902, and of Devonport, 1906 to 1908.

The papers were presented to the Museum by Major Barlow in 1956. They include logs, 1863 to 1867, 1876 to 1880 and 1889 to 1892; a journal and a report on the Burma War; some papers concerning the opening of the Kiel Canal, 1899, and official papers for both dockyards. (1½ft; 46cm)

8   BAX, Bonham Ward, *Captain*, 1837-1877

Bax was the son of Henry Bonham Bax (*q.v.*). He entered the Navy in 1851 and specialized in surveying. From 1871 to 1875 Bax commanded the survey ship *Dwarf* on the China Station and published an account of the voyage. From December 1876 until his death in July 1877, he commanded the *Sylvia*, also on the China Station.

He published *The Eastern Seas* (London, 1875).

The papers were presented by Admiral R.N. Bax in 1964. They consist of Captain Bax's logs of the *Dwarf*, 1871 to 1874, and his letterbook in the *Sylvia*. (3 vols)

9   BAX, Henry Bonham, *Commander* (H.E.I.C.), 1798-1869

Bax was in the Navy from 1813 to 1817, after which he entered
the service of the East India Company. In 1844 he became an
Elder Brother of Trinity House.

See Arthur Nesham Bax, *A Bax Family of East Kent* (published
privately, 1951).

The papers, presented by Admiral R.N. Bax in 1956, consist
of an illustrated list of buoys and light vessels owned by
Bax as an Elder Brother of Trinity House. (1 vol)

His illustrated book of lighthouses and a journal kept in the
Mulgrave are in the Department of Pictures, on loan from
Canon A.N. Bax since 1953.

10   BAX, Robert Nesham, *Admiral*, 1875-1969

Bax was the son of Bonham Ward Bax (*q.v.*). He joined the
Britannia in 1889, rose to captain in 1913 and saw active
service in World War I. He was promoted to admiral on the
retired list in 1932.

The papers were presented by Admiral Bax in 1956. They consist of a rough notebook kept in the training ship *Cruiser*
and an annotated notebook of examination questions of the
Training Squadron, 1894. (2 vols)

11   BAYNES, Henry Compton Anderson, *Rear-Admiral*, 1852-1922

Baynes, son of Robert Lambert Baynes (*q.v.*), joined the Navy
in 1866 and became a lieutenant in 1877. He served in the
Pembroke, 1893 to 1895, and was promoted to captain in 1897.
After attending gunnery and torpedo courses, his first active
service as captain was briefly in the *Minerva*, 1899, and
then in the *Mildura*, Australian Station, in 1900. He retired
in 1902, advancing to the rank of rear-admiral in 1907.

The papers were presented in 1936 by Mrs H.C.A. Baynes and
Miss Nias, both of whom were daughters of Admiral Sir Joseph
Nias (*q.v.*). Another family link is that at the Battle of
Navarino, 1827, Admiral Nias and Robert Lambert Baynes were
First Lieutenant and Second Captain respectively in the *Asia*.
This collection includes official service documents, 1866 to
1901; an article on 'Armament of Battleships', undated; a

letter, 1888, concerning Whitehead torpedoes; a few letters
about Baynes's fishery protection work in the North Sea in
the 1890s and three night order books, 1893, 1895 and 1901.
(1 box)

12   BAYNES, *Sir* Robert Lambert, *Admiral*, 1796-1869

Baynes entered the Navy in 1810, serving in the *Blake* under
Sir Edward Codrington (*q.v.*) and in the *Tonnant* and *Tartar*
in North America. He was commissioned as lieutenant in 1818,
serving as First Lieutenant in the *Vigo* in South America until
1826 when he joined the *Asia*, flagship of Admiral Sir Edward
Codrington (*q.v.*). It was in the *Asia* that he was present at
the Battle of Navarino. In 1828 he was promoted to captain.
After ten years on half-pay he joined the *Andromache* in Nova
Scotia during the rebellion in Canada, after which he commanded
he on the Cape Station, 1840 to 1841. In 1847 he was in
the *Bellerophon* off the coast of Tuscany, when Leghorn was
taken by the Austrians, and in 1855 was on Particular Service
with the blockading fleet in the Baltic. He became Commander-
in-Chief in the Pacific in 1857, remaining there until 1860
and was promoted to admiral in 1865.

The papers were presented in 1936 by Mrs H.C.A. Baynes and
Miss Nias. They consist of official service documents,
details of ships on the Pacific Station 1854 to 1860, an
autobiographical outline of his career, 1810 to 1857, invitations to social events, and other personal papers. (1 box)

13   BAYNTUN, *Sir* Henry William, *Admiral*, 1766-1840

Bayntun was a lieutenant of 1783. Apart from a short interval
in 1796, he served in the West Indies from 1794, the year in
which he was promoted to captain, until 1804. On his return
to England he was appointed to the *Leviathan* and sent to the
Mediterranean to join Nelson. He then took part in the pursuit of the French to the West Indies and in the Battle of
Trafalgar, 1805. From 1806 to 1808 he served in the
Africa on the Cape Station, returning for a period in home
waters in 1808. In 1809 he was appointed to the *Milford* and
three years later reached the rank of rear-admiral, after
which he saw no more active service. He was made an admiral
in 1837.

The papers were presented in 1952 by Mr R.J. Bayntun Kipperley. They consist of notes, memoranda and various letters relating largely to the *Milford*, as well as some navigational notes. In 1964 Mrs C.L.F. Mackay Brown presented Bayntun's letterbook for the *Leviathan*, 1804 to 1805, and the *Africa*, 1806 to 1808. (1 vol, 1 file)

14   BEAVER, Philip, *Captain*, 1766-1813

Beaver joined the Navy in 1777, serving in the Channel and the West Indies before his promotion to lieutenant in 1783. For ten years after the American War he was on half-pay, broken only by brief service during the mobilizations of 1790 and 1791. In 1795 Beaver sailed as First Lieutenant of the *Stately* and served at the reductions of the Cape of Good Hope and of Ceylon. In 1796 he was transferred to the *Monarch* for the journey home. After a short spell in the *Queen Charlotte*, he served in the *Formidable*, *Foudroyant* and *Barfleur*, in the Channel Fleet, and at Cadiz between 1798 and 1799. Between 1799 and 1802 he served in the Mediterranean in the *Dolphin*, *Aurore*, *Minotaur* and *Foudroyant*. He was at the bombardment of Genoa and in Egypt. In 1801 on his promotion to captain, he transferred to the *Determinée* and was sent to Constantinople. Beaver then had a period ashore but in 1806 was appointed to command the *Acasta*, in which ship he went to the West Indies, where, in 1809, he took part in the reduction of Martinique. He then returned home, was appointed to the *Nisus* and sailed for the East Indies in June 1810, where he took part in the capture of Mauritius and Java. After a year in Mozambique and on the coast of Madagascar, he died suddenly at the Cape on his return home.

A useful source is W.H. Smyth, *The Life and Services of Captain Philip Beaver* (London, 1829) and his own *African Memoranda* (London, 1805).

The papers form part of the collection transferred from the Royal United Service Institution in 1968. They consist of eleven volumes of logs, which cover all Beaver's career at sea between 1795 and his death. (1½ft; 46cm)

15   BEDFORD, *Sir* Frederick George Denham, *Admiral*, 1838-1913

Bedford entered the Navy with a cadetship awarded by the Naval School at New Cross. In 1854 he was at the Crimea as a midshipman in the *Sampson*. However, he went to the Baltic in March 1855, when he was appointed to the *Vulture*, and he took part in the destruction of the Russian fortress at Sveaborg. He was promoted to lieutenant in 1859, to commander in 1871 and to captain in 1875 into the *Serapis*, which took the Prince of Wales to attend ceremonies proclaiming Queen Victoria Empress of India. Bedford was next appointed to the *Shah*, 1876, as Flag-Captain to Rear Admiral de Horsey (1827–1922), Commander-in-Chief, Pacific Station. In this ship he was engaged in the duel with the Peruvian ironclad *Huascar*. As a consequence of this action, the ironclad *Triumph* replaced the *Shah* and Bedford transferred to her. In 1880, on his return home, he attended the torpedo course at Portsmouth. Bedford then joined the Board of Admiralty, 1889 to 1892. In 1895 he became Second Sea Lord and was appointed Commander-in-Chief of the North American and West Indies Station, 1899 to 1903. From 1903 to 1909 he was Governor of Western Australia.

See F.G.H. Bedford, *The life and letters of Admiral Frederick George Denham Bedford* (published privately, 1960).

The papers were presented by Mr F.G.H. Bedford in 1952. There are logs, 1852 to 1858; diaries, 1875 to 1879, and letters concerning the *Huascar* incident. There are no papers for Bedford's later career. (1½ft; 46cm)

In the Department of Pictures are six albums containing watercolours and photographs. Two of them cover his service in the *Shah*, 1876 to 1878, and the third his career in the *Triumph*, 1879.

16   BELCHER, *Sir* Edward, *Admiral*, 1799–1877

Belcher entered the Navy in 1812, became a lieutenant in 1818 and a commander in 1829. After early experiences surveying in Arctic regions and a lengthy survey of the Pacific, he was given post-rank and a knighthood in 1841. From 1842 to 1847 he commanded the *Samarang*, in which he surveyed the coasts of Borneo, the Philippines and Formosa (Taiwan). In 1852 he was appointed to the *Assistance* to search for Sir John Franklin (*q.v.*). He was court-martialled for abandoning his ships but acquitted; one, however, was recovered the following year. He saw no more active service and reached the rank of admiral in 1872.

The papers were acquired in two parts. The first came to the Museum in the 1930s and consists of 110 letters from Belcher to Sir John Phillipart (1784–1874) between 1850 and 1863. The second was deposited on loan by Mr J.R. Belcher, in 1964.

This consists of letter and order books, 1843 to 1847 and
1852 to 1854. There is a watch and signal book, undated,
and some official service documents. (2 vols, 2 files,
1 box)

17 BERRY, *Sir* Edward, *Rear-Admiral*, 1768-1831

Berry went to sea as a volunteer in 1779 and served in the
guardship *Magnificent* between 1787 and 1788. He was promoted to lieutenant in 1794. He later served in the *Agamemnon*
and the *Captain* with Nelson (*q.v.*), 1796 to 1797 and was then
promoted to captain. After service with Nelson at the battle
of the Nile, 1798, he commanded the *Foudroyant* and captured
the *Généreux* and *Guillaume Tell*. He was appointed to the
Agamemnon in 1805 and fought at Trafalgar. Subsequent
commands took him to the West Indies and in 1812 he was
appointed to the *Barfleur*. Berry commanded the royal yacht
Royal Sovereign, 1813 to 1814. He was promoted to rear-
admiral in 1821.

The papers were bequeathed to the Museum in 1953 by Mrs K.E.
Maunsell. They consist of logs, 1787 to 1788, 1796 to 1797,
1799 to 1806, 1812, 1813 to 1814, and twenty-five letters
from Nelson, 1797 to 1805. (5 vols, 1 file)

18 BETHUNE, Charles Ramsay Drinkwater, *Admiral*, 1802-1884

Bethune was the son of the army officer and historian
Colonel John Drinkwater (d. 1844) and it was not until 1837
that he took the name Bethune. He entered the Navy in 1815
as a first-class volunteer in the *Northumberland* and sailed
in her from 1815 to 1816 on the voyage taking Napoleon to
exile in St Helena. In 1817 he joined the *Leander* in North
America; he then went to South America, where he served in
the *Superb* and the *Creole* from 1819 until 1823. Still on
this station, he was promoted to lieutenant, 1823, and joined
the *Doris* and then the *Barham* until promoted to commander in
1828. From 1828 to 1829 he commanded the *Espiègle*, Jamaica
Station. He was promoted to captain in 1830. At Palmerston's
request, in 1835, he joined the Embassy of the Earl of Durham
(1792-1840) to Russia to report on the naval installations
in the Black Sea. Later he served in the East Indies and in
the China War. He was made rear-admiral in 1855, vice-
admiral in 1862, admiral in 1866 and retired in 1870.

The papers were presented in 1958 by Captain R.M. Roberts. They consist of letters, written mainly by Bethune to his family, 1815 to 1835, and a number of watercolours. (4 vols)

19   BETHUNE, Henry, *Captain*, 1858-1939

Bethune entered the Navy in 1871 and served from 1873 to 1877 in the *Topaze*, Detached Squadron. In 1878 he was appointed to the *Alexander*, flagship in the Mediterranean, leaving her in order to join the *Agincourt*, flagship, Channel, 1881 to 1882. He was commissioned lieutenant in 1882, in the *Constance*, remaining in her on the Pacific Station until 1886. Still a lieutenant, he retired in 1903 and was promoted on the retired list.

The papers were presented by Mrs Holdsworth, daughter of Captain Bethune, in 1957. They consist of a series of logs for the above ships and a notebook on navigation and steam, (1ft; 30cm)

20   BLAKE, *Sir* Geoffrey, *Admiral*, 1882-1968

Blake entered the Navy in 1897, was made a lieutenant in 1904, specializing in gunnery and was promoted to commander in 1914. Between 1914 and 1918 he served in the Grand Fleet flagships *Iron Duke* and *Queen Elizabeth* as Fleet Gunnery Commander and Executive Officer respectively. In 1918 he was promoted to captain and served as Naval Attaché in Washington between 1919 and 1921. From 1921 to 1923 he commanded *Queen Elizabeth* and from 1923 he served on the staff of the War College for two years. Between 1925 and 1929 he was Deputy Director and then Director of the Royal Naval Staff College, after which, for three years, he was Commodore in command of the New Zealand Station and First Naval Member of the New Zealand Naval Board. In 1931 he was made rear-admiral. He became Fourth Sea Lord in 1932 and was promoted to vice-admiral in 1935. His last active command was that of the Battle Cruiser Squadron. He retired because of ill-health in 1938, was recalled in 1940 and served on the Board of Admiralty as Assistant Chief of Naval Staff. From 1942 to 1945 he was Flag Officer, Liaison, with the United States Navy in Europe.

The papers were deposited on loan by Sir Geoffrey Blake's son-in-law, Mr John Ehrman, in 1969. Access to them is restricted. They cover Blake's career from 1914 but not in great depth. There are official service documents; photographs of his service in the First World War and official papers relating to his period in America; papers covering affairs in Samoa, 1930, and other items relating to the New Zealand appointment. In addition, there are semi-official and personal letters, 1937 to 1940, from Admirals Sir Dudley Pound (1877-1943), A.B. Cunningham (*q.v.*), Sir Charles Little (1882-1973), and Admiral Stark (1880-1972), United States Navy, 1945, as well as post-war correspondence with Admiral Stark, Lord Louis Mountbatten (1900-   ), General Lord Ismay (1887-1965) and Professor Marder (1910-   ). There are also some notes on the attack on Oran, 1940, and on Operation Torch, 1942. (1ft; 30cm)

21 BLAKE, William Hans, *Captain*, 1832-1874

Blake entered the Navy as a cadet in 1846, was promoted to lieutenant in 1854 and to commander in 1860. After two years in the *Alecto* in South America, 1863 to 1865, he was on the Pacific Station in the *Mutine* in 1865, when Chile was at war with Spain. He then commanded the *Falcon*, 1866 to 1867, on the Australian Station. Blake was promoted to captain in 1867 and, as Captain of the *Druid*, was in command of the Naval Brigade during the Second Ashanti War, 1873 to 1874, when he died.

The papers were bequeathed to the Museum by Miss H. Blake, Captain Blake's daughter, in 1954. Apart from official service documents, they refer chiefly to the latter part of his career, there being letterbooks, 1863 to 1867; diaries, 1867, 1873 to 1874 and official letters and orders from the Admiralty and senior officers. There is also a letter, 1865, of appreciation from the British residents in Valparaiso. (6 vols, 2 files)

22 BLANE, Arthur Rodney, *Captain*, 1834-1891

Blane, a grandson of Sir Gilbert Blane (*q.v.*), entered the Navy in 1848. In the *Niger* he served in the Second Chinese War, 1857 to 1859, and on receiving his commission as lieutenant in 1858, transferred to the *Drake* as her commander. He retired from active service in 1866 and was promoted to captain on the retired list in 1881.

The papers were presented by Lady Royds in 1939. Apart from some commissions for his early service, they concern Blane's activities in China. There are charts of Canton, orders from the Admiralty and copies of contemporary newspapers. (2 files)

23   BLANE, *Sir* Gilbert, 1st Bt. (Physician of the Fleet), 1749–1834

Blane studied medicine in Edinburgh and, in 1779, sailed to the West Indies. It was during this and subsequent expeditions to the West Indies that he impressed upon the Admiralty the importance and the success of anti-scorbutic measures. He was appointed Physician Extraordinary to the Prince of Wales in 1785, the year in which he produced the first edition of his work on the diseases of seamen. From 1795 until 1803 he was one of the Commissioners for Sick and Wounded Seamen.

See Christopher Lloyd *ed.*, *The Health of Seamen* (Navy Records Society, 1965), pp. 132–211.

The papers were presented by Lady Royds in 1939. They consist of memorials, notes and letters from Tsar Paul of Russia (1754–1801), 1799, the Prince Regent, later King George IV (1762–1830), 1802, Prince William Henry (1765–1837), undated, Spencer Perceval (1762–1812), 1809, Lord Palmerston (1784–1865), 1810, Sir Edward Pellew (later Viscount Exmouth) (*q.v.*), 1799, Earl St Vincent (*q.v.*), 1800, Lord Keith (*q.v.*), 1808, and other public figures, kept largely for their autograph value. (2 files)

24   BOND, Francis Godolphin, *Rear-Admiral*, 1765–1839

Bond, whose mother, Catherine, was a half-sister of William (later Admiral) Bligh (1754–1817), entered the Navy as a captain's servant in 1774. In 1779 he was promoted to midshipman and in 1782 to lieutenant. On the recommendation of Bligh he was appointed First Lieutenant of the *Providence* in 1791 and accompanied him on the second breadfruit voyage, 1791 to 1795. He held various further appointments as lieutenant, was made a commander in 1800 and a captain in 1802. He was made a rear-admiral in the general promotion of 1837.

The documents have been used in George Mackaness *ed.*, *Fresh light on Bligh* (published privately, 1953).

The papers were purchased in 1958 through the Caird Fund
from Lieutenant-General Sir Leopold Bond. They consist
of forty letters from Bligh to Bond, twenty-eight of which
deal with the voyage of the *Providence*, three with the
mutiny on the *Bounty* and the remainder with Bligh's efforts
to promote Bond's career. There are also letters from
others in the *Providence* and some notes by Bond on the
voyage about Bligh. (4 files)

25 BOSANQUET, Henry Theodore Augustus, *Captain*, 1870-1959

Bosanquet entered the Navy in 1883 and served on the Cape of
Good Hope Station, 1885 to 1887, in the *Raleigh*, going out
in the *Wye* and returning in the *Himalaya*. Between 1888 and
1892 he served in the *Iron Duke*, *Active*, *Thames* and *Anson*,
all in home waters. He became a lieutenant in 1892. In the
Paluma he went to Australia and there joined the *Crescent*,
Katoomba and *Iphigenia*, returning to England in 1894. Because
of ill-health he retired as lieutenant in 1898. During the
two World Wars he worked at the Admiralty and was advanced
to captain on the retired list. He was Secretary of the
Marine Society, 1900 to 1914, was then on the Committee
between 1917 and 1948 and was also active in the Society for
Nautical Research.

The papers were presented by Captain Bosanquet between 1953
and 1958. These include seven volumes of personal papers
and newspaper cuttings, 1879 to 1955. Bosanquet's service
afloat is covered by logs and watchbills, 1883 to 1894.
Bosanquet's notes on historical and technical subjects are
elsewhere in the Museum manuscript collections. (3ft; 92cm)

26 BOUGAINVILLE, Louis Antoine de (Admiral, French Navy), 1729-
1811

Bougainville served in the French army in Canada, where he
was aide-de-camp to Montcalm (1712-1759). In 1763 he sailed
on a private enterprise to colonize the Falkland Islands with
French Canadian refugees but when France sold her interest in
the islands to Spain in 1766, he sailed to the South Seas and
in the next three years circumnavigated the world. He subsequently proposed undertaking a voyage towards the North
Pole but his scheme was dropped when the Duc de Choiseul (1719-
1785) was dismissed in 1770. In 1775 Bougainville was granted
naval rank and was second-in-command to de Grasse (1722-1788)

in the West Indies during the American War of Independence.
In 1791 he was offered the post of *Ministre de la Marine* but
refused it. He narrowly escaped the guillotine and he
later enjoyed the patronage of Napoleon. In 1796 he was
elected to the *Institut National*. He was also a member of
the *Bureau des Longitudes* and a Fellow of the Royal Society
of London.

See Jean Etienne Martin-Allanic, *Bougainville, navigateur et
les découvertes de son temps* (Paris, 1964).

The papers were purchased through the Caird Fund from the
sale of the Bougainville collection at Sotheby's in 1957.
They comprise a personal memoir on navigation between Europe
and Canada by an unknown seaman, a draft by Bougainville
concerning the Duc de Choiseul and the proposed voyage to
the North Pole and a collection of notes made during
Bougainville's completion of his "Essai historique sur les
navigations anciennes et modernes dans les hautes latitudes
septentrionales", *Mémoires de l'Institut National des Sciences
et Arts: Sciences morales et politiques*, Tome 3, An 9. (1 box)

27 BOYLES, *Sir* Charles, *Vice-Admiral*, 1756-1816

Boyles became a lieutenant in 1777 and a captain in 1790.
During the French wars he served in the West Indies, the
Channel and the Mediterranean. He became a rear-admiral in
1809 and from 1810 to 1812 served in the Mediterranean, in
the *Trident* and the *Canopus*. He became a vice-admiral in
1814.

The papers are part of the Hawker collection, purchased
through the Caird Fund from Sotheby's in 1955. They consist
of an out-letterbook, 1810 to 1811, and copies of letters
to the Sicilian court, 1811. (2 vols)

28 BRACKENBURY, John William, *Admiral*, 1842-1918

Brackenbury entered the Navy in 1857, served in the
Marlborough on the Mediterranean Station, 1862 to 1863, was
promoted to lieutenant in 1865, to commander in 1876 and in
1879 commanded the *Shah*'s naval brigade during the Zulu war.
He became a captain in 1881 and served in the *Thalia* during
the Egyptian campaign of 1882. From 1886 until 1887 he commanded
the *Hyacinth*, South American Station, and the *Turquoise*, East
Indies, from 1888 until 1891, during which time he took

part in the operations against the Sultan of Vitu. In 1893 he was captain of the *Edinburgh* and witnessed the collision of the *Victoria* and *Camperdown*. From 1894 to 1896 he was in charge of naval establishments at Bermuda. He was promoted to rear-admiral in 1896 and in 1898 served as second-in-command of the Channel Squadron in the *Magnificent*. Brackenbury received his commission as admiral in 1905. He married Frances Mary Francklyn in 1880.

The papers were presented in 1966 by Mrs Olive Story, Admiral Brackenbury's daughter. The bulk of the collection is a series of letters written by Brackenbury to his wife, 1870 to 1902. Other than these there are logs, 1862 to 1863, 1879; a diary, 1888; official service documents; official correspondence, 1879, 1881 to 1882, 1884, 1887 to 1892 and 1896; letters from other naval officers, 1879 to 1912, and papers relating to the Vitu operations and the *Victoria* and *Camperdown* disaster. (3ft; 91cm)

29 BRENT, Harry Woodfall, *Vice-Admiral*, 1834-1911

Brent entered the Navy as a cadet in 1848, was promoted to lieutenant in 1854 and to commander in 1866. Between 1867 and 1870 he served in the *Bellerophon* in the Channel and the Mediterranean. He was promoted to captain in 1875 and commanded the troopship *Himalaya* from 1879 to 1881, running between Great Britain and the Mediterranean. For a short period he was Director of the Royal Indian Marine but resigned and after further seagoing appointments retired in 1889. He was made a vice-admiral in 1896.

The papers were acquired from the Navy Records Society in the early days of the Museum. They consist of two volumes of official service documents, 1851 to 1887; an order book of the *Bellerophon*; a volume of correspondence relating to the *Himalaya* and a log of the *Monarch*, 1886, Channel Station, kept by Henry Dacres Menzie Brent. (5 vols)

30 BRIDGE, *Sir* Cyprian Arthur George, *Admiral*, 1839-1924

Bridge joined the Navy in 1851, was commissioned lieutenant in 1859 and from 1874 until 1877, when he was promoted to captain, served in the *Audacious* on the China Station. He went to Australia in command of the *Espiègle*, 1881 to 1885, and when he was promoted to rear-admiral in 1894 became Commander-in-Chief there. As a vice-admiral he was Commander-in-Chief of the China Station, 1901 to 1904, during which time the Anglo-Japanese treaty was signed. At the end of this commission he retired.

He published *Some Recollections* (London, 1918).

The papers were presented by Mr J.S.C. Bridge, Admiral Bridge's nephew, in 1932. They include a few watch bills and other papers relating to the *Audacious*, 1874 to 1877; out-letterbooks, 1881 to 1885 and 1898; private letters received, 1895 to 1898, 1901 to 1904, and admiral's journals, 1895 to 1898. (3ft; 91cm)

31 BROUGHTON, William Robert, *Captain*, 1762-1821

Broughton served as midshipman on the North American and East Indies Stations and was promoted to lieutenant in 1782. He was appointed in 1790 to command the *Chatham* to accompany George Vancouver (1758-1798) on his voyage of discovery and was for some time employed on the survey of the Columbia river on the west coast of North America. In 1793 he travelled overland from San Blas in the North Pacific to Vera Cruz on his way home with despatches. In October 1793, he was made Commander of the *Providence*, once again being sent to the north-west coast of America to rejoin Vancouver. On his arrival he found that Vancouver had left. He then decided to carry out a close survey of the Chinese and Japanese coasts, which took four years. After the *Providence* was wrecked off the coast of Formosa in May 1797, Broughton continued the survey until May 1798, when he returned to England. He was made a captain in 1797 and after further service in the East Indies ended his career in 1812.

The papers form part of the collection of naval manuscripts transferred from the Royal United Service Institution in 1968. They consist of logs mainly relating to the surveying voyage of 1795 to 1797 and his overland crossing of 1793. There is also a section covering the earlier surveying voyage of 1792. (1ft; 30cm)

32 BROWN, Francis Clifton, *Vice-Admiral*, 1874-1963

Brown entered the Navy in 1890 and served in the *Dreadnought* in the Mediterranean until 1893, when he joined the *Tourmaline* in the West Indies. He then joined the *Volage* in the Training Squadron and took part in the summer cruise of 1896. His next ship was the *Trafalgar*, Mediterranean and Channel

Stations, and between 1900 and 1902 he served in the *Argonaut* on the China Station. Brown was promoted to commander in 1905, to captain in 1912 and held a succession of cruiser appointments during the First World War. He then served as head of the naval mission to Greece between 1917 and 1919 and was made rear-admiral in the Royal Hellenic Navy in 1918. In 1922 he was promoted to rear-admiral, placed on the retired list and in 1927 was advanced to vice-admiral.

The papers were presented by Mrs Clifton Brown in 1963. They consist of a continuous run of logs, 1890 to 1900, diaries, 1890 to 1902, notebooks and loose papers, including some relating to his period as naval attaché in Greece. There are also some comprehensive photograph albums, 1890 to 1911. There are no papers for Brown's First World War service. (3ft; 91cm)

33 BROWN, *Sir* Harold Arthur, *Vice-Admiral*, 1878-1968

Brown entered the Navy in 1894 as an engineer student at Devonport Dockyard, qualifying in 1899 as a Probationary Assistant Engineer. He became an engineer lieutenant in 1900, engineer lieutenant-commander in 1912, engineer commander in 1917 and engineer captain in 1924. Between 1921 and 1925 he was Assistant Naval Attaché in Washington. In 1930 he became engineer rear-admiral and in 1932 was appointed vice-admiral and Engineer-in-Chief of the Fleet, until his retirement in 1936.

The papers were presented in 1969 by his daughter, Mrs Ann Arnold-Foster, and consist of certificates, 1899 to 1929, appointments, 1894 to 1932, and letters, including those from the Foreign Office and British Embassy (Washington) in appreciation of his service, 1925, and those from Vice-Admiral Dalton (1904-   ) about substituting 'Chief Naval Engineer Officer' as a title for the former 'Engineer-in-Chief of the Fleet', 1959. (1 file)

34 BURT, Turner Warner (Mate, Indian Navy), 1839-*ca*.1920

Burt entered the Indian Navy as a volunteer in 1855 and was appointed midshipman in the following year. He served in the *Assaye, Constance, Clive, Georgiana, Auckland, Lady Canning, Ajdaha* and *Falkland* between 1856 and 1861. He was promoted to mate in 1861, but in 1862 the service disbanded. He died in New Zealand.

The papers are part of the collection of naval manuscripts transferred from the Royal United Service Institution in 1968. They consist of midshipman's logs, 1856 to 1861. (5 vols)

35 BURTON, Alfred, *Captain* (Royal Marines), 1787-1840

Burton was commissioned as first lieutenant in the Royal Marines in 1806. From 1811 to 1812 he served in the *Rota* in the Channel. He was promoted to captain in 1827 and served in the Mediterranean in the *Alfred*, 1831 to 1834.

The papers were purchased for the Museum in 1957 by Sir Eric Miller from a dealer, Edward Hall of Gravesend. They consist of letters, 1811 to 1812, 1831 to 1834, including a series of twenty-nine to his mother for the latter period. (2 files)

36 BURTON, Cuthbert Ward, *Major-General* (Royal Marines), 1832-1890

Son of Captain Alfred Burton (*q.v.*), Burton was commissioned as first lieutenant in 1853. He served in the *Winchester* and *Calcutta* from 1853 to 1858 and took part in the Second China War. In 1858 he was temporarily attached to the Canton Constabulary. On his return home he was stationed at Plymouth, 1859 to 1860. Burton was promoted to captain in 1861 and to major in 1862. He served in the *Phoebe* in the Mediterranean from 1862 to 1865 and was in the marine battalion in Japan attached to the *Iron Duke*, flagship on the China Station, 1870 to 1873. He retired in 1884 with the rank of Major-General.

The papers were purchased for the Museum in 1957 by Sir Eric Miller from a dealer, Edward Hall of Gravesend. They consist of two series of letters. The first is of eighty-four letters written by Burton to his mother during his service on the China Station, 1853 to 1858, and the second is to his family, 1859 to 1860, 1862 to 1865 and 1871 to 1873. (3 files)

37 CALDWELL, *Sir* Benjamin, *Admiral*, 1737-1830

Caldwell entered the Navy in 1754 and was made a lieutenant
in 1760. After service in the Channel during the Seven Years
War, he became a commander in 1762 and a post captain in 1765.
He then commanded the *Rose* in North America, 1768 to 1771,
and the *Emerald*, 1775 to 1779, on that station and on convoy
duties. He was appointed in 1780 to the *Hannibal* and convoyed
the East India Company ships home. In April 1781 he was
transferred to the *Agamemnon* in the Channel; she then sailed
with Admiral Rodney (1719-1792) to the West Indies and was
present at the battle of the Saints, 1782. The *Agamemnon*
remained on the West Indies and North American Stations until
1783. Caldwell commanded the *Alcide* in 1787 and the *Berwick*
during the mobilization of 1790. In 1793 he was promoted to
rear-admiral and served in the *Cumberland* under Admiral Howe
(*q.v.*). He transferred his flag in 1794 to the *Impregnable*
and took part in the battle of First of June. In July of the
same year he became a vice-admiral and was sent to the Leeward
Islands in the *Majestic* under Admiral Jervis (*q.v.*); shortly
after this Jervis returned home and Caldwell acted as Commander-
in-Chief. His active career ended in 1795 and he was promoted
to admiral in 1799.

The papers were presented in two sections. The first, by Mrs
C.B.H. Caldwell in 1938, was given together with the papers
of Admiral Henry Osborn (*q.v.*). A further collection was
presented by Mrs Joan Cooper in 1969, together with the papers
of Captain Henry Caldwell (*q.v.*). Mrs Cooper's husband,
Captain Derek Cooper, was a great-great-grandson of Admiral
Caldwell. The papers in the first collection consist of logs,
1768 to 1771, 1775 to 1777, 1780 to 1782, 1794 to 1795;
letterbooks, 1776 to 1782, 1788, 1793 to 1795, and order
books 1775 to 1783, 1788, 1794 to 1795. There is an account
of the battle of the Saints. The second collection includes
in-letters, 1775 to 1779, 1794 to 1795; a prize book, 1777 to
1795; documents relating to the *Agamemnon*; Lord Howe's signals,
1790; letters relating to the disagreements after the battle
of First of June, and a personal signed copy of Rodney's
defence of his conduct at St. Eustatius, 1781. (2ft; 61cm)

38 CALDWELL, Henry, *Captain*, 1815-1868

Caldwell, grandson of Sir Benjamin Caldwell (*q.v.*), entered
the Navy in 1828 as a volunteer on board the *Dartmouth* and
became a midshipman in the *Prince Regent* in 1830. He served
for the next five years on the coast of South America in the

Clio, *Spartiate* and *Hornet* and then in the *Pembroke* and
Vanguard on the Mediterranean Station. After this he spent
three years in the brigs *Pantaloon* and *Rapid*, tenders to the
Royal George yacht. Caldwell was promoted to lieutenant in
1841 and for two years attended courses in the *Excellent* on
gunnery and at the Royal Naval College on steam. He then
served in the *Inconstant* on the Mediterranean Station from
1843 until 1846, when he joined the *Excellent* and *Prince
Regent*, home waters. From the latter ship he was promoted
to commander in 1847. In 1848 he joined the *Powerful* on the
Mediterranean Station and returned to the *Prince Regent* in
1851. He was promoted to captain in 1853 and after studying
steam at Woolwich dockyard, became Flag Captain to Rear-
Admiral Hon. R.S. Dundas (1802-1861), Commander-in-Chief
Baltic, in the *Duke of Wellington*, and remained in her until
1857. Caldwell joined the *Mersey* in 1859 for three years,
serving in the Channel and on the North American and West
Indies Station. After a short period in the *Royal Adelaide*
at Devonport, he joined, in 1864, the *Asia*, guardship of the
steam reserve at Portsmouth. Finally Caldwell was aide-de-
camp to Queen Victoria from 1866 until his death.

The papers were presented in 1969 by Mrs Joan Cooper. Captain
Derek Cooper, Mrs Cooper's husband, was the great-grandson of
Henry Caldwell. There is one letter to Mary Caldwell, Henry's
sister, written in 1865. Other than this the papers include
watch bills 1848 to 1851, 1856; a night order book, 1859 to
1862; printed papers; exercise books for the period at the
Royal Naval College and remark books and notes relating to
his various ships. (1½ft; 46cm)

39 CAREW, *Sir* Benjamin Hallowell, *Admiral*, 1760-1834

This officer, known throughout his naval career as Hallowell,
took the additional name of Carew in 1828. In 1783 he was
a lieutenant, becoming a commander in 1790. He served off
Africa and was in the Mediterranean as one of Nelson's 'Band
of Brothers'. In 1812 he hoisted his flag in the *Malta*,
again in the Mediterranean, where he remained until the peace.
He was Commander-in-Chief on the coast of Ireland, 1816 to
1818, and at the Nore, 1821 to 1824. Attaining the rank of
vice-admiral in 1819, he was advanced to admiral in 1830.

The papers were acquired in several parts. Some loose papers,
which came to the Museum in 1934, are of unknown provenance,
while Sir James Caird presented a signal book in 1933. A
further collection of papers was purchased at Sotheby's in
1973. Almost all the papers cover the period 1812 to 1814

and include letters, mainly received by Hallowell, and his
out-letter drafts. There are a number of documents relating
to the Peninsular War, in particular to the siege of
Tarragona, 1813, and also a small collection of letters from
Sir Edward Codrington (*q.v.*), 1827 to 1828. (5 files)

40 CARTERET, Philip, *Rear-Admiral*, *ca.*1733-1796

When he entered the Navy, in 1747, Carteret joined the
Salisbury and then served from 1751 to 1755 under Captain
John Byron (1723-1786). Between 1757 and 1758 he was in the
Guernsey on the Mediterranean Station. As a lieutenant in
the *Dolphin* he accompanied Byron during his voyage of circumnavigation, 1764 to 1766. On his return Carteret was
commissioned for another exploratory voyage, this time
commanding the *Swallow*, which expedition was led by Captain
Samuel Wallis (1728-1795) in the *Dolphin*. The ships separated
early in the voyage and Carteret made many independent
discoveries. When he returned home he was on half-pay for
a time and joined the movement pressing for an increase in
the half-pay allowance. In 1779, Carteret was appointed to
the *Endymion* and after a few months in the Channel went to
the west coast of Africa before sailing for the West Indies
to join Admiral Rodney's (1719-1792) fleet. He returned to
England in 1781, had no further employment and was made
rear-admiral in 1794.

The papers were purchased from Maggs Bros. in 1933. They
include logs of the *Guernsey* and *Endymion*; a letterbook,
1779 to 1780, and a large number of loose papers including
letters from Byron and others and various notes on his ships
and voyages. The *Endymion* is the only ship for which there
is much material, there being but few notes about his voyages
of circumnavigation. His private journals for the years 1779
to 1789 cover the period in considerable detail and there
are many letters relating to the movement for the increase
in half-pay. The collection includes letters from Carteret's
son, Samuel, to his mother, 1794 to 1796, some written from
the *Expedition* at Plymouth, and the remainder from the
Mediterranean and the West Indies. There are also letters
from his other son, Philip (later Silvester, *q.v.*), relating
to his voyage in the *Lion* with Lord Macartney's Embassy to
China, 1794 to 1796. (1ft; 30cm)

41　CHAMBERS, William Wylly, *Captain*, *ca.*1810-1860

Chambers entered the Navy in 1823 and served in the West
Indies from 1824 until 1829, the year in which he became a
lieutenant.　He went again to the West Indies in 1833 when
he was appointed First Lieutenant of the *Racer* and in 1836
was given charge of the Portuguese prize brigantine *Vigilanti*.
In 1837 he transferred to the *Wellesley*, flagship in the
East Indies, and in 1840 was acting captain firstly of the
Alligator, then of the *Pelorus* which was stationed at Port
Essington, Australia.　When the *Pelorus* was sold at Singapore
in 1841, Chambers returned to the *Wellesley* as her First
Lieutenant and took part in the latter stages of the First
China War, 1839 to 1842.　For this service he was promoted
to commander and became captain in 1846.

The papers were deposited on loan in 1963 by Messrs Harward
and Evers, Solicitors, through Mr H.J. Haden.　They include
official service documents, 1826 to 1843; logs, 1836, 1839
to 1841; letterbooks, 1836, 1840 to 1841; order books, 1827
to 1837; books of expenses for various stores and other
ship's papers, mainly for the *Pelorus*.　(1½ft; 46cm)

42　CHATFIELD, Alfred Ernle Montacute, *Admiral of the Fleet,
1st Baron Chatfield*, 1873-1967

Chatfield entered the Navy in 1886, was promoted to lieutenant
in 1894 and to captain in 1909.　He was captain of the
Medina during the Royal Tour of King George V and Queen Mary
to India, 1911 to 1912, and later Flag-Captain to Admiral
Beatty (1871-1936), 1913 to 1919, combining this duty with
responsibility for fleet gunnery in the *Queen Elizabeth*, 1917
to 1919.　He was a delegate to the Washington Naval Conference
of 1920, becoming a rear-admiral in that year and he subsequently held a variety of Admiralty and sea-going
appointments.　He was promoted to vice-admiral in 1926.　In
1929 he was Commander-in-Chief of the Atlantic Fleet and of
the Mediterranean Fleet from 1930 to 1932.　He was First Sea
Lord, 1933 to 1938, became Admiral of the Fleet in 1935 and
was made a baron in 1937.　He was appointed Minister of Co-
ordination of Defence, with a seat in the War Cabinet, by
Neville Chamberlain in 1939, after serving as chairman of a
committee which reported on the defence of India.　In April
1940 he resigned as he felt the post was rendered redundant.
During the rest of the war he was appointed to various civil
defence committees.

He wrote two autobiographical works: *The navy and defence* (London, 1942) and *It might happen again* (London, 1947).

The papers were presented in 1973 by the family. They consist mainly of semi-official and private letters, 1932 to 1940, from Churchill (1874-1965), Lord Lothian (1882-1940), Admirals Sir Roger Backhouse (1878-1939), Sir Frederic Dreyer (1878-1956), Sir W.W. Fisher (*q.v.*), Lord Beatty (1871-1936), Sir John Kelly (*q.v.*), Sir (William) Howard Kelly (*q.v.*), Sir Charles Little (1882-1973), Sir Eric Fullerton (*q.v.*), Sir Dudley Pound (1877-1943) and other commanders-in-chief. The topics referred to in this correspondence include the battle of Jutland, 1916, the Invergordon Mutiny, 1931, the Naval Disarmament Conference, 1935, the Abyssinia crisis, 1935, the Spanish Civil War, 1936, the problems of defence and rearmament during the 1930s, international relations and control of the Fleet Air Arm. There are also photograph albums relating to the Royal Tour of India, the Mediterranean Command and the India Mission. (4½ft; 122cm)

43 CHATFIELD, Henry (Master Shipwright), *fl.*1820-1860

Chatfield attended the School of Naval Architecture at Portsmouth. He was Assistant Master Shipwright at Deptford, 1848 to 1853, and Master Shipwright between 1853 and 1860. He was a member of the Dockyard Committee of Enquiry, which concluded its report in 1861 and to which he attached a minority report.

The papers, deposited on loan by Captain A.B. Sainsbury in 1965, include notes on ordnance and shipbuilding and on the sailing trials between the *St. Vincent* and the *Queen*, 1844. There are two letters relating to the Dockyard Committee of Enquiry, 1858 to 1859, and a copy of Chatfield's dissension from its Report. There are also printed copies of Parliamentary Reports relating to the dockyards, 1805 and 1860, and a pamphlet written by Chatfield in 1834, *An elementary essay on the principles of masting ships*. (2 boxes)

44 CHILDERS, William Henry, *Lieutenant*, 1837-1869

Childers, first cousin of Hugh Childers (1827-1896), the politician, entered the Navy as a cadet in 1850 on board the *Queen*. From 1852 he was in the *Britannia* at the Crimea until late 1854, being present at the battles of Alma and Sebastopol. He then joined the *Tribune*, Mediterranean Station, and was in her in 1857 at the beginning of the Second China War, when she went to the Canton River, before crossing the Pacific to British Columbia in 1859. In 1860 he became a lieutenant and served in the *Victorious* and *Firebrand*, both in the Channel Fleet. Between 1861 and 1863 Childers went round the world in the *Charybdis*. After a gunnery course and a short period in the *Canopus* in 1867, he was appointed Transports Officer for the Abyssinian expedition in the *Black Prince*. His final appointment was the command of the *Flirt* in the North Sea, 1868 to 1869.

The papers were presented to the Museum in 1959 by Childers's granddaughter, Mrs L.L. Ogier. They consist mainly of family letters describing his experiences, 1850 to 1869, written to his parents in Jersey and their replies. There is a diary, 1867 to 1868, an out-letterbook, 1868 to 1869, and official service documents, 1852 to 1869. (1ft; 30cm)

45 CLARKE, *Reverend* Thomas Brooke (Auditor, Naval Asylum), *fl.* 1800-1821

Clarke, a graduate of Trinity College, Dublin, held livings in Ireland in which he was non-resident. He was a confidant of Nicholas Vansittart, Lord Bexley (1766-1851), and tutor to the Duke of Cumberland's illegitimate son, George Fitzernest. Clarke was appointed Auditor of the Naval Asylum at Greenwich, which position he held from 1805 to 1821. His appointment and those of the Secretary and Chaplain were later criticized by Sir Charles Pole (*q.v.*) in the House of Commons on the grounds that none of them had ever had any sea service.

The papers, sixty-six letters, were purchased in 1959 through the Caird Fund from a dealer, Edward Hall of Gravesend. They refer to Dr Clarke's appointment, to the renting of a house in Greenwich, the building of an asylum house, to glebe land of Pinner and produce of Harrow. There are also a series of letters from his son at Trinity Hall, Cambridge, 1812 to 1814, and some from George Fitzernest while at Magdalen College, Oxford. (1 box)

46 CLEMENTS, Michael, *Rear-Admiral*, *ca.*1735-*ca.*1796

Between 1748 and 1749 Clements served in the East Indies in the *Syren*. He was in the *Unicorn* firstly in the Mediterranean and

later in the Western Squadron, from 1755, when he became a
lieutenant, until 1757, when he was promoted to captain and
given command of the *London* buss. In 1758 he was posted into
the *Actaeon* in home waters and from 1759 to 1763 he commanded
the *Pallas* , at first under Admiral Hawke (*q.v.*) in the
Channel and later in the Mediterranean. He was at Portsmouth
in the *Dorsetshire* in 1770 and in the Channel in the *Vengeance*
in 1778. He became a rear-admiral in 1790.

The papers were presented by Mrs Hopton in 1942, via the Art
Gallery, Hereford. They consist of logs, 1748 to 1771, letter
and order books, 1757 to 1771, sailing and fighting instructions,
1747 to 1778, and notes and personal papers, 1759 to 1780.
There are also some of Clements's charts in the Department of
Navigation and Astronomy. (2ft; 62cm)

47 COCHRANE, Archibald, *Rear-Admiral*, 1874-1952

Cochrane entered the Navy in 1888 and first went to sea in
the *Bellerophon* in 1890, going to North America and the West
Indies. He then joined the Channel Squadron in the *Royal
Sovereign*, 1892 to 1893, and went out again to the West Indies
in the *Volage* until 1894. Later he served in the Mediterranean
and the Home Fleet and was on the China Station when war broke
out in 1914. In 1918 he was promoted to captain and retired
with the rank of rear-admiral in 1929.

The papers were presented to the Museum by Mrs Cochrane in
1952, together with the Owen papers, and consist of two
midshipman's logs, 1890 to 1894. (2 vols)

48 COCKBURN, *Sir* George, 10th Bt., *Admiral of the Fleet*, 1772-
1853

Cockburn went to sea in 1786, became a lieutenant in 1793 and
then served in the Mediterranean under Lord Hood (*q.v.*) and
Nelson (*q.v.*). He was promoted to captain in 1794. In 1796 he
commanded the *Minerve* and was sent to relieve the garrison at
Elba; he continued in the Mediterranean until 1802. His next
command was of the *Phaeton* in which he went to North America
and India. He returned to England in the *Howe* in 1805.
Afterwards he served in the *Captain*, *Aboukir* and *Pompée*,
playing a major part in the reduction of Martinique, 1809, and
then returning to England in the *Belleisle*. At the taking of
Flushing, 1809, he was in the *Plover* and commanded a flotilla
as the army retreated from the Scheldt. Then he resumed

his command of the *Belleisle*. In 1810 Cockburn was active off
the coasts of France and Spain in the *Implacable* and was later
appointed a commissioner in what resulted in an attempt
to mediate between Spain and her South American colonies. He
was promoted to rear-admiral in 1812 and hoisted his flag in
the *Marlborough*; in her he was sent to North America, 1813,
where he was engaged in the destruction of shipping and the
harrying of the settlements of the south and middle states and
also took part in the burning of Washington. When the peace
was concluded he returned to England. After the battle of
Waterloo, 1815, Cockburn conveyed Napoleon to St. Helena in
the *Northumberland* and stayed there as Governor and Commander-
in-Chief of the Cape Station until 1816. He was made vice-
admiral in 1819, admiral in 1827 and Admiral of the Fleet in
1851. He also held the posts of junior Lord of the Admiralty,
1818 to 1830, 1834 to 1835, and First Naval Lord, 1841 to
1846. He was a Member of Parliament for various constituencies,
1818 to 1828 and 1841 to 1847.

The papers were presented by Mr Travers Buxton in 1941. They
relate largely to Napoleon's transportation and imprisonment
in St. Helena and there is also a very detailed personal diary,
1797 to 1818. There are no papers for his later career.
(4 files)

49   CODRINGTON, *Sir* Edward, *Admiral*, 1770-1851

Codrington entered the Navy in 1783 and served in the *Leander*,
Ambuscade and *Formidable* in North America and the Mediterranean
until 1791. In 1794 he was Earl Howe's (*q.v.*) Flag Lieutenant
in the *Queen Charlotte* and subsequently commanded the fireship
Comet and the sloop *La Babet* in home waters. In 1796 he was
appointed captain of the *Druid*, again in home waters, but was
unemployed from 1797 until 1805. In this year he commissioned
the *Orion* and was present at Trafalgar. From 1807 he commanded
the *Blake* for six years in the Mediterranean, during the
Walcheren expedition, 1809, and off the coast of Spain. He
was then appointed to the *Tonnant*, going to the North American
Station where he organized the supplies of the army at the
capture of Washington. He was promoted to rear-admiral in
1814, remaining on the station until 1815. It was not until
1826 that he again saw active service when he was appointed
Commander-in-Chief, Mediterranean, flying his flag aboard the
Asia, and during this command he undertook operations against
the pirates in the Levant. He subsequently took a leading part
in the interpretation of allied policy in the Greek War of
Independence. These operations culminated in the Battle of
Navarino, 1827; this secured Codrington's fame while it also

ensured his recall in 1828. After a short period of unemployment, he was appointed to command the Channel Squadron in 1831.
He then became Member of Parliament for Devonport, 1832 to 1839,
when he was appointed Commander-in-Chief, Portsmouth, a post
he held until 1842.

The papers have been used by Lady Bourchier, Codrington's
daughter, in *Memoir of the life of Admiral Sir Edward
Codrington*... (London, 1873, 2 vols) and in C.G. Pitcairn Jones,
ed., *Piracy in the Levant* (Navy Records Society, 1934).

The papers were presented by Colonel G. Codrington between 1946
and 1950. They include logs, 1786 to 1791, 1794 to 1797, 1808
to 1813 and 1827 to 1828; an admiral's journal, 1831; official
letter and order books, 1809 to 1815 and 1828 to 1848; private
letterbooks, 1828 to 1848; muster books, 1808 to 1813; despatches
and reports, 1801 to 1815, 1827 to 1828, and loose papers.
Among these are letters to Codrington from the Duke of Clarence
(later King William IV), Sir Pulteney Malcolm (*q.v.*), ministers,
consuls, Greek government officials and various captains of the
ships under Codrington's command, 1827 to 1828, and from Sir
James Graham (1792-1861), in 1831. A small collection of
additional material relating to Nelson and Codrington was deposited
on loan by the family in 1974. (12ft; 366cm)

50   CODRINGTON, *Sir* Henry John, *Admiral of the Fleet*, 1808-1877

Codrington, third son of Sir Edward Codrington (*q.v.*), joined
the Navy in 1823 and spent the early years of his service in
the Mediterranean, being Signal Midshipman in his father's
flagship, *Asia*, at the battle of Navarino, 1827, where he was
severely wounded. He was made a lieutenant in 1829 and
commander in 1831. His first command was the *Orestes*,
Mediterranean Station, 1834 to 1836. As Captain of the
Talbot he took a leading part in the operations culminating
in the siege of Acre, in 1840. In 1846 he was again sent to
the Mediterranean in the *Thetis* where the circumstances
leading to the revolutions of 1848 involved him in various
diplomatic missions. At the outbreak of the Crimean War,
1854, Codrington was in the Baltic in the *Royal George*,
moving to the *Algiers* after the war. He became a rear-
admiral in 1857 and was Admiral Superintendent of Malta
Dockyard, 1858 to 1863. He was Commander-in-Chief at Plymouth,
1869 to 1872, but never hoisted his flag afloat. He was made
Admiral of the Fleet in the year of his death.

The papers have been used by Lady Bourchier, Codrington's
sister, in *Selections from the letters, private and professional,*

of Sir Henry Codrington, Admiral of the Fleet (London, 1880).

The papers were presented by Colonel G. Codrington between
1946 and 1950. They include logs, 1825 to 1831, 1834 to 1835,
1839 to 1841, 1846 to 1850 and 1854 to 1856; letter and order
books, 1834 to 1850, 1853 to 1856, 1858 to 1872, and loose
papers, among which are personal letters from Codrington to
his family, 1831 to 1855. (6ft; 183cm)

51 COLES, Cowper Phipps, *Captain*, 1819-1870

Coles entered the Navy in 1838 and was promoted to lieutenant
in 1846. He served in the Mediterranean and was made a
commander in 1854 and a captain in 1856. His experiences in
the Crimean War led him to experiment with defensive armour
and turrets for ships, which he developed often at his own
expense. The *Captain*, launched in 1869, was built to Coles's
design against the view of the Surveyor of the Navy. She
capsized off the coast of Spain with Coles on board in 1870.

The papers were presented by Mrs Sherard Cowper-Coles in 1936.
They consist of three large albums of newspaper cuttings which
relate to the Navy and to ship design and were collected by
Coles himself between 1862 and his death. There are a number
of later cuttings to 1878. (3 vols)

52 COLLINGWOOD, Cuthbert, *Vice-Admiral, 1st Baron Collingwood*,
1750-1810

Collingwood entered the Navy in 1760 and was promoted to
lieutenant in 1775. After serving in the Mediterranean
and in American waters, he spent most of the American War in
the West Indies, becoming a captain in 1780. He did not
return to England until 1786. It was during this period
that he became a firm friend of Nelson. From 1793 to 1795 he
commanded the *Prince* and took part in the battle of the
First of June 1794. He was then in the *Excellent*, 1795 to
1798, Mediterranean Fleet, distinguishing himself at the
battle of St. Vincent in 1797. Between 1799, when he
became rear-admiral, and 1802 he was in the Channel
in the *Triumph* and the *Barfleur*, returning there on the
renewal of the war in 1803. After Trafalgar, 1805, when
he was second-in-command to Nelson (*q.v.*), he succeeded to
the command of the Mediterranean Fleet, which appointment
he held until his death.

Among a number of biographes there are G.L. Newham Collingwood, *A selection from the private correspondence of Vice-Admiral Lord Collingwood* (London, 1828) and Oliver Warner, *The life and letters of Vice-Admiral Lord Collingwood* (London, 1968). The papers have been used in Edward Hughes *ed.*, *The private correspondence of Admiral Lord Collingwood* (Navy Records Society, 1957).

The papers were purchased in the main by Sir James Caird from Sotheby's in 1935. Two letterbooks, however, which contain private letters received between 1793 and 1809, were presented in 1928 by Mr C.H.B. Caldwell. The rest of the collection is composed of official letterbooks. There is one for the *Prince* and one for the *Excellent*; ten others form part of the records for the Mediterranean command. Several, however, are clearly missing. There is an admiral's journal, 1801 to 1804, and another for the latter part of the Mediterranean command. A secret letterbook, kept between 1805 and 1808, has been very recently acquired from the Library, California State University, Hayward. There are no papers for Collingwood's early life. ($2\frac{1}{2}$ft; 76cm)

53 COLLINSON, *Sir* Richard, *Admiral*, 1811-1883

Collinson entered the Navy in 1823. From 1831 to 1833 he served in the survey ship *Aetna* off the west coast of Africa and in the Mediterranean. He was commissioned as lieutenant in 1835 and in September of that year was appointed to the *Sulphur*, surveying vessel, Pacific, under Captains Frederick Beechey (1796-1856) and Edward Belcher (*q.v.*). He was promoted to commander in 1841 and the following year was appointed to the *Plover*, surveying vessel, in which he made the first survey of the China coast. He remained in the *Plover* until 1846, having been promoted to captain in 1842. Collinson is known chiefly for his voyage of 1850 to 1855 in the *Enterprise*, during which he spent three years exploring the Arctic beyond Point Barrow in a fruitless search for Sir John Franklin (*q.v.*) and his ships the *Erebus* and *Terror*. It was, however, his second-in-command, Robert McClure (*q.v.*), who went ahead in the *Investigator*, who, while equally unsuccessful in the Franklin search, achieved the transit of the North West Passage, the goal of British Arctic exploration since Elizabethan times; though losing his ship in the process, he received the major share of public acclaim. Collinson was annoyed that his work had not received more attention and that he was not given any official reward. He never again applied for employment under the Admiralty, although he attained his flag in 1862, became vice-admiral in

1869 and an admiral on the retired list in 1875. He was an
Elder Brother and Deputy Master of Trinity House, 1862 to
1883, and an active member of the Royal Geographical Society.

The papers were purchased from Maggs Bros. in 1965. There are
private journals for 1836, 1850 to 1855, logs, 1843 to 1846, a
remark book, 1850 to 1851, and letterbooks, 1845 to 1846 and
1850 to 1854. There is a large amount of material relating
to Collinson's survey work, in particular to China and to the
voyage of the *Enterprise*. It includes numerous records of
observations and calculations on navigation, magnetic
variation, meteorology and tides. There is also a large
body of official, semi-official and private correspondence,
1835 to 1855, together with copies of some letters and
memoranda by Collinson. His correspondents included Sir
Francis Beaufort (1774-1857), Hydrographer to the Admiralty,
Peter la Trobe (1795-1863), Horatio T. Austin (*ca.* 1800-
1865) and John Barrow the younger (1808-1898). The only
items relating to his later career are notebooks on his work
for Trinity House and printed papers, mainly official
publications. (6½ft; 197cm)

54 COPE-CORNFORD, Leslie (journalist), 1867-1927

Cope-Cornford was an architect who turned to writing. His
contributions to the *National Observer* attracted the attention
of Rudyard Kipling (1865-1936), who was to remain a lifelong
friend. In 1905 he went to Berlin to gather material on
the Imperial German Navy. He became naval correspondent and
leader writer of the old *Standard* and, on its demise, joined
the staff of *The Morning Post* as naval correspondent,
becoming second leader writer in 1915. He was a critic of
Admiral Fisher's (1841-1920) policies. He wrote many
articles for *Punch*, edited the *Memoirs of Admiral Lord
Beresford by himself* (London, 1914) and wrote a number of
books on naval and maritime subjects.

The papers were acquired from Mrs Cope-Cornford in 1932.
They consist of letters, 1902 to 1927, received by Cope-
Cornford from Rudyard Kipling and others, thanking him
for copies of his books, discussing the politics of the
day and personal matters. The correspondence with Professor
Sir Geoffrey Callender (1875-1946), refers to a scheme to
establish a national maritime museum and there are many
letters from Callender to Mrs Cope-Cornford, 1928 to 1938.
(1½ft; 46cm)

55 CORNWALLIS, *The Hon. Sir* William, *Admiral*, 1744-1819

Cornwallis entered the Navy in 1755 and served in the
Newark in North America and the *Dunkirk* in the Channel,
1759 to 1760. He became a lieutenant in 1761 and a
commander in 1762, the year he took the *Swift* to the West
Indies where he remained until 1765, when he was promoted
to captain. His next ship was the *Guadeloupe*, Mediterranean,
to which he was appointed in 1768, going in her to
Newfoundland in 1769 and thence to the West Indies until
1773. From 1774 to 1776 he went on two commissions to West
Africa and Jamaica in the *Pallas*. Between 1777 and 1778
he commanded the *Isis* in North America and in 1779 was
appointed to the *Lion*, remaining in her until 1781, in the
West Indies. He was present at the battle of Grenada, 1779,
and was at both the battles of St. Kitts, 1782, and the
Saints, 1782, in the *Canada*. In 1788 he became Commander-
in-Chief, East Indies, in the *Crown* and towards the end of
his command reduced Pondicherry. He was promoted to rear-
admiral in 1793 and to vice-admiral in 1794, when he was
appointed to the *Excellent* in the Channel, from which he
moved quickly to the *Caesar* and then to the *Royal Sovereign*.
In 1796 he commanded an expedition to the West Indies but
after a collision Cornwallis turned back: he was court-
martialled but acquitted. In 1799 he was made an admiral
and in 1801 succeeded Earl St. Vincent (*q.v.*) to the command
of the Channel Fleet. With the exception of the period of
peace he maintained the blockade of Brest in the *Ville de
Paris* until he was superseded by St. Vincent in 1806. He
saw no further active service. Cornwallis was Member of
Parliament for Eye in Suffolk from 1768 to 1774, 1782 to
1784 and 1790 to 1807 and for Portsmouth from 1784 to 1790.

The papers were used by John Leyland *ed.*, *Dispatches and
letters relating to the blockade of Brest* (Navy Records
Society, 1898, 1901). There is a biography by G.
Cornwallis-West, *The life and letters of Admiral Cornwallis*
(London, 1927).

The papers were purchased in three sections in 1932, 1934
and 1948. The first two sections were acquired from the
Wykeham-Martin family and these have been examined by the
Historical Manuscripts Commission (*Various Collections*,
vol. VI, 1909, pp. 297-434). The greater part of the
present collection was purchased at the Harmsworth sale
at Sotheby's in 1948 and includes logs, 1759 to 1760, 1789
and 1792 to 1793; admiral's journals, 1794 to 1796 and 1801
to 1806; letterbooks, 1768 to 1771, 1777, 1788 to 1794 and
1795 to 1815; order books, 1789 to 1791 and 1801 to 1806
and a purser's wine book, 1789 to 1795. The loose papers
are mainly letters from the family, 1761 to 1779, 1790 to

1799 and 1800 to 1818 and there are some from Nelson (*q.v.*),
1788 and 1803, Lord Hood (*q.v.*), 1790 to 1791 and other
naval officers, 1770 to 1818.   (7ft; 213cm)

56   COWAN, *Sir* Walter Henry, 1st Bt., *Admiral*, 1871-1956

Cowan entered the *Britannia* as a naval cadet in 1884. He
was promoted to lieutenant in 1892 and commanded the *Redbreast*
between 1893 and 1895 in the Red Sea. In 1895 he was
appointed to the *Barrosa*, Cape Station. He saw active service
during the Brass River and Benin expeditions in 1897 and in
1898 commanded the gunboat flotilla on the Nile during the
operations in the Sudan. Cowan was promoted to commander in
1901 and to captain in 1906. After almost two years in the
post of Assistant to the Admiral of Patrols, Cowan was sent
in 1914 to the *Zealandia*, Grand Fleet. He joined the
Princess Royal in 1915 and in her was present at Jutland,
1916. He was appointed Commodore commanding the First Light
Cruiser Squadron, Grand Fleet, in 1917 and reappointed after
his promotion to rear-admiral in 1918. He continued to
command it as well as the naval force in the Baltic during
the anti-Bolshevik operations in 1920, for which he became
well-known. In 1921 he took command of the Baltic Cruiser
Squadron. After a year as Commanding Officer on the coast
of Scotland, Cowan became, in 1926, Commander-in-Chief,
North America and West Indies, and it was during his two
years there that his Station was extended to include South
America. Cowan was promoted to admiral in 1927, was
appointed First and Principal Aide-de-Camp to the King in
1929 and retired in 1930. At the age of sixty-eight, he
persuaded the Admiralty to employ him for the duration of
the war in the rank of commander. He served as liaison
officer with a commando brigade in the eastern Mediterranean
during 1941 and was then attached to an Indian regiment in
the Western Desert. He was captured at Bir Hakeim in 1942
and repatriated the following year. After further active
service he retired in 1945.

See Lionel Dawson, *Sound of the guns* (Oxford, 1949) and
Geoffrey Bennett, *Cowan's war* (London, 1964).

The papers were presented by Admiral Cowan's daughter, Miss
M.C.B. Cowan, in 1956 and 1962. The collection contains two
logs, 1893 to 1897, an order book, 1914, and charts and
photographs. There are also many semi-official letters
received, 1896 to 1947, in particular from Admirals of the
Fleet Viscount Cunningham (*q.v.*) and Sir Roger Keyes (1872-
1945). There are also Cowan's letters to Admiral Sir

Rudolph Bentinck (1869-1947), which were returned to
Cowan; they are of a private rather than of an official
nature. There are, however, some official papers relating
to the Baltic campaign and a draft autobiography. (3ft; 91cm)

57 CUNNINGHAM, Andrew Browne, *Admiral of the Fleet, 1st
Viscount Cunningham*, 1883-1963

Cunningham entered the Navy in 1898. He became a lieutenant
in 1904, a commander in 1915, captain in 1919, rear-admiral
in 1934, vice-admiral in 1936, admiral in 1941 and Admiral
of the Fleet in 1943. He was Deputy Chief of Naval Staff,
1938 to 1939, Commander-in-Chief, Mediterranean, 1939 to 1942
and 1943, naval Commander-in-Chief, Expeditionary Force,
North Africa, 1942, and First Sea Lord and Chief of Naval
Staff, 1943 to 1946. He was created a viscount in 1946.

See Cunningham's autobiography, *A sailor's odyssey* (London,
1951) and Oliver Warner, *Cunningham of Hyndhope, Admiral of
the Fleet* (London, 1967).

The papers were presented in several parts by Cunningham's
widow, Lady Cunningham, in 1963 and 1964. They relate mostly
to the period after his retirement. There are seven copies
of the *Tenedos Times*, 1914 to 1915, notes and drafts of
speeches, and papers relating to the many honours bestowed
on Cunningham and to his membership of various societies
and institutions. The bulk of Cunningham's papers went to
the British Museum (now the British Library). (6ft; 183cm)

58 CUNNINGHAM, *Sir* Charles, *Rear-Admiral*, 1755-1834

Cunningham entered the Navy from the merchant service in 1775
and served in the West Indies throughout the American War.
He was made lieutenant in 1782 and commanded the *Admiral
Barrington* brig in that year. In 1788 he went to the East
Indies and in 1790 was made commander of the *Ariel*. He
became a captain in 1793 and went to the Mediterranean,
returning with Lord Hood's (*q.v.*) despatches. His next
appointment was in 1796 to the *Clyde* which was refitting at
the Nore at the outbreak of the mutiny: he acted decisively
and after seventeen days managed to bring his ship safely
away. He was appointed, in 1803, a Commissioner of
Victualling and, in 1806, Commissioner of Deptford and
Woolwich dockyards. In 1823 he went to Chatham dockyard and
retired with the rank of rear-admiral in 1829. In this year

he published *A Narrative of...the Mutiny at the Nore* (Chatham, 1829).

The papers were presented in 1932 and 1941 by Mrs Drogo Montagu. Apart from official service documents, there is a log, 1796 to 1798, and a manuscript account of the Nore Mutiny. There is also a transcript of this made by Mr Granville Proby in the 1940s. The loose papers consist of correspondence received between 1799 and 1832 from, among others, William, Duke of Clarence, when Lord High Admiral, Earl St. Vincent (*q.v.*), Sir Evan Nepean (*q.v.*), Lord Spencer (1758-1834), Sir William Cornwallis (*q.v.*), the Hon. Charles Philip Yorke (*q.v.*), Sir John Barrow (1764-1848) and the 2nd Viscount Melville (*q.v.*). There is also material relating to Cunningham's period at Chatham. (3 vols, 1 box)

59 CURZON-HOWE, *the Hon. Sir* Assheton Gore, *Admiral*, 1850-1911

Curzon-Howe entered the Navy in 1863. From 1868 to 1871 he went round the world in the frigate *Galatea*. He was made lieutenant in 1872 while serving in the *Hercules*. It was not until 1888 that he was on active service again, when he was promoted to captain and appointed to the *Boadicea*, which became the flagship of Sir Edmund Fremantle (*q.v.*) on the East Indies Station. Here, as Flag-Captain and Chief of Staff, Curzon-Howe took part in the operations against the Sultanate of Vitu. In the *Cleopatra*, in 1892, he spent a period as Senior Officer, Newfoundland, reporting on the fishing question. In 1894 he was called south to Bluefields to protect the Mosquito Indians, whose reservation had been invaded by the Nicaraguans. He subsequently returned to Newfoundland and remained there until 1895, when he went to the Mediterranean in the *Revenge*, staying on the Station until 1900. In 1901 he was promoted to rear-admiral and became second-in-command of the Channel Fleet in the *Magnificent* until, in 1903, he went out to the East in the *Albion* to become second-in-command of the China Fleet. Curzon-Howe returned to the Channel in 1905 and in 1907 was given command of the Atlantic Fleet. From 1908 to 1910 he was Commander-in-Chief, Mediterranean, and then Commander-in-Chief, Portsmouth, until his death.

The papers were presented in 1963 by Mrs J. Curzon-Howe-Herrick, daughter-in-law of Admiral Curzon-Howe. They consist of logs, 1868 to 1873, fishery reports, Newfoundland, 1892 to 1895, memoranda, 1888 to 1893, 1909 to 1910, and notes on manoeuvres, 1895, 1899. (1½ft; 46cm)

60   DANNREUTHER, Tristan, *Captain*, *ca*.1872-1963

Dannreuther entered the Navy in 1885 in the *Britannia*. In
1887 he went to sea as midshipman in the *Garnet* in the East
Indies. He was in the *Inflexible*, Mediterranean, in 1891,
after which he specialized in navigation. From 1892 to 1894
he served in the *Iris* and *Foxhound* in home waters. He was
appointed lieutenant of the *Melita* in 1894, serving in the
Mediterranean and the Red Sea, and took part in the Dongola
expedition of 1896. Dannreuther was in the *Leander* in the
Pacific from 1897 to 1900. He subsequently served in the
Ariadne and the *Hood*, Mediterranean, the *Leviathan*, China
Station, and the *Bacchante*, *Roxburgh* and *Vindictive* in home
waters. He was promoted to commander in 1905 and served in
the *Leviathan* and *Amphitrite* on the Home Station from 1906
to 1907 and in the *Kent* on the China Station, 1907 to 1909.
In 1911 he was appointed to command the *Intrepid*, one of
the early minelayers, and from 1914 to 1915 was engaged in
the same capacity in the *Mars*. In 1915 he commanded the
Kinfauns Castle at the Cape of Good Hope and, from 1916 to
1919, the *Patuca*, on convoy escort duties in northern waters.
He was promoted to captain in 1918. Dannreuther's last
appointment was as one of the Assistant Directors of Naval
Intelligence from 1919 to 1921.

The papers were presented in 1963 by Rear-Admiral H.E.
Dannreuther, excepting the letters from Captain Dannreuther
to his mother which were presented by Captain H.M.
Dannreuther in 1973. The collection contains logs, 1887
to 1891, night order books, 1911 to 1917, notebooks, 1890
to 1891, diaries, 1887 to 1958, and remark books, 1893 to
1912. There are numerous letters from Dannreuther to his
mother written between 1885 and 1919, except for the years
1909 to 1914, and official documents relating to the ships
under his command. (8ft; 243cm)

61   DARE, Joseph Stafford (First Mate), 1863-1951

Dare first went to sea in 1878 as an apprentice with
Shallcross and Higham of Liverpool and much of his early
service was spent on the west coast of South America. He
took his second mate's certificate in 1883, but was
dogged by ill health and did not take the first mate's and
master's certificates until 1891 and 1894. He then went into
steam, sailing first with the Bedouin Steam Navigation
Company and later with F. Leyland & Company, both of
Liverpool. Failing health finally forced him to leave the

sea in 1901 and he retired to his home town of Leicester.

The papers were presented by Mr M.P. Dare in 1955. They consist of fifty-five certificates of discharge, 1883 to 1901, showing a complete record of his service. There are also testimonials and indentures, diaries, 1885 to 1888, 1898 to 1901, and a notebook of cargoes, loaded and unloaded, in the *Athenian*, 1900. Collections of pictures and printed books were presented at the same time. (6 vols)

62 DAVISON, Alexander (naval agent), 1750-1829

Davison started his career as a merchant and shipowner in the Canadian trade. He first met Nelson (*q.v.*) in 1782 and remained a life-long friend as well as his prize agent. Davison flourished as a government contractor, and, eventually, after obtaining the prize agency for the Nile Fleet, as a banker. His fortunes dwindled after dabbling with politics and after Nelson's death.

The papers were purchased in 1952 through the Caird Fund. They consist of forty-five letters concerning prize money, 1804 to 1814, including those from Admirals Collingwood (*q.v.*), Robert Digby (1732-1815), Sir Thomas Graves (*ca.*1747-1814), Thomas Hardy (1769-1839), Samuel, Viscount Hood (*q.v.*) and Sir James Saumarez (1757-1836). They deal largely with Davison's expectations of the fleet agency which were disappointed after Nelson's death. (1 box)

63 DAWKINS, Richard, *Rear-Admiral*, 1828-1896

Dawkins entered the Navy in 1841. After becoming a lieutenant in 1848 he served in the *Rattler* and was given charge of two Brazilian slavers as prizes in 1849. He then served in the *Modeste* and in the *Glatton*, a floating battery which went to the Crimea, 1855 to 1856. After this he was in the *Esk* commanded by Sir Robert McClure (*q.v.*) in a cruise to the Far East, and was present in the *Bittern* at the attack on Canton in 1857. He returned home in the *Comus*. He was commander in the *Mars*, Channel Squadron, in 1859, was promoted to Captain in 1863 and in 1866 went to the Pacific in command of the *Zealous*. In 1873 he was appointed to the *Vanguard*, which in September 1875 sank after colliding with the *Iron Duke*. At the subsequent court martial Dawkins was held responsible for the accident. After 1875 Dawkins made several unsuccessful applications to the Admiralty for employment and for a reconsideration of his case. He was promoted to rear-admiral in 1878 on the retired list but the finding of the court martial was never reversed.

The papers had been arranged by Dawkins himself and were further arranged by Mr J.M. Dawkins, his son, at the time of their presentation in 1958. There were two small additions in 1961 and 1963, both given by Mr Dawkins. The papers for Admiral Dawkins' early career consist of official service documents and three diaries, 1851 to 1858. Those concerned with the loss of the *Vanguard* consist of some official publications, such as the findings of the court martial, a large collection of press cuttings, some private letters and Dawkins' own account of the disaster. (1½ft; 46cm)

64   D'EYNCOURT, *Sir* Eustace Tennyson, 1st Bt.   (Director of Naval Construction), 1868-1951

Probably the leading naval architect of his day, Tennyson D'Eyncourt was trained at Armstrong's yard at Elswick and at the Royal Naval College, Greenwich. On completion of his apprenticeship, he remained with Armstrong's until 1898 when he became naval architect to Fairfields on the Clyde. In 1902 he returned to Armstrong's and made a reputation both for technical competence as well as skill in securing foreign orders. In 1912, d'Eyncourt was appointed Director of Naval Construction and thereby became responsible for the British wartime shipbuilding programme, as well as for the development of tanks and airships. He retired in 1924 and rejoined Armstrong's until they amalgamated with Vickers in 1927. Afterwards he acted as a consulting naval architect and was connected with numerous institutions such as the National Physical Laboratory, the Worshipful Company of Shipwrights and the Royal Institution of Naval Architects.

He published an autobiography, *A shipbuilder's yarn; the record of a naval constructor* (London, 1948).

The papers were presented by the widow of Sir Eustace's son, Lady Pamela Tennyson d'Eyncourt, in 1972. The majority are loose papers, 1898 to 1939. Many are copies of official memoranda on particular ships, the development of the tank and on general topics, while there are subject files of correspondence for the post-1924 period. (4½ft; 137cm)

65 DE VITRE, *Reverend* John Durham Denis (Chaplain, Royal Navy),
ca. 1870-*ca.* 1949

De Vitre, a naval chaplain who joined the service in 1898,
served in the Mediterranean before the First World War and
in the *Canopus* in the Dardanelles. He later retired to a
parish in Berkshire.

The papers were presented in 1938 by the Reverend de Vitre.
They consist of letters and drafts of letters concerning his
service but most of the collection is concerned with his
family, which originated in Canada with Mathew Theodosius,
Marquis de Vitre (d.1771) and his son John Denys de Vitre,
who entered the Royal Navy in 1771. There is a mathematical
work book belonging to the latter. (1 box)

66 DEWAR, Kenneth Gilbert Balmain, *Vice-Admiral,* 1879-1964

Entering the service in 1893, Dewar specialized in gunnery.
He was a lieutenant in 1900 and became a commander in 1911.
In 1912 he won the Royal United Service Institution Gold
Medal for his essay on the influence of overseas commerce on
the operations of war and its past and present effects. He
was Assistant Director of the Plans Division of the Admiralty
in 1917, was promoted to captain in 1918 and commanded
cruisers on the North America and West Indies Station, 1922
to 1924. Between 1925 and 1927 he was Deputy Director,
Naval Intelligence Division. His command of the *Royal Oak*
in the Mediterranean in 1928 ended in the notorious 'incident'.
In 1929 he became a rear-admiral, was retired the following
day and advanced to vice-admiral in 1934. During the Second
World War, however, he served again at the Admiralty. He
stood as Labour candidate for Portsmouth in 1931. Dewar
was one of the founder members of *The Naval Review* and a
strong advocate of naval reform and of improved staff
training.

He wrote an autobiography, *The navy from within* (London, 1939).

The papers were presented in 1966 by Dewar's widow, Mrs
Gertrude Dewar. They consist mainly of letters received,
including some from Admiral Sir Herbert Richmond (*q.v.*)
and drafts and memoranda relating to Dewar's Admiralty
service, there being little official or other correspondence
relating to his career afloat. Private and family letters,
and papers concerning the court-martial arising out of the
Royal Oak affair, were presented subject to certain conditions

and access to them remains restricted. There are also rough
diaries kept for both the First and Second World Wars and
official service documents. (5ft; 153cm)

67 DIXIE, *Sir* Alexander, 9th Bt., *Captain*, 1780-1857

Dixie entered the Navy in 1795 as a first-class volunteer
and was captured by the French in 1797. After ten months in
captivity he joined *La Pomone*, serving in the Mediterranean,
and then joined the *Orion* in the West Indies. In 1804 he was
with Nelson (*q.v.*), who confirmed him as a lieutenant; he was
present at the battle of Trafalgar, 1805. Until 1814 he was
in North America. He retired in 1815 and in 1851 was
promoted to captain on the retired list.

The papers were purchased from the family in 1953 through
the Caird Fund and consist of three logs, 1799 to 1801, and
twenty-four service documents. (1 box)

68 DOMVILE, *Sir* Barry Edward, *Admiral*, 1878-1971

Domvile entered the Navy in 1892 and served in the *Royal
Sovereign* in the Channel. From 1895 to 1897 he went to the
Crescent, flagship in North America, followed by a period in
the *Active*, Training Squadron. After promotion to lieutenant
in 1898, Domvile was in the *Revenge* in the Mediterranean
before taking the specialist gunnery course in *Excellent*,
after which he was a staff officer there. From 1903 to 1907
he was on the Mediterranean Station, firstly as gunnery
officer in the *Montagu* and then in the *Leviathan*. His next
appointment was with the Home Fleet, from 1907 to 1901. It
was at this time that he ran foul of Sir John (later Lord)
Fisher (1841-1920) over an essay which won the Gold Medal of
the Royal United Service Institution in 1907. Promoted to
commander at the end of 1909, Domvile commanded the
destroyers *Bonetta* and *Rattlesnake* in home waters, 1910 to
1912, after which he became Assistant Secretary to the
Committee on Imperial Defence until 1914. He spent the whole
war with the Harwich Force in command of the *Miranda*,
Lightfoot, *Arethusa*, *Carysfort*, *Centaur* and *Curacoa*, the
latter four being Admiral Tyrwhitt's (1886-1951) flagships.
Domvile was Director of the Plans Division at the Admiralty
from 1919 to 1922, then Chief of Staff to the Commander-in-
Chief, Mediterranean, between 1922 and 1925. He commanded
the *Royal Sovereign* in the Atlantic Fleet, 1925 to 1926.

In 1927 he reached flag rank and became Director of Naval Intelligence from 1927 until 1930. After commanding the Third Cruiser Squadron in the Mediterranean between 1931 and 1932, he ended his service career as President of the Royal Naval College, Greenwich, 1932 to 1934. Subsequently he became known for his pro-German views and in June 1940 was detained under the Defence Regulations. He was released from Brixton Prison in 1943.

Domvile wrote two autobiographical works: *By and large* (London, 1936) and *From admiral to cabin boy* (London, 1947).

The papers were left to the Museum in 1972. They consist mainly of a series of detailed diaries extending from 1892 almost until Domvile's death. There is also a collection of paper cuttings and photographs relating to the Greenwich Pageant of 1933 and to Anglo-German relations. (11ft; 335cm)

69 DOUGHTY, Frederick Proby, *Rear-Admiral*, 1834-1892

Doughty entered the Navy as a cadet in 1847 in the *Victory*. He went to the Mediterranean in the *Rodney* and remained there firstly in the *Howe* and then in the *Bulldog*. From 1850 to 1854 he was in the *Portland* on a voyage to Pitcairn Island and, still on the Pacific Station, he joined the *Centaur* in 1855, the year in which he became a lieutenant. From 1860 Doughty was in the Mediterranean as First Lieutenant of the *Foxhound* until 1864. He was appointed to command the *Weazel* in 1866 on the China Station and returned to the Shannon in 1868 to take up coastguard duties in the *Valiant*. His next commission was to the East Indies in the *Magpie*, 1870 to 1872, and he was promoted to captain in 1875. Between 1878 and 1881 he commanded the *Crocodile*, an Indian troopship, until he was sent to the *Constance* on the Pacific Station, 1882 to 1886, during which time he court-martialled his first lieutenant. The *Revenge*, the flagship at Queenstown, was his last command, in 1887, and he was placed on the retired list as rear-admiral in 1890.

The papers were presented by Doughty's daughter, Mrs Drogo Montagu, in 1942. They include logs, 1847 to 1854; journals, 1860 to 1864, 1878 to 1883; official letterbooks, 1866 to 1872, 1882 to 1887; a personal letterbook, 1867 to 1876; an order book, 1860 to 1864, and notes and drawings on torpedoes compiled in 1868. Although Doughty's career was comparatively uneventful, he was a man of wide interests and his journals are of more than official interest. (1½ft; 46cm)

70   DOUGLAS, *Sir* James, 1st Bt., *Admiral*, 1703-1787

Douglas saw early service in the *Ipswich*, 1734 to 1735, and
in the *Salamander*, 1739. He became a lieutenant in 1732, a
captain in 1744 and in 1745, in the *Vigilant*, was present
at the capture of Louisburg. In 1760, in the *Dublin*, he
commanded a squadron in the Leeward Islands and in the
following year led a successful expedition to capture the
island of Dominica. When Admiral Rodney (1719-1792) relieved
him in the Leeward Islands in 1761, he was given command of
the Jamaica Squadron and was with Rodney as his second-in-
command at the capture of Martinique, 1762. He was made
rear-admiral in the same year and became a vice-admiral in
1770. From 1773 to 1776 he was Commander-in-Chief,
Portsmouth, flying his flag in the *Barfleur* and the *Resolution*
and was made an admiral in 1778. Douglas was Member of
Parliament for Orkney and Shetland, 1754 to 1768.

The papers were purchased by Sir James Caird at Sotheby's in
1938 and are said to have come from the library of Sir
George Douglas of Springwood Park. There are logs, 1734 to
1735, 1739, 1741, 1745, 1760 to 1762; order books, 1760 to
1763, 1774 to 1777; letterbooks, 1760 to 1762; a private
account book for Douglas's estates, 1766 to 1770, and a list
of dispositions for the ships of the squadron, 1760 to 1761.
(1½ft; 46cm)

71   DUCKWORTH, *Sir* John Thomas, 1st Bt., *Admiral*, 1748-1817

Duckworth went to sea in 1759 and became a lieutenant in
1771. He saw service in North America during the War of
American Independence. He was made Commander of the *Rover*
in 1779 and a captain in 1780, serving in the West Indies
until 1781. He commanded the *Bombay Castle* during the
mobilization of 1790. In 1793 he was appointed to the *Orion*,
under Lord Howe (*q.v.*) in the Channel fleet, and fought at
the battle of the First of June 1794. In 1795 he returned
to the West Indies as Captain of the *Leviathan* and commanded
the fleet for a time in 1796. After a short period in home
waters, he joined Earl St. Vincent (*q.v.*) in the Mediterranean
and was in command of the naval forces at the capture of
Minorca, 1798. He was promoted to rear-admiral in 1799 and
continued to serve in the Mediterranean until 1800. He
then took command of the blockading squadron off Cadiz,
captured a Spanish convoy, and in the same year was appointed
Commander-in-Chief, Leeward Islands Station. He received a
knighthood for his services against the colonies

of the Northern Confederation in 1801. In 1803 he was
appointed Commander-in-Chief, Jamaica, and brought about
the surrender of the French army in San Domingo. He was
promoted to vice-admiral in 1804. After Trafalgar, he was
ordered to join Collingwood (*q.v.*) in the blockade of Cadiz
and when there, heard that a French squadron had escaped; he
defeated it at San Domingo on 6 February 1806. Afterwards
he returned to Cadiz and the Mediterranean. In February and
March 1807 he commanded the squadron which forced the passage
of the Dardanelles. The ineffectual outcome of this mission
caused Duckworth to be severely criticized. He was ordered
to join the Channel fleet. Subsequently he remained in home
waters until 1810 when he was promoted to admiral and
appointed Commander-in-Chief and Governor of Newfoundland,
returning home in 1813. He was elected Member of Parliament
for New Romney in 1812. Shortly before his death he was
appointed Commander-in-Chief at Plymouth.

The papers probably originate from the 1937 sale of Duckworth's
papers, but were acquired in five separate parts. Four of
these were purchased from Sotheby's between 1937 and 1939
and in 1966. The fifth is of unknown provenance since 1937.
The collection consists of a log, 1779 to 1780; letterbooks,
1800 to 1807 and 1812; order books, 1800 to 1806; an
admiral's journal, 1807 to 1808; two rough journals, 1805
and 1810 to 1812, and correspondence. The loose papers cover
the years 1790 to 1813. They consist of official and some
private correspondence; reports and orders, including series
from Lords Howe (*q.v.*), 1790, and Collingwood (*q.v.*), 1805 to
1806; an account of the battle of the First of June 1794; correspondence relating to Duckworth's Mediterranean command, 1799 to
1800, in particular to naval hospitals; correspondence with
Sir Robert Calder (1745-1818), 1800 to 1805, mostly on their
dispute over prize money, and other papers relating to the
West Indies; congratulatory addresses on San Domingo;
correspondence relating to the Dardanelles affair and letters
and papers received as Governor of Newfoundland. (3½ft;
110cm)

In addition the Museum holds copies of some of Duckworth's
papers held at Yale University. There are letterbooks, 1793
to 1798 and 1804 to 1813, order books, 1793 to 1798, 1807
to 1811, and miscellaneous papers. There is also a copy of
Duckworth's journal, 1809 to 1811, which belongs to the
Newfoundland Archives.

72 DUDMAN, Joseph, *Commander* (H.E.I.C.), *ca.*1790-1865

After serving his time as a midshipman, Dudman joined the
Cumberland as fifth officer in 1808. On his next voyage,
in 1812, he left her at Whampoa to join the *Inglis*. He
stayed with this ship until 1834, having taken command of
her in 1828. Dudman's family owned a shipyard at Deptford
which built warships and East Indiamen and two other
commanders of East India Company ships also came from the
family. In 1836 Dudman went into partnership with Thomas
Bush, a hop and seed merchant of Southwark.

The papers, purchased from Messrs Kegan, Paul, Trench and
Trubner in 1971, contain Dudman's logs, 1808 to 1834;
accounts for the *Inglis*, 1816 to 1820, 1827 to 1834;
chronometer rate books, 1827 to 1834, and a hold book with
entries in 1815, 1817 and 1822. There are also account
books for the shipbuilding business of the Dudman family,
1812 to 1815, and logs for the East India Company ships
Northumberland, 1795 to 1797, and *Warley*, 1811 to 1812 and
1815 to 1816. Finally, there are some loose papers
relating to shares and probate of members of the Dudman
family in the mid-nineteenth century. (3ft; 92cm)

73 DUFF, *Sir* Alexander, *Admiral*, 1862-1933

Duff entered the Navy in 1875, passed as a sub-lieutenant in
1881 and as a lieutenant in 1884, after which he specialized
in torpedo duties. He was promoted to commander in 1897
and to captain in 1902. In 1911 he became Director of Naval
mobilization and two years later was promoted to rear-admiral.
During the first half of the war he was second-in-command of
the Fourth Battle Squadron, flying his flag in the *Emperor
of India* in 1914 and in the *Superb* at Jutland, 1916. Duff
was then appointed as Director of the Anti-Submarine Division.
In 1917 he was made Assistant Chief of Naval Staff. He was
promoted to vice-admiral in 1918 and from 1919 to 1922 was
Commander-in-Chief on the China Station. He retired in 1925.

The papers were presented in several sections by Lady Duff
between 1948 and 1969. The main part, consisting of letters
received from Lord Jellicoe (1859-1935) and Sir Charles
Madden (*q.v.*), 1916 to 1933, and a few letters from Jellicoe
to Lady Duff, 1934, came to the Museum in 1948. A series of
notes and letters, 1914 to 1919, on the convoy system were
presented in 1953 and 1954. There are also papers on
mercantile shipping, conferences and convoys, 1918, and some

of Duff's retrospective views on convoys written in 1931, presented between 1963 and 1969. Finally, there is a private diary kept between 1914 and 1916 in this latter section. (1 box)

74 DUFF, Robert, *Vice-Admiral*, *ca*.1720-1787

Duff was promoted to the command of the *Terror* bomb vessel off the coast of Scotland in 1744 and then to the *Anglesea* between 1747 and 1748 off the coast of Ireland. In 1755 he was appointed to the *Rochester* in the Channel. He contributed to the victory of Quiberon Bay, 1759, by leading the French in pursuit of his small squadron to bring them within range of the main British fleet. His next command was the *Foudroyant* in the West Indies where he was present at the reduction of Martinique, 1762. In 1775 he was promoted to rear-admiral and appointed Governor and Commander-in-Chief, Newfoundland. His last command was as Commander-in-Chief, Mediterranean, in the *Panther* between 1777 and 1780. He was promoted to vice-admiral in 1778.

The papers were presented by Lieutenant-Colonel Scott Duff of Fetteresso in 1947. A further section was bequeathed by Miss Gladys Duff in 1965. There are logs, 1744 to 1747, 1749 to 1762 and for part of 1779; letter and order books, 1745 to 1762, 1775 to 1780; a register of Newfoundland fishing vessels, 1775; a list of ships, 1770; various signals and sailing directions and a family account book, 1769 to 1778. An extensive collection of charts was also presented by Lieutenant-Colonel Duff in 1947 and is held by the Navigation Department. (5ft; 152cm)

75 DUNCAN, Adam, *Admiral*, *1st Viscount Duncan*, 1731-1804

Duncan entered the Navy in 1746 and served in the Channel and the Mediterranean during the early part of his career. He was made a lieutenant in 1755 and a post-captain in 1761, after which he played a distinguished part in the Channel and West Indies, particularly in the *Valiant* during the Belleisle and Havana operations of 1761 to 1762. After the peace he was not employed again until 1778 when he was appointed to the *Suffolk*, in the Channel, and then to the *Monarch*, in which ship he took part in the Moonlight Battle of 1780 and the subsequent relief of Gibraltar. In 1782 he commanded the *Blenheim* and was present at the final relief of Gibraltar. Between 1783 and 1786 he commanded the *Edgar*, guardship at Portsmouth. After another period of unemployment, he was appointed admiral and Commander-in-Chief, North Sea Station, in 1795. This involved the task of blockading the Dutch Fleet in the Texel, made particularly difficult by the mutinies of 1797. He eventually defeated the Dutch at the battle of Camperdown, 1798, and in the following year the Helder batteries were captured and the Dutch fleet surrendered. He retired from active service in 1800.

There is a biography by the Earl of Camperdown, *Admiral Duncan* (London, 1898).

The papers were deposited on loan by the family in 1945. They have been finely bound and consist of four main groups. The first comprises thirteen volumes of official papers for his service 1778 to 1787 and 1794 to 1800. The second is of ten volumes arranged by subject or correspondent, 1794 to 1800, and contains mostly private letters, including those to Earl Spencer (1758-1834) and Charles Middleton (*q.v.*), prize cases, sailing orders and a narrative of the 1797 mutinies. Thirdly there are a series of logs, 1754 to 1783, and some signals. Finally there are a number of items acquired by Duncan which include a navigational log of the *Centurion* during Anson's voyage, 1743 to 1746, possibly by Piercy Brett (1709-1781); the log of *H.E.I.C.S. Walpole*, 1745 to 1747, and of *H.E.I.C.S. Prince Edward*, 1749 to 1751. (6ft; 182cm)

76 DUNDAS, Henry, *1st Viscount Melville* (First Lord of the Admiralty), 1742-1811

Dundas was admitted to the Scottish Bar in 1763, was appointed Solicitor-General for Scotland in 1766 and Lord Advocate in 1775. He represented Edinburghshire, 1774 to 1782, Newtown, Isle of Wight, 1782, Edinburghshire, 1783 to 1790 and Edinburgh, 1790 to 1802. He first held office in 1782 when he was appointed Treasurer of the Navy for a short time under Shelburne and resumed office under Pitt in December, 1783, holding it continuously until June 1800. He was also Home Secretary, 1791 to 1794, and Secretary of War, 1794 to 1801. In 1804 he was made First Lord of the Admiralty. When the Commission of Naval Enquiry published its tenth report dealing with the office of Treasurer of the Navy, Dundas resigned from office. He was impeached in 1806 and, although acquitted, it was clear that he was guilty of negligent supervision during his term of office. He held no further appointment.

The papers were bought at Sotheby's in 1931, 1932 and 1960. They consist of miscellaneous letters and documents relating to Dundas's official career as a naval administrator, 1760 to 1811. A further section was purchased from Madame Elisabeth La Serre in 1976. It consists of letters received between 1794 and 1806, from, among others, Admirals Cornwallis (*q.v.*), Duncan (*q.v.*), Orde (*q.v.*), Keith (*q.v.*), and Hallowell (*q.v.*), as well as a number of ship lists. (4 boxes)

The main Dundas collections are held in the Scottish Record Office and the National Library of Scotland.

77   DUNDAS, *Sir* James Whitley Deans, *Admiral*, 1785–1862

Born James Whitley Deans, he took the name of Dundas on marrying his cousin in 1808. He entered the Navy in 1799, served in the Mediterranean and Channel fleets and was made lieutenant in 1805. For the rest of the Napoleonic War he served in the Baltic or the North Sea. After a succession of peacetime commands, he was made rear-admiral in 1841, and briefly, a member of the Board of the Admiralty. From 1846 to 1847 he was Second Naval Lord and was First Naval Lord from 1847 to 1852. He was Member of Parliament for Greenwich, 1832 to 1834 and 1841 to 1852 and for Devizes, 1836 to 1838. In 1852 he was made Commander-in-Chief, Mediterranean, and a vice-admiral. He was in command when the Crimean War started and his responsibilities included the transport of the army to the Crimea and support of the allies in the battle of Alma and at Sebastopol. Having completed the usual term of command he was relieved in January 1855. He was promoted to admiral in 1857 but saw no further service.

The papers were bought in two separate lots in 1960 from Sotheby's and from Messrs Francis Edwards. They consist of bound volumes of official and private correspondence for Dundas's Mediterranean command, 1851 to 1854. There are also letters, reports and memoranda of diplomatic importance in this period. (2ft; 61cm)

78   DUNDAS, Robert Saunders, *2nd Viscount Melville* (First Lord of the Admiralty), 1771–1851

Robert Dundas, only son of Henry Dundas, 1st Viscount Melville (*q.v.*), entered Parliament as representative for Hastings, 1794 to 1796, Rye, 1796 to 1801 and Edinburghshire, 1801 to

1811. He first came into prominence when he defended his father against impeachment in 1806. In 1807 he was made President of the Board of Control. In 1809 he was briefly Irish Secretary before resuming his former office. From 1812 to 1827 he was First Lord of the Admiralty, resigning because he refused to serve under Canning. He held the office again from 1828 to 1830.

The papers were bought at Sotheby's in 1931, 1932 and 1960. They consist of a small collection of letters for the period during which Dundas was First Lord. In addition, there are some papers concerning Lord Cochrane's secret plan of 1812 which were presented by Admiral P.W. Brock in 1964. A further section was purchased from Madame Elisabeth La Serre in 1976. It consists of letters received, 1812 to 1830, from naval officers, including Admirals Sir Charles Rowley (*q.v.*), Sir David Milne (*q.v.*), Sir Graham Moore (1764-1843) and Captain Sir George Grey (*q.v.*). (4 boxes)

The main Dundas collections are in the Scottish Record Office and the National Library of Scotland.

79 EDGELL, Harry Edmund, *Vice-Admiral*, 1809-1876

Edgell was promoted to lieutenant in 1828, to commander in 1837 and to captain in 1846. He was appointed to command the *Tribune* in 1855 when she was in the Crimea. During this commission she went to the Pacific and finally to China. In 1857 Edgell was the Senior Naval Officer at Hong Kong and he transferred into the *Bittern* tender commanding the gun boats on the Canton River during the hostilities with the Chinese. In 1858 he was given command of the squadron in Indian waters, during which time he commanded the *Chesapeake* and later the *Retribution*. The latter returned to England and was paid off in 1860. Edgell had no further active employment and was promoted on the retired list, reaching the rank of vice-admiral in 1871.

The papers were presented by Vice-Admiral Sir John Edgell in 1931. They consist of offical letterbooks, 1855 to 1860, and two folders of offical letters, 1857 to 1858. (1ft; 30cm)

80   EGGINS, Douglas George (Master Mariner), 1894–

Born in Bristol, Eggins spent several years at sea and in
1922 gained a master's ticket. In that year he became a
Falmouth pilot, retiring in 1958.

The papers were presented by Mr Eggins in 1968. They consist
of eight day books, forming a continuous record between 1922
and 1958 of all the ships which he piloted in and out of
Falmouth Bay and Harbour, together with the fees charged.
There is also a typescript of the scheduled times of
movement of craft before D–Day, 1944. (8 vols)

81   ELIOTT, George Augustus, *General*, *1st Baron Heathfield*,
1717–1790

George Eliott, son of Sir Gilbert Eliott, 3rd Bt., of Stobs,
descended through four generations from a younger branch of
the Minto family, received a French military academy training
and fought on the Continent at an early age with the
Prussian army. After training as a field engineer, he served
during the War of 1739 to 1748 in the British army, becoming
a captain in 1745 and a lieutenant-colonel in 1754. During
the Seven Years War he was present at the capture of Havana.
In 1774 he was made Commander-in-Chief of the forces in
Ireland and the following year he went out, as Governor, to
prepare Gibraltar for the threatened attack from Spain.
This did not come until 1779. From then until 1783 the
Rock was under constant siege, being relieved on three
occasions. For his skilful defence Eliott was raised to the
peerage in 1787.

The papers, part of the Minto collection, were purchased by
Sir James Caird in 1941 from the Earl of Minto. They consist
of three cases of orders and letters relating mainly to the
siege of Gibraltar. (1ft; 30cm)

82   ELKINS, *Sir* Robert Francis, *Vice-Admiral*, 1903–

After attending the Royal Naval Colleges at Osborne and
Dartmouth, Elkins joined the Atlantic Fleet, 1921 to 1923, as a
midshipman in the *Hood*, *Wryneck* and *Wild Swan* successively. He
was promoted to lieutenant in 1924, qualified as an Interpreter
(German) in 1928 and specialized in gunnery in 1929. During

the Invergordon incident of 1931 he was the lieutenant in
charge of the *Valiant*'s shore patrol on the evening when
the trouble began. In 1937 he became a commander and in
1939 took command of the *Bideford* in China and the
Mediterranean. As Naval Liaison Officer he was sent to
assist the intended evacuation of the 51st Highland Division
from St. Valéry-en-Caux but fog prevented the main with-
drawal. Elkins was captured but he and Captain Lesley Hulls
of the Gordon Highlanders escaped and sailed to England.
After this Elkins served in the *Renown* which was one of the
four ships that bombarded Genoa in February, 1941. Elkins
was appointed to the Naval Ordnance Department at Bath and
was promoted captain in 1942. He then went to the *Dido*,
Home Fleet (Tenth Cruiser Squadron) in 1944 and was at
Copenhagen when the Germans surrendered. In 1952 Elkins
was aide-de-camp to King George VI and to Queen Elizabeth
II, becoming a rear-admiral in that year and a vice-admiral
in 1955. From 1955 to 1956 he was second-in-command on the
Far East Station and then, from 1956 to 1958, was Flag
Officer, British Joint Staff Mission, Washington. He
retired in 1959.

The papers have been presented to the Museum by Vice-Admiral
Elkins in two groups. The larger, presented in 1967,
comprises Elkin's midshipman's journal, 1921 to 1923, his
summaries and reports on Invergordon, 1931, and a later
report written in 1967 for Captain Stephen Roskill's
(1903-   ) use in his history on *Naval Policy between the
Wars* (London, 1968) as well as Elkin's wartime 'Line' books.
These include accounts (as well as his official report, 1947)
of his escape from St. Valéry, and of the proceedings for
the surrender of the German squadron at Copenhagen. The
draft of Elkin's reminiscences is closed to readers, by
Admiralty direction, until 2004 A.D. The remainder of this
group consists of arrangements for ceremonial Royal occasions,
1948 to 1951, and a selection of sea shanties, arranged for
orchestra. The second group, presented in 1974, relates to
the publication of Len Wincott's book *Invergordon mutineer*
(London, 1974) and the publicity given to his visit to
England, also in that year. (1ft; 30cm)

83   ELLIOT, *Sir* Gilbert, 3rd Bt. (Treasurer of the Navy), 1722-
1777

Gilbert Elliot was called to the Scottish Bar in 1743. He
entered Parliament in 1753 as Member for the county of Selkirk,

but from 1765 until his death sat for the county of Roxburgh.
In 1756 he was appointed a Lord of the Admiralty until 1761
when he became a Lord of the Treasury. He also became Treasurer
of the Chamber in 1762 and, in 1766, Keeper of the Signet in
Scotland. In 1770 he was made Treasurer of the Navy, which
post he held until his death.

The papers, part of the Minto collection, were purchased by
Sir James Caird from the Earl of Minto in 1941. Their content
is mainly official and consists of account rolls of the
Treasurer of the Chambers, 1762 to 1770, and an account made
as Treasurer of the Navy, 1776 to 1777. There are some
miscellaneous papers and a few letters, some personal and some
official, relating to the settlement of Elliot's naval accounts.
(1ft; 30cm)

There are other papers relating to Elliot as Treasurer of the
Navy and as Lord of the Admiralty in the National Library of
Scotland.

84 ELLIOT, Gilbert, *1st Earl of Minto* (diplomat), 1751-1814

Gilbert Elliot, eldest son of Sir Gilbert Elliot, 3rd Bt.
(*q.v.*), was called to the English Bar in 1774 and entered
Parliament two years later as the Member for Morpeth, transferring to Roxburghshire in 1777. He gave independent
support to the government during the War of American Independence, only going over to the Opposition in 1782. Having
lost his seat in 1784, he was returned for Berwick in 1786.
In 1790 he was returned for Helston, Cornwall, and in 1793
transferred his allegiance to Pitt's government. In this
year he was appointed Civil Commissioner at Toulon and
served as Viceroy of Corsica between 1794 and 1796. He
attempted to make Corsica the centre of British power in the
Mediterranean and it was through him that Nelson (*q.v.*)
attacked Porto Ferraio. In September 1796 he was ordered to
withdraw from Corsica to Naples, after which he returned to
England in March 1798. In 1799 he was appointed Envoy
Extraordinary to the Court of Vienna and was Governor-
General of India, 1806 to 1813. He was created Baron Minto
in 1797 and Earl of Minto in 1813.

See Countess of Minto *ed.*, *Life and letters of Sir Gilbert
Elliot, first Earl of Minto...* (London, 1874)

The papers, part of the Minto collection, were purchased by
Sir James Caird in 1941 from the Earl of Minto. The
collection comprises sixty-two volumes and covers the
official correspondence of Lord Minto when he was Commissioner
at Toulon and Viceroy of Corsica. In addition, there is an

account of the attack and defence of Toulon, 1793, a journal for March 1794, a few loose papers and some correspondence between Elliot, Nelson and Lady Hamilton. (15ft; 454cm)

Further naval papers of the First Earl form part of the Minto collection in the National Library of Scotland.

85 ELLIOT, Gilbert, *2nd Earl of Minto* (First Lord of the Admiralty), 1782-1859

Gilbert Elliot was the eldest son of Gilbert Elliot, first Earl of Minto (*q.v.*) and was trained for the diplomatic service. He was a Member of Parliament for Ashburton, 1806 to 1807 and for Roxburghshire, 1812 to 1814. He supported the Whigs and in 1832 was appointed Ambassador to Berlin. In 1835 he succeeded Lord Auckland as First Lord of the Admiralty and served as such until 1841. In 1846 Minto became Lord Privy Seal. He left office in 1852, after which he took no further part in politics.

The papers, part of the Minto collection, were purchased by Sir James Caird in 1941 from the Earl of Minto. They consist of correspondence and papers covering the period when he was First Lord of the Admiralty. There are forty volumes of in-letters and some draft replies in his own hand including the letters from commanders connected with the events of the Carlist war, 1836 to 1841. There are also loose papers which consist of reports and memoranda and correspondence on a wide variety of naval topics. (6ft; 183cm)

Further naval papers of the 2nd Earl form part of the Minto collection in the National Library of Scotland.

86 ELLIOT, Hugh (diplomat), 1752-1830

After an early period of military service abroad, Hugh Elliot, second son of Sir Gilbert Elliot (*q.v.*), had a varied diplomatic career until, in 1803, he was appointed to Naples. Here he encountered a complicated situation. The Queen of Naples wished, and so influenced Elliot, that the English army should remain to defend Naples. However, the British military commander insisted that the army should go to Sicily, the Fleet duly escorted the Royal Family there and Elliot was recalled. He was later appointed Governor of the Leeward Islands and finished his career as Governor of Madras.

See Countess of Minto, *A memoir of the Right Honourable Hugh Elliot* (Edinburgh, 1868).

The papers, part of the Minto collection, were purchased by Sir James Caird in 1941 from the Earl of Minto. They consist of diplomatic correspondence, 1803 to 1806, and contain sixty-two letters from Nelson (*q.v.*), together with drafts and copies of Elliot's replies and correspondence with Admiral Collingwood (*q.v.*). There are also intelligence reports and other material which throw light on the diplomacy of the Neapolitan Court. (1ft; 30cm)

There are further papers relating to Hugh Elliot in the National Library of Scotland.

87 ELLIOT, John, *Admiral*, 1732-1808

John Elliot, brother of Sir Gilbert Elliot 3rd Bt., (*q.v.*), went to sea in the *Augusta* in 1745. He was made a lieutenant of the *Scarborough* in 1756 and gained promotion to command the *Hussar* in the following year under Hawke (*q.v.*) and then under Anson. In 1758 he commissioned the *Aeolus* and in 1760 captured the small French squadron which was attempting a raid on Belfast. He was appointed to the *Gosport*, a forty-gun ship, but soon went back to his frigate off Brest. In 1761 he went to the Mediterranean in the *Chichester*. During the peace he commanded several ships and in 1777 was appointed to the *Trident* which carried the Peace Commission of Lord Carlisle to Philadelphia. From the end of 1779 he commanded the *Edgar* and was present at the first relief of Gibraltar. This was then followed by service in the Channel and in 1781, under Kempenfelt (1718-1782), he assisted in the capture of the French convoy. In 1782 Elliot went to the *Romney*. From 1786 to 1789 he was Governor and Commander-in-Chief, Newfoundland, and in 1787 was made rear-admiral. He became a vice-admiral in 1790 and hoisted his flag in the *Barfleur*. Although promoted to admiral in 1795, he saw no further service.

The papers, part of the Minto collection, were purchased by Sir James Caird in 1941 from the Earl of Minto. They consist only of one volume, containing a biographical note and seventy-two letters sent mostly by Elliot to his father or brother, 1745 to 1805. There are also letters received, including some from Lords Sandwich (*q.v.*) and Barham (*q.v.*). Also included is a description by Captain Erasmus Gower (*q.v.*) of Lord Macartney's Embassy to China in 1793 and another of the First of June, 1794. (1 vol)

88 ELLIOT, *the Hon.* William, *Lieutenant*, d. 1811

William Elliot was the fourth son of Gilbert Elliot, first
Earl of Minto (*q.v.*). He served in the *Ardent* and *Medusa* in
the Channel between 1803 and 1806 and in the *Aurora* and *Modeste*
in the East Indies under his brother, George, later Admiral Sir
George Elliot (1784-1863). He was promoted to lieutenant in
1808 and on the same station served in the *Procris* between
1808 and 1810 and in the *Bucephalus* until his death in India.

The papers are part of the Minto collection, purchased by Sir
James Caird in 1941 from the Earl of Minto. They consist of
three logs kept between 1803 and 1810. (3 vols)

89 ELPHINSTONE, George Keith, *Admiral, 1st Viscount Keith*, 1746-
1823

Elphinstone entered the Navy in 1761, became a lieutenant in
1770 and in 1772, having been promoted to commander, went to
the Mediterranean in the *Scorpion*, where he remained until
1775. As a captain he then went to North America and commanded,
in succession, the *Romney*, 1775 to 1776, the *Perseus*, 1776 to
1780, and the *Warwick*, 1780 to 1782, being present at the
reduction of Charleston in 1780. Between 1782 and 1793
Elphinstone was unemployed until he took command of the
Robust during the occupation and evacuation of Toulon. He
was promoted to rear-admiral in 1794 and served in the Channel
Fleet until, in 1795, he was appointed to command the expedition
against the Cape of Good Hope. After the successful capture
of the Cape he returned home, to encounter a French invasion
force in Bantry Bay. He also received a peerage as Baron
Keith, 1797. His next task was to assist in suppressing the
mutinies at the Nore and Plymouth. In 1799 he was second-in-
command to Earl St. Vincent, Mediterranean Fleet, succeeding
to the command in the same year and holding it until 1802.
When war broke out again, in 1803, Lord Keith became Commander-
in-Chief of the North Sea Station where, until 1807, his prime
concern was the protection of the English coasts against
invasion. From 1812 to 1814 he commanded the Channel Fleet
and again took this office during the Hundred Days. Finally,
he was responsible for organizing the safe passage of Napoleon
to St. Helena. He was made Viscount Keith in 1814.

The only biography is by Alexander Allardyce, *Admiral Lord
Keith* (London, 1882). The Navy Records Society published *The
Keith Papers* in 1926 (*ed.* W.G. Perrin), 1950 and 1955 (*ed.*
C.C. Lloyd).

The papers were presented by Lord Lansdowne in 1930. They consist of 168 volumes and 350 boxes of loose papers all of which include letters, orders and memoranda received between 1772 and 1815. Keith's active career, before he commanded a station, is well covered by correspondence. From 1796, however, the papers become very extensive. There is considerable material on the reduction of the Cape of Good Hope and on other matters during the Cape command (15 vols, 7 boxes). As Commander-in-Chief, Mediterranean, he received letters from Lords Nelson (*q.v.*), Minto (*q.v.*) and Elgin (1766-1841), Sir Sidney Smith (*q.v.*) and a number of Turkish potentates (80 vols, 100 boxes). The papers covering his North Sea Command illustrate strategic and day-to-day problems and there are a large number of letters from Admiral Sir Bartholomew Rowley (d. 1811) at the Nore, Admiral Holloway (d.1826) in the Downs, Commodore Edward Owen (*q.v.*) in Boulogne and others (55 vols, 185 boxes). No less comprehensive are the records for the final Channel command with correspondence from Sir Home Popham (1762-1820), the Duke of Wellington (1769-1852) and some letters relating to Napoleon's surrender (25 vols, 50 boxes). Keith's private papers form only a very small part of the collection but as a flag-officer he kept the most routine of letters: for each major command, particularly that of the Mediterranean, there are numerous accounts and returns which provide a detailed picture of victualling and the other general problems of an overseas fleet. There are also complete lists of ships' dispositions for all his major commands. (124ft; 3,780cm)

90   FIOTT, William Edward, *Lieutenant*, 1786-1849

Fiott joined the Navy as a volunteer in 1798 and was present at the battle of Copenhagen, 1801. He took part in the Walcheren expedition of 1809 and in 1810 was made a lieutenant but court-martialled in the same year for using seditious language, dismissed his ship and put to the bottom of the Lieutenants' List. Soon afterwards, however, he was appointed to the *Marlborough* and served in the West Indies. After two years on half-pay he bought the *Queen*, a trading vessel, which was lost in 1818. From then until 1827 he owned the *Retrench*, sailing as master while still on half-pay until 1823. In this year the *Retrench* was attacked by Spanish pirates off Cuba. When he received a commission in 1823 to command *H.M.S. Renegade* in the West Indies, he employed another half-pay naval captain on the *Retrench*, which was wrecked in 1824 but salvaged and, in 1827, sold. In 1824 he was court-martialled again on various charges including that

of mistreating his crew but was acquitted. From 1827 Fiott
lived on the continent and remained there until his death.

The papers are part of the collection from Hartwell,
Buckinghamshire, sold by Mrs Benedict Eyre at Sotheby's in
1939. Fiott's life is fully covered by this collection, which
is composed largely of loose papers. These consist of
official service documents, material on Walcheren, both his
courts martial, papers covering the *Renegade* period and a log,
1823 to 1824. There are extensive papers and volumes for
the period when he was merchant ship master and owner,
including legal agreements, crew lists and account and freight
books. Finally, there are private letters received, 1809 and
1848, and yearly diaries, 1837 to 1847. (4ft; 123cm)

91 FISHER, *Reverend* George (astronomer), 1794-1873

Owing to the death of his father, Fisher had to go out to
work at an early age. However, his interest in science won
him recognition and in 1817 he was able to go to Cambridge
University. In 1818 he sailed as astronomer with the naval
expedition to Spitsbergen commanded by Captain David Buchan
(d. *ca.* 1839) in the *Dorothea* and the *Trent*. He then returned
to Cambridge. In 1821 he graduated and was ordained. In
that year he sailed with Captain W.E. Parry (1790-1855), on
his second expedition, 1821 to 1823, to search for the North-
West Passage, in the double capacity of chaplain and astronomer.
During both these expeditions he made astronomical and
magnetic observations and did some pioneer work on the
physical, chemical and physiological consequences of the Arctic
climate. In recognition of his work he was elected a Fellow
of the Royal Society in 1825. From 1828 to 1832 he served in
the Mediterranean as chaplain in the *Spartiate* and *Asia* and
continued his work on astronomy and magnetism. From 1834 to
1863 Fisher was Headmaster of the Greenwich Hospital School,
where he continued his scientific work and established an
observatory.

The papers were presented by Fisher's grand-daughter, Miss
Darnell, in 1958. The earliest items are two books of
mathematical theorems, 1811 and 1813. There are volumes of
notes and observations for both Fisher's Arctic voyages and
for his period in the Mediterranean, accounts of later
scientific work and abstracts of observations made by other
scientists. This is the material which formed the basis of
the scientific papers which he published in the *Philosophical
Transactions* and elsewhere. There are letterbooks for

Greenwich Hospital School from 1836 to 1863 (excepting the years 1858, 1859 and 1860) and other reports and papers relating to the School. There are a number of items collected by Fisher. The most important are Peter Puget's journal for March to May 1793 in the *Chatham*, storeship for Vancouver's expedition; a meteorological log also giving details of ship arrivals and and departures at Madras, 1815 to 1816; Franklin's (*q.v.*) lunar observations on board the *Trent* in 1818 and Parry's (1790-1855) meteorological journal on his first two voyages in search of the North-West Passage in 1819 to 1820 and 1821 to 1823. (5ft; 152cm)

Fisher's scientific instruments were presented to the Museum in 1958 and are held in the Navigation Department.

92 FISHER, *Sir* William Wordsworth, *Admiral*, 1875-1937

Fisher entered the Navy in 1888 and served as a sub-lieutenant and lieutenant in the Mediterranean. In 1903 he was appointed a senior staff officer of the Gunnery School on Whale Island. He was made a commander in 1906 and a captain in 1912. After more than four years with the Grand Fleet he was called in May 1917 to the Admiralty as Director of the then recently-formed Anti-Submarine Division. In 1919 he commanded the *Iron Duke*, flagship, Mediterranean Fleet, and was then Chief of Staff to Admiral Sir John De Robeck (1862-1928), in both the Mediterranean and Atlantic Fleets. Fisher became rear-admiral in 1922, commanded the First Battle Squadron, Mediterranean Fleet, in 1924 and in 1926 was appointed Director of Naval Intelligence. He joined the Board of the Admiralty as Fourth Sea Lord in 1927 and, after rising to vice-admiral, became in April 1928 Deputy Chief of Naval Staff. In the autumn of 1930 he was appointed second-in-command, Mediterranean Fleet, until April 1932. He was then promoted to admiral and returned to the Mediterranean as Commander-in-Chief in October. His command covered the period which included the Abyssinian crisis of 1935. His final appointment was Commander-in-Chief, Portsmouth.

There is a biography by Admiral Sir William James, *Admiral Sir W.W. Fisher* (London, 1943).

The papers were presented by Fisher's daughter, Lady Coleridge, in 1967. This small collection of memoranda and letters, 1912 to 1936, consists of Fisher's ideas and opinions on policy rather than of material closely related to his career. The subjects covered include First World War operations, anti-submarine warfare, the Disarmament Conference, 1929 to 1930, comments on Invergordon, 1931, and papers concerning relations with Egypt and the Fleet in the Eastern Mediterranean, 1919 to 1922, and in 1936. (1 box)

93 FLINDERS, Matthew, *Captain*, 1774-1814

Flinders joined the Navy in 1790 and went on the second breadfruit voyage in the *Providence* from 1791 to 1793. On his
return, Flinders went to the *Bellerophon* and was present at
the battle of the First of June 1794. He then served in the
Reliance, taking the new Governor to New South Wales and used
the opportunity to explore the coastline firstly in the *Tom
Thumb* and then in the *Francis* with the surgeon, George Bass
(d. *ca.* 1812). They charted the coast of Van Diemen's Land
(Tasmania) between 1798 and 1799 in the *Norfolk* and proved
that it was an island. On his return home in 1800 Flinders
convinced Sir Joseph Banks (1743-1820) of the need to chart
the whole of Australia; he was promoted to commander and sent
out in the *Investigator*, 1801, with a team of scientific
assistants. While surveying the southern coast of Australia
as far as Port Phillip (the site of Melbourne), Flinders
encountered the French ships *Le Géographe* and *Le Naturaliste*
which were also engaged in charting the continent. He later
travelled northwards, amplifying and correcting the work of
Cook, but had to abandon his work in 1803 as the *Investigator*
appeared to be rotten. On his return voyage to England he
was detained at Ile de France (Mauritius) by the French
governor there and held prisoner for over six years. He was
released in 1810 and survived only long enough to complete
and publish, in 1814, his *Voyage to Terra Australis*.
Flinders also made an important contribution to the knowledge
of the variation of the mariner's compass.

Among the many biographies written about Flinders, the latest
is by James Decker Mack, *Matthew Flinders* (London, 1966).

The papers are the residue of those presented to the Public
Library of Victoria, Melbourne, by Sir William Flinders Petrie
(1853-1942). Together with books and relics of Matthew
Flinders, they were deposited on temporary loan for
cataloguing in 1958 and were formally transferred on permanent
loan in 1960 by Miss A.F. Petrie and Mr J.F. Petrie. They
consist of three main groups: the first, the papers of Flinders
himself, are charts and original journals, 1791, 1793 to 1794
and 1796, and copies, 1798, 1801 to 1803; narratives of his
voyages; service papers, 1797 to 1810, and technical notes on
subjects in which he was particularly interested, such as
terrestrial magnetism; there is a wide range of original
correspondence including letters from Sir Joseph Banks and Sir
John Franklin (*q.v.*). Mrs Flinders' papers make up the
second group: these consist mainly of letters, 1799 to 1812,
including those from Flinders written during the *Investigator*'s
voyage, 1801 to 1803, and correspondence with French residents
in Mauritius about her husband's captivity. The final group

is Professor Flinders Petrie's collection of biographical
material, notes, memoirs, newscuttings, etc, on his grandfather's career and correspondence with J.F. Shillinglaw
about a biography of Flinders, which work Shillinglaw failed
to complete. (3ft; 92cm)

94 FOLEY, *Sir* Thomas, *Admiral*, 1757-1833

Foley entered the Navy in 1770 and after early service in
Newfoundland and the West Indies was promoted to lieutenant
in 1778. During the American War he saw service in the
Channel, North America and the West Indies. In 1782 he was
promoted to commander and in 1790 to captain. After a period
on the Home Station, he was Flag-Captain in the *Britannia*
at the battle of Cape St. Vincent, 1797, and in the *Goliath*
he led the Fleet into action at the Nile, 1798, In 1800 Foley
was appointed to the *Elephant* in the Channel Fleet, going
later to the Baltic, where he served at the battle of
Copenhagen, 1801. Foley was then ill and unfit for service
for several years until his appointment as Commander-in-Chief
in the Downs from 1811 to the peace, 1815. He had been promoted to rear-admiral in 1808, became a vice-admiral in 1812
and in 1825 an admiral. In 1830 he was appointed Commander-
in-Chief at Portsmouth, where he served until his death.

There is a privately printed biography by John Beresford
Herbert, *The life and services of Admiral Sir Thomas Foley,
G.C.B., Rear-Admiral of Great Britain* (Cardiff, 1884).

The papers were purchased in 1953 from Christie's through the
Caird Fund. They consist of about 630 letters received by
Foley between 1797 and 1832. Much of the correspondence
concerns the promotion of young officers. There are
approximately 140 correspondents; those with more than a
few letters include Prince William Henry, Admiral Sir Richard
Bickerton (1759-1832), Admiral Sir Richard Keats (*q.v.*),
Robert Saunders Dundas, Lord Melville (*q.v.*), Earl St.
Vincent (*q.v.*), Admiral Sir Robert Stopford (*q.v.*),
Admiral Sir William Young (1751-1821) and Vice-Admiral Sir
William Hope (1766-1831). (2ft; 62cm)

95 FRANKLIN, *Sir* John, *Captain*, 1786-1847

Franklin entered the Navy in 1800. He served as midshipman
under his cousin, Captain Matthew Flinders (*q.v.*) from 1801

to 1803, surveying the coasts of Australia. He began his
Arctic career as second-in-command to Captain David Buchan
(d. *ca* 1839) during the Spitsbergen expedition of 1818. From
1819 to 1822 he commanded an expedition down the Coppermine
River of Canada to the Arctic Ocean. From 1825 to 1827 he
commanded a second expedition to the Arctic Ocean down the
Mackenzie River. He was knighted in 1829. Franklin was in
the Mediterranean from 1830 to 1833 and between 1833 and 1844
was Lieutenant-Governor of Van Diemen's Land (Tasmania). In
1845 at the age of fifty-nine, he took command of an expedition
in search of the North-West Passage in the *Erebus* and *Terror*.
He died on board the *Erebus* off King William Island.

See Sir J. Franklin, *Narrative of the journey to the shores
of the Polar Seas in the years 1819, 1820, 21 and 22* (London,
1823) and *Narrative of a second expedition to the shores of
the Polar Sea, in the years 1825, 1826 and 1827* (London, 1828).
Among a number of biographies is Richard J. Cyriax, *Sir John
Franklin's last Arctic Expedition* (London, 1939).

The papers were purchased by Sir James Caird in 1938. They
consist of a volume of bound letters written by Sir John
Franklin between 1820 and 1845 to his niece Mary Anne Kay and
to Lieutenant Edward Kendall, R.N., whom she later married.
Several letters refer to Franklin's second overland expedition.
His last letter was written in 1845 at the Whale Fish Islands.
There are other letters relating to exploration and some Arctic
material including prints and manuscript copies of the New
Georgia Gazette of 1819. (1 vol)

96 FRASER, Gordon Colquhoun, *Captain*, 1866-1952

Fraser entered the Navy in 1880. As a midshipman he served
in the *Monarch* and the *Agincourt*, Mediterranean Station,
between 1882 and 1885 and then in the *Active* between 1885
and 1886 mostly in the East Indies. Having attended the Royal
Naval College, Greenwich, he was promoted to lieutenant in
1888. In 1890 he was appointed to the *Kingfisher* in the East
Indies, after which he specialized in torpedo duties, serving
at the torpedo school *Vernon* in 1894 and again between 1897
and 1900. He organized the illumination of the Fleet at the
opening of the Kiel Canal in 1899, probably the first time
this had been done by electricity. After promotion to
commander in the same year, he joined the *Vindictive* in the
Mediterranean. During this period he became seriously ill
and had eventually to be invalided, retiring as captain in
1907. During the First World War he served in the Torpedo
and Mining Division of the Admiralty, specializing in defensive
mining.

The papers were presented by Fraser's widow, Mrs Claire Fraser, in 1960. They include his midshipman's logs, some rough logs for his lieutenant's service and descriptions of his service in the East Indies. There is also a rough journal of part of his *Vindictive* commission and several notebooks of the Greenwich and *Vernon* periods, some of which contain printed question papers of that time. Some notes on the illumination of the Fleet at Kiel, letters of 1918 and printed material relating to defensive mining, complete the collection. (1ft; 30cm)

97 FRASER, John (marine painter), 1858-1927

Fraser was a marine painter who collaborated extensively with the Commendatore Eduardo de Martino (1838-1912), Marine Painter-in-Ordinary to Queen Victoria. Martino also enjoyed special favour with Edward VII, who never went to sea without him, but although Fraser hoped to succeed to this position at Martino's death, he was disappointed.

The papers were presented by Fraser's widow, Mrs E.M. Fraser, in 1957 and 1959 and consist of letters about his paintings and family matters, 1893 to 1927. The Department of Pictures has a large collection of his works. (2 boxes)

98 FREMANTLE, *the Hon. Sir* Edmund Robert, *Admiral*, 1836-1929

Edmund Fremantle, grandson of Vice-Admiral Sir Thomas Fremantle (*q.v.*), entered the Navy in 1849 in the *Queen* on the Mediterranean Station. From 1852 he served in the *Spartan* on the East Indies and China Stations and was involved in the Burma War. He was promoted to lieutenant in 1857. He next served in the *Orion* and *Royal Albert* on the Mediterranean and Channel Stations and from 1860 in the *Neptune*, with Captain Sir Geoffrey Phipps Hornby (*q.v.*), on the Mediterranean Station, until his promotion to commander in 1861. Fremantle then commanded the despatch vessel *Eclipse* on the Australian Station, 1864 to 1867, and saw service in the Maori War, 1864 to 1866. He was promoted to captain in 1867. He commanded the *Barracouta* between 1873 and 1874 on the Cape Station, after which he served in the *Doris* between 1874 and 1876 as part of the Detached Squadron. From 1877 he commanded

the *Lord Warden* for a year on coastguard service and then
went to the *Invincible* in the Mediterranean, 1879 to 1881.
He was Senior Naval Officer at Gibraltar from 1881 to 1883.
His next command was the *Dreadnought* in 1884. After his
promotion to rear-admiral in 1885, he was second-in-command
of the Channel Squadron with his flag in the *Agincourt*.
He was Commander-in-Chief, East Indies, from 1888 to 1891,
on the China Station from 1892 to 1895 and at Devonport
from 1896 to 1899. He was promoted to vice-admiral in
1890 and admiral in 1896.

Fremantle published *The Navy as I have known it* (London,
1904). See also Anne Parry, *The Admirals Fremantle*
(London, 1971).

The papers were presented in 1956 by Admiral Sir Sydney
Fremantle. They cover Fremantle's career well, especially
the Maori and Ashanti war periods. They include logs,
1849 and 1859, 1856 to 1857 and 1873 to 1881; letterbooks,
1862 to 1876, 1879 to 1880; personal letters written mainly
between 1864 and 1866 and papers relating to his commands,
1889 to 1895. There is also a section which deals with
his court martial for grounding the *Eclipse* in 1866.
(4ft; 122cm)

99   FREMANTLE, Stephen Grenville, *Captain*, 1810-1860

Fremantle was the youngest son of Vice-Admiral Sir Thomas
Fremantle (*q.v.*). He entered the Royal Naval Academy,
Portsmouth, in 1823 and afterwards served as midshipman
in the *Challenger*, 1828, and the *Pallas*, 1828 to 1829,
on the Home Station. He was promoted to lieutenant in
1829 and to commander in 1836, when he commanded the *Clio*,
Southampton and *Wanderer* at the Cape of Good Hope and on
the South American Station and in China respectively.
He was promoted to captain in 1842 while in the *Wanderer*.
After service in North America, he was appointed to the
Arrogant, 1852 to 1853, on the Home Station and then the
Juno on the Australian Station, 1853 to 1857. He was
accused of over-strict discipline in the *Juno* and had
no further employment.

The papers were presented in 1956 by Admiral Sir Sydney
Fremantle. They consist of logs, 1828 to 1829, 1839 to
1841; letter and order books, 1839 to 1842, 1852 to 1857,
and a private record of letters sent and received, 1847
to 1848. There is also a privately-printed statement in
answer to the charges made against him as Captain of the
Juno. (1ft; 31cm)

100 FREMANTLE, *Sir* Sydney Robert, *Admiral*, 1867-1958

Eldest son of Admiral Sir Edmund Robert Fremantle (*q.v.*), Sydney Fremantle entered the Navy in 1881. He was promoted to lieutenant in 1887, to commander in 1889 and to captain in 1903. After a distinguished career afloat he was made Head of the War Division at the Admiralty in 1910 and President of the Signal Committee at Portsmouth in 1912. He became a rear-admiral in 1913 and was made Head of the Signals Division at the Admiralty in 1914. He was second-in-command of the Third Battle Squadron in 1915, and was appointed to command the Ninth Cruiser Squadron in 1916 and the Second Cruiser Squadron in early 1917. In August of that year he was in command of the British Aegean Squadron. In January 1918 he was made Deputy Chief of Naval Staff, was promoted to vice-admiral and in May 1919 was appointed to command the First Battle Squadron. Fremantle was promoted to admiral in 1922 and was Commander-in-Chief, Portsmouth, from 1923 to 1926. He retired in 1928.

See Fremantle's autobiography, *My Naval Career* (London, 1949).

The papers were presented by Admiral Fremantle in 1956. They consist of a memorandum on the war in the Aegean, 1916 to 1917, detailed minutes compiled while he held office as Deputy Chief of Naval Staff and other papers relating to this post. There are also collected essays and articles written by Fremantle, 1904 to 1919. (2ft; 61cm)

101 FREMANTLE, *Sir* Thomas Francis, *Vice-Admiral*, 1765-1819

Thomas Fremantle entered the Navy in 1777 and after service in the West Indies was promoted to lieutenant in 1782. He was promoted to captain in 1793 when he commissioned the *Tartar* frigate and went to the Mediterranean. He led the way into Toulon in 1793 and in the following year served under Nelson at the siege of Bastia, after which he commanded the *Inconstant*, in which he took part in the action off Toulon, March 1795, and in the blockade of the North Italian coast. In 1797 he accompanied Nelson to the attack on Santa Cruz where both were severely wounded. Fremantle took part in the battle of Copenhagen in 1801 and was also at Trafalgar. He returned to England in 1806, was made a Lord of the Admiralty until his appointment as Captain of the Royal Yacht in 1807. In 1810 he was promoted to rear-admiral and to a command in the Mediterranean, and in 1812 took command of the squadron in the Adriatic. In 1818 he was appointed Commander-in-Chief, Mediterranean, and died at Naples.

See Anne Parry, *The Admirals Fremantle* (London, 1971).

The papers were presented by Admiral Sir Sydney Fremantle in 1956. They consist of three logs, 1793 to 1796, two signal notebooks, undated, two memoranda on naval discipline, 1806, and some printed material relating to the French and Spanish navies. (1ft; 30cm)

102 FULLER, *Sir* Cyril Thomas Moulden, *Admiral*, 1874-1942

Fuller entered the Navy in 1887 and was promoted to lieutenant in 1893. He specialized in gunnery and served on the staff of the *Excellent* in 1902. Two years later he was promoted to commander and became a captain in 1910. After service in China, Fuller took command of the *Cumberland*, 1914, and in the latter part of that year was Senior Naval Officer in the campaign against the German territories in Togoland and the Cameroons. He continued on this service in the *Challenger* and the *Astrea* and saw the successful termination of the operation in 1915. Fuller subsequently had a distinguished career, becoming Director of the Plans Division of the Naval Staff, 1917, Head of the British Naval Section at the Peace Conference in Paris, 1919 to 1920, and Second Sea Lord in 1932. He retired in the same year.

The papers were presented by Captain D. Fuller, R.N. in 1948. The major part of the collection consists of volumes of letters, orders and signals relating to the campaign in Togoland and the Cameroons. There are also maps and surveys of the Cameroons, some printed material in German and some chapters on the campaign, in proof, for the *Official History of the War [Naval Operations]*. In addition there are loose memoranda and technical notes on gunnery, 1902 to 1904. (4½ft; 137cm)

103 FULLERTON, *Sir* Eric John Arthur, *Admiral*, 1878-1962

Fullerton entered the Navy in 1895, became a lieutenant in 1900 and a commander in 1910. In 1908 he married Dorothy Fisher, daughter of Admiral Sir John (later Lord) Fisher

(1841-1920). At the beginning of the First World War he commanded monitors off the Belgian coast; for this he was specially commended and promoted to captain in 1914. As Senior Officer of the Monitor Squadron in 1915 he commanded the inshore operations in East Africa and took part in the destruction of the German cruiser *Königsberg*. From 1916 to 1918 he commanded the *Orion* in the Grand Fleet as Flag Captain to Rear-Admiral Goodenough (1867-1945). Between 1921 and 1923 he was Captain of the Fleet on the staff of Admiral Sir Charles Madden (*q.v.*) in the Home Fleet, was then Commodore commanding the Royal Naval Barracks at Chatham and, for a few months in 1925, was aide-de-camp to King George V. Having been promoted to rear-admiral the previous year, in 1927 Fullerton was appointed Naval Secretary to the First Lord of the Admiralty, the Rt. Hon. (later Viscount) W.C. Bridgeman (1864-1935), and in 1929 went out to the East Indies Station as Commander-in-Chief. On his return he was Commander-in-Chief at Plymouth, 1932 to 1935, was promoted to admiral in 1935 and retired the following year. During the Second World War Fullerton served in the Royal Naval Reserve between 1940 and 1942.

The papers were presented in 1973 by Mrs G.C. Howard, Admiral Fullerton's daughter. They are mostly personal letters written between 1901 and 1955 to both Sir Eric and Lady Fullerton; the correspondents include Admirals Lord Fisher, Sir William Wordsworth Fisher (*q.v.*), Sir William Goodenough, Lord Jellicoe (1859-1935), Earl Beatty (1871-1936), Sir John de Robeck (1862-1928), the Rt. Hon. W.C. Bridgeman and Captain Godfrey-Faussett, the King's Equerry (1896-1970), In addition, there are some letters received by Lord Fisher, including those from Lord Balfour (1848-1930) and Lord Charles Beresford (1848-1930). (1 box)

104 GANZ, W.H. (teacher of dancing), 1867-*ca.*1946

Miss Ganz taught dancing at Mr Littlejohn's Navy School between 1888 and 1898. Later she took pupils, many of whom were from the Royal Naval College, Greenwich.

The papers were presented by Miss Ganz in 1939 and 1946. They consist of diaries and papers relating to her dancing classes and letters from pupils at the Royal Naval College, 1890 to 1910. (1 vol, 1 box)

105 GEARY, *Sir* Francis, 1st Bt., *Admiral*, 1709-1796

Geary entered the Navy in 1727, became a lieutenant in 1734, a captain in 1742 and served through the War of Austrian Succession. During the early part of the Seven Years War he was in North America and then returned, in 1757, to take command at the Nore for a few months, in the *Princess Royal*. In 1758 he moved into the *Lenox*, Channel Fleet, and in the following year served on the same station in the *Resolution* and then in the *Sandwich*. It was in the latter ship that he hoisted his flag in 1759 as rear-admiral and commanded detached squadrons in the Channel until late in 1760. After this he became Commander-in-Chief at Portsmouth until 1762, when he became vice-admiral. His next service was in the same command between 1769 and 1771. Having been promoted to admiral in 1775, in 1780 he took up his last appointment as Commander-in-Chief of the Channel Fleet.

The papers were presented by Sir William Geary in 1937 and consist of letter and order books, 1757 to 1762, and 1769 to 1771. (1ft; 31cm)

106 GODDEN, William (fisherman), *fl.* 1812-1854

After serving an apprenticeship of seven years to William Brown of Gillingham, William Godden of Chatham became a Fisherman and Dredgerman of the City of Rochester in 1821.

The papers were presented by Mr A.L. Godden in 1965. They consist of William Godden's apprenticeship indenture of 1812, the oath of Fisherman and Dredgerman, 1821, the transfer of registry of the smack *Betsy*, 1848, oyster fishing accounts, 1853, and some notes on ships and fishing. (1 box)

107 GOODSALL, Walter (Master Mariner), 1848-*ca.* 1900

Goodsall entered the merchant service in 1863 and in 1867 joined the Bombay Shipping Company as second mate. His submarine telegraph work began as Third Officer in the cable ship *Kangaroo* with the Telegraph Construction and Maintenance Company, laying a cable from Singapore to Hong Kong. As Second Officer in the Company's ship *Vanessa* between 1872 and 1873, he participated in the laying of the duplicate Placentia-St.Pierre-Sydney cable. Late in 1873 he was Third

and Navigating Officer in the *Great Eastern*, working on the
cable from Valentia to Newfoundland. He subsequently commanded
other cable ships, including the *Chiltern*, which was employed
in the Red Sea, 1883 to 1884.

The papers were deposited on loan by Mr R.H. Goodsall in 1965.
They consist of a biographical note of his early life and
diary extracts up until 1876. There is a full account for
1881. There are also logs, 1870, 1872, 1883 to 1884, and a
technical pamphlet. (1 box)

108 GOWER, *Sir* Erasmus, *Admiral*, 1742-1814

Gower entered the Navy in 1755. He was promoted to lieutenant
in 1762 and took part in two voyages of circumnavigation
early in his career. He was promoted to captain in 1780 and
served on the East Indies and Newfoundland stations. In 1792
he was appointed to command the *Lion* in which he took the
embassy of Earl Macartney (1737-1806) to China. In November
1794, he was appointed to command the *Triumph* and was with
Admiral Sir William Cornwallis (*q.v.*) during the 'Cornwallis
retreat' in 1795. He was involved in the mutiny at the Nore
when he commanded the *Neptune*, one of the ships commissioned
for the defence of the Thames, and continued to serve in her,
in the Channel Fleet, until his promotion to rear-admiral in
1799. In 1804 Gower became a vice-admiral and in 1809 an
admiral.

The papers were purchased at Sotheby's in 1955 from Mrs Pedler,
daughter of Brigadier C.J. Hawker, together with some papers
of Admiral Edward Hawker (*q.v.*) and Vice-Admiral Charles
Boyles (*q.v.*). They consist of a log, 1792 to 1794, with one
watercolour sketch; two volumes of 'Nautical Observations on
a Voyage to China', illustrated with views of coasts and
harbours; a letterbook, 1794 to 1798, and a signal notebook,
1801. (1ft; 31cm)

109 GRANT, Samuel (Purser) *fl.*1778-1803

Grant, son of an Aberdeen merchant, entered naval service as
a clerk in 1778. In 1794 he was appointed to the *Lutine* as
Purser, and in 1795 to the *Dido*. Two years later he was
appointed to the *Goliath* and was present at the battle of the
Nile. In 1799 he applied for an exchange to home service for
health reasons and returned with the *Goliath* at the end of the

year. He remained in England until 1801 when he rejoined his ship and went to the West Indies. His health became so bad that he was invalided back to England.

The papers were presented in 1949 by Messrs. Coutts. They consist of detailed diaries, 1793 to 1803 (some of them in shorthand), and correspondence and naval papers connected with his work as a purser, 1781 to 1803. These include passes, indentures for a clerk, certificates, financial papers, lists of stores and lists of ships. There are also some financial and legal papers relating to the family property in Pembroke. (2ft; 62cm)

110 GRAVES, Thomas, *Rear-Admiral*, 1677-1755

Graves was promoted to commander in 1709 and captain in 1713. In the summer of 1711 he was in command of the *Winchester* for a few months. From 1711 to 1714 he commanded the *Dunwich*, stationed mainly in home waters but was sent in 1713 to take news of the conclusion of the Treaty of Utrecht to Bermuda and the American colonies. He was unemployed from 1714 to 1728, in which year he took command of the *Assistance*, guardship, at Plymouth. In 1733 he was appointed to command the *Swallow* and the next year was with Sir John Norris (*ca.* 1670-1749) at the Tagus. In 1738 he was Captain of the *Princess Louisa* and in November of the same year commissioned the *Norfolk*. In 1740 he was sent to the West Indies and took part in the attack on Cartagena. Still in the *Norfolk*, he was ordered to the Mediterranean in 1742 where he transferred to the *Marlborough*. After 1743 he had no further service and became a rear-admiral in 1747.

The papers were purchased from the family in 1932. They consist of logs, 1738 to 1744, an official letterbook, 1711 to 1738, a private letterbook, 1721 to 1740, and two order books, 1711 to 1728 and 1739 to 1741. There are some commissions and an abstract of orders received, 1739 to 1743. (2 boxes)

111 GRAVES, Thomas, *Admiral 1st Baron Graves*, 1725-1802

Graves was the second son of Rear-Admiral Thomas Graves (*q.v.*) and first cousin to Admiral Samuel Graves (1713-1787). He was with his father in the *Norfolk* at the attack on Cartagena in 1741 and went with him to the Mediterranean and transferred

into the *Marlborough* in 1742. In 1743 he was appointed
Lieutenant of the *Romney* and was present at the action off
Toulon in February 1744. In 1746 he was in the *Princessa*
at the attack on L'Orient and he then served in the
Monmouth under Anson and Hawke (*q.v.*) in the Channel. Between
1751 and 1754 he made two voyages to Africa. In 1754 he
was given command of the *Hazard* in home waters. He was
made a captain in 1755 and appointed to the *Sheerness*, but
in 1757 was court-martialled for refusing an engagement
with an enemy ship, which appeared to be of superior force,
and sentenced to be reprimanded. Graves was appointed to
the *Unicorn* in 1758 and served in the Channel under Anson
and Rodney. In 1761, as Captain of the *Antelope*, he was
Governor and Commander-in-Chief, Newfoundland. On his
arrival he found there had been a French invasion and he
organized a relief expedition which drove them from the
island. On his return home he was made Captain of the
Téméraire in 1764 and in 1765 was sent to the west coast
of Africa to investigate charges of maladministration in
the British forts. He served as Member of Parliament for
East Looe, January to May, 1775. In 1778 he commanded the
Conqueror in North America and the West Indies, returning
home the next year on his promotion to rear-admiral when he
served as second-in-command of the Channel Fleet. He was
sent to America as Commander-in-Chief in 1780 and led the
British fleet at the action off the Chesapeake in March
1781 which resulted in the surrender of Cornwallis at
Yorktown. Graves sailed for home from the West Indies in
1782 but lost several ships in a storm. He was made a
vice-admiral in 1787 and in 1788 Commander-in-Chief, Plymouth.
He hoisted his flag in the *Cambridge* in 1790. In 1793 he
was appointed second-in-command of the Channel Fleet under
Lord Howe (*q.v.*). He was promoted to admiral in 1794. He
was raised to the Irish peerage for his part in the battle
of the First of June 1794 but received a wound which forced
him to give up his command and he saw no further service.

The papers were purchased from the family in 1931 and 1932.
They include logs, 1742 to 1744, 1746 to 1748 and 1779 to
1782; a letterbook, 1793 to 1794; order books, 1788 to 1793;
a book of sailing directions with some orders, 1755 to 1756;
letters and a volume on courts martial, 1771 to 1780 and
1786 to 1787. There are some loose papers which relate to
Graves' court martial and to his Governorship of Newfoundland.
The latter contain some documents on hydrographic surveys,
among which is a letter of 1764 to Graves from Captain James
Cook (1728-1779). There are also some commissions, official
letters and drafts, 1764 to 1767, 1777 to 1782, a few private
letters, 1782 to 1797 and a biography of Graves up to 1790.
Some papers of Admiral Sir Thomas Graves (*ca.* 1747-1814)

another cousin of Lord Graves are also in the collection. They are orders received as Captain of the *Savage*, North American Station, 1779 to 1781, and official letters received, 1800 to 1804. (2ft; 62cm)

112 GREENE, *Sir* William Graham (Secretary of the Admiralty), 1857-1950

Greene entered the Admiralty as a Higher Division Clerk in 1881. From 1887 to 1892 he was Private Secretary to successive First Lords and became Principal Clerk in the Secretary's department in 1902. He was Assistant Secretary of the Admiralty, 1907 to 1911, in which year he became Permanent Secretary. Considerable changes in the constitution of the Admiralty Board and other departments were made in 1917 and Greene became Secretary of the Ministry of Munitions, which post he held until his retirement in 1920.

The papers were presented in 1950 by Sir William's nephew, Dr Raymond Greene. They form a substantial collection of notes, letters, reports, and government papers concerning Greene's work and interests. Those relating to his own career range between 1913 and 1936, of which the large section of letters and memoranda written during the First World War include drafts to Lloyd George and Churchill. There are letters and articles on Lord Alfred Douglas' (1870-1945) libel suit against the *Morning Post*, 1923, and on the sinking of the *Lusitania* 1915. On post-war technical subjects there are letters from Sir James Thursfield (*q.v.*) and Sir Eustace Tennyson D'Eyncourt (*q.v.*) and on historial topics from Sir Oswyn Murray (1873-1936) and Lord William Cecil (1854-1943). Among the extracts, notes and printed papers on naval administration are lists of naval officials, dating back to the ninth century, notes on the battle of Trafalgar and on the Seven Years War. (3 boxes)

113 GREET, Thomas Young, *Admiral*, 1854-1948

Greet entered the Navy in 1867 and was promoted to midshipman in 1869. He served in the Pacific in the *Zealous* and *Fawn* and was made a sub-lieutenant in 1874. He served in the *Juno*, China Station, 1876 to 1877, and was promoted to lieutenant in 1878. He then spent the usual period at the Royal Naval College, Greenwich, before his appointment to the *Tenedos* in 1882. In 1887 he served in the *Iron Duke*, Channel, and in the following year he was appointed to the *Champion*, Pacific Station. He was promoted to commander in 1891, served in the Channel and, from 1896, at a training establishment, and was promoted to captain in 1897. He retired with the rank of rear-admiral in 1907 and became an admiral on the retired list in 1916.

The papers were presented in 1966 by Mrs T.Y. Greet. They consist of logs, 1869 to 1875, watch bills, 1888 and one from the *Empress of India*, 1890, and notebooks on various subjects written at sea and at the Royal Naval College, Greenwich, 1872 to 1882. (1ft; 30cm)

114 GREIVE, William Samuel, *Vice-Admiral*, ca.1830-1892

Greive was born William Samuel Brown. He changed his name to Greive late in life as the result of an inheritance. He entered the Navy in 1845 and served in the *Styx* on the West African Station from 1845 until 1847. From 1851 to 1852 he was mate in the *Spiteful* in the Mediterranean. He went out to Bermuda in the *Espiegle* in 1853 and served for some months in the *Cumberland* at Halifax. He was promoted to lieutenant and appointed to the *Penelope* in 1854 and served in the Baltic during the Crimean War. In 1855 the *Penelope* went out to the Cape of Good Hope and Brown served on that station in several ships until promoted to commander in 1860. From 1861 to 1865 he served on the North American Station and, following his promotion to captain in 1866, returned there in the *Danae* from 1871 to 1874. He was Naval Officer-in-Charge, Jamaica, from 1880 to 1882. He was promoted to rear-admiral in 1884, to vice-admiral in 1889 and retired in the same year.

The papers form part of the Wrey family collection which was presented to the Museum in 1956 by Commander Windham Mark Phipps Hornby (*q.v.*), executor of Mrs Wrey. They contain logs, 1845 to 1847, and 1851 to 1855; a letterbook, 1871 to 1874; commissions, 1851 to 1884, and a few single documents. (3 vols, 1 box)

115 GREY, *The Hon. Sir* George, 1st Bt., *Captain*, 1767-1828

Grey was made a lieutenant in 1781 and served in the West Indies and in home waters. In 1793 he was promoted to captain and commanded the *Boyne*, in which Sir John Jervis (*q.v.*) had his flag. The *Boyne* was lost through fire at Spithead in 1795 but Grey was acquitted of responsibility at his court martial. From 1795 to 1797 he was Captain of the *Victory*, in which Jervis again had his flag, and was present at the battle of Cape St. Vincent in 1797. Later in the same year he took command of the *Ville de Paris* but left the ship at the end of 1798. In April 1800 he returned to the *Ville de Paris*, once again as Jervis' Flag Captain, and served in her until March 1801. He then commanded the Royal Yachts. In 1804 he was appointed Commissioner of Sheerness Dockyard and in 1806 was transferred to Portsmouth Dockyard where he remained until his death. He was created a baronet in 1814.

The papers were presented in 1945 by Captain Sir Cecil Graves, nephew of Lord Grey of Fallodon, and great-great-grandson of Sir George Grey. They consist of logs, 1795 to 1798 and 1800 to 1801, letter and order books, 1795 to 1801, and an order book, 1795 to 1801. There are some loose papers, including an account of the loss of the *Boyne* and of Grey's court martial. In addition there are extracts copied from the journal of Sir George Rooke (1650-1709), 1692 to 1704; a volume of copies of General James Wolfe's (1727-1759) orders issued in 1759; and a volume with copies of correspondence exchanged between Admiral Sir Benjamin Hallowell (q.v.) and General Donkin (1773-1841) concerning a proposed duel, 1813 to 1815. (2ft; 61cm)

116 GRIFFIN, Thomas, *Admiral*, *ca.*1699-1771

Griffin served in the Baltic Fleet, 1716 to 1717, in the *Weymouth* and then in the *Panther*. He became a lieutenant in 1718 and was in the *Barfleur* and *Orford*, Mediterranean Station, until 1720; from 1727 to 1730 he served in the *Gibraltar*, the *Princess Louisa* and the *Falmouth* on the same station. He was promoted to captain in 1731, served in the West Indies in the *Shoreham* from 1731 to 1733 and on the Channel Station under Sir John Norris (*ca.*1670-1749) from 1735 until 1740 in the *Blenheim*, *Oxford* and *Princess Caroline*. It was in the latter ship that he sailed to join Admiral Vernon's fleet in the West Indies in October 1740. During the abortive attack on Cartagena in 1741 he commanded the *Burford*. Griffin was then at Portsmouth until 1743 in the *St. George*. It was during his service in the *Captain*, 1744 to 1745, that he was accused of an error of judgement, court-martialled but acquitted. He was made rear-admiral, in 1747, when he hoisted his flag in the *Princess Mary* and went to the East Indies. In the following year he was promoted to vice-admiral and, on his arrival back in England, found himself the object of criticism over an alleged failure to attack eight French ships: he requested a court martial, was found guilty of negligence and suspended from his rank. Although reinstated in 1752, he had no further active employment.

The papers were deposited on permanent loan in 1934 by Mr F.J. Griffin. They consist of a full run of logs from 1716 to 1749, letterbooks, 1732 to 1749, with letters inserted in 1751, 1755 and 1757, and books of orders received and issued, 1735 to 1745. There is also a purser's account book, 1742 to 1743. (3ft; 91cm)

117 GROHMAN, Harold Tom Baillie, *Vice-Admiral*, 1888-

Baillie Grohman joined the Navy in 1903, becoming a lieutenant in 1909. He served in the Mediterranean and on the China station, and during the First World War on the east coast, in the Dover Patrol and in minesweepers. In 1922 and 1923 he served in the Persian Gulf and the Red Sea, and was made commander in the latter year. He then became Senior Officer, First Minesweeping Flotilla, 1923 to 1924. He was promoted to captain in 1930 and between 1931 and 1933 was Senior Officer of a British Naval Mission to China. He then served in the Mediterranean, commanded a training establishment and at the beginning of the Second World War was again in the Mediterranean. He was promoted to rear-admiral in 1941 and in the same year was attached to the staff of the General Officer Commanding, Middle East. In 1942 he was nominated as Naval Force Commander for the Dieppe Raid, but, although he took part in the planning of the raid, he did not command it. Afterwards he became Flag Officer, Harwich, and in 1943 was promoted to vice-admiral, retiring in 1946.

The papers were presented by Vice-Admiral Baillie Grohman in 1967. The collection can be divided into two groups of files of official papers. The larger relates to the Naval Mission to China, 1931 to 1933, and the second is concerned with the preparations for the Dieppe Raid, 1942. There are restrictions on access to the second section. In addition, there is a small number of personal letters. (2ft; 62cm)

118 HAMILTON, Archibald, *Commander* (H.E.I.C.), 1778-1848

Archibald Hamilton, younger brother of John Hamilton (*q.v.*),
served in the East India Company's ship, *Bombay Castle*, as
Fourth Mate in 1798. He was given command of a French prize
La Médée, which was captured off Brazil in 1800. He then
succeeded his brother in the command of the *Bombay Castle*, 1802,
and made two voyages in her to Bombay and China. His ship was
one of the East India Company's China fleet under Sir Nathaniel
Dance (1748-1827) when the French squadron was beaten off in
1804, off Pulo Aor, in the Straits of Malacca. A court of
enquiry into charges of misconduct was held during the final
voyage of the *Bombay Castle*. Her successor, the *Bombay*, made
four voyages with Hamilton commanding between 1810 and 1820;
the first two were to China and the latter two to Bombay and
China.

The papers are part of the Hamilton (East India) collection,
presented between 1965 and 1968 by Lieutenant-Commander John
Hamilton, R.N. They consist of journals, owners' instructions,
accounts of stores, navigational work books, cash books, as
well as accounts of the engagement off Pulo Aor and the
subsequent court of enquiry. There are also private and
general trade accounts and several items of economic interest,
including a fabric pattern sample book of 1819. A few of the
papers relate to Montgomerie Hamilton, younger brother of
Archibald. There are a number of logs of other East India
Company ships, 1765 to 1785, and some papers of William Reid,
relating to trade with North America, 1734 to 1735.
(6ft; 186cm)

119 HAMILTON, *Sir* Frederick Tower, *Admiral*, 1856-1917

Hamilton entered the Navy in 1869 and served in the *Bristol*
in the West Indies, 1870 to 1871, and then in the *Ariadne* in
the Mediterranean, 1872. From 1877 to 1878 he served in the
Martin training brig on a cruise to the West Indies. In 1878
he joined the *Liffey* which sailed to Coquimbo where the crew
took over the *Shah*. On the return voyage Hamilton thus found
himself as part of the Naval Brigade in the Zulu War of 1879,
for which service he was mentioned in despatches. He was
also made a lieutenant in this year. He then served in the
Mediterranean in the *Thunderer* until 1881. In 1892 he was
made a commander and appointed to the *Hood*, 1893 to 1896, in
the Mediterranean. He was promoted to captain in 1898. In
1907 he was made rear-admiral and from 1914 to 1916 was
Second Sea Lord. He then became Commander-in-Chief, Rosyth,

in which command he died.

The papers were presented by Admiral Hamilton's daughter, Miss Jean Hamilton, in 1957. They consist of logs, 1870 to 1872, 1877 to 1881, 1885 and 1915 to 1916, and semi-official letters received, 1914 to 1917, including some from Admirals Lord Fisher (1841-1920), Jellicoe (1859-1935), Beatty (1871-1936), Sir Charles Madden (*q.v.*) and Prince Louis of Battenburg (1854-1921). In addition, there is detailed material on the resignation of Lord Fisher in 1915. There are also a large number of private papers and letters received, 1889 to 1917, letters to his son Louis Henry Keppel Hamilton (*q.v.*). 1906 to 1915, scrap and photograph albums, official service documents, notes on manoeuvering the *Hood*, 1893 to 1894, and reports and memoranda, 1917. (6ft; 152cm)

120 HAMILTON, Henry George, *Captain*, 1808-1879

Hamilton entered the Navy in 1822 and became a lieutenant in 1829. Between 1826 and 1830 he served in the *Cambrian* in the Mediterranean and on the South American Station. From 1839 he spent four years sheep farming in Australia. He was promoted to captain on the retired list in 1856.

The papers were presented by Miss Jean Hamilton in 1957. They consist of official service documents, letters to his family, 1822 to 1830, and from Australia, 1839 to 1843. (1 box)

121 HAMILTON, John, *Commander* (H.E.I.C.), 1763-1837

John Hamilton, elder brother of Archibald Hamilton (*q.v.*), and nephew of Alexander Montgomerie (*q.v.*), first went to sea in the service of the East India Company. He took command of the *Bombay Castle* for three voyages between 1795 and 1801, when the ship was managed by Alexander Montgomerie (*q.v.*). The first two of these voyages were to Bombay and China. The destination of the third was to China direct and it was during this voyage, when the *Bombay Castle* was one of six East Indiamen under convoy of Captain Rowley Bulteel (*fl.*1780-1820) in *H.M.S. Belliqueux*, that three French frigates and a prize schooner were sighted off the coast of Brazil. *La Médée* was captured by Hamilton and by Captain Meriton (H.E.I.C.) of the *Exeter* and command of her was given to John's brother, Archibald Hamilton (*q.v.*).

The papers are part of the Hamilton (East India) collection, presented between 1965 and 1968 by Lieutenant-Commander John Hamilton, R.N. They consist of very full records for all of the *Bombay Castle*'s voyages, including expenses, signal books, lists of passengers, and accounts of the French prize. There is also an extract from the *Castle Huntly*'s log, 1819. (1ft; 31cm)

122 HAMILTON, *Sir* Louis Henry Keppel, *Admiral*, 1892–1957

Hamilton (known throughout his career as 'Turtle'), son of Admiral Sir Frederick Tower Hamilton (*q.v.*), entered the Navy in 1903. After Dartmouth he served on the Mediterranean Station, 1908 to 1910, in the *Albemarle* and the *Prince of Wales*. Between 1910 and 1911 he was in the *Vanguard* in the Channel and went in the *Venus* to the Indian Durbar of 1911. He was made lieutenant in 1913, after which he went to the *Cumberland* and took a prominent part in the Cameroons operations, 1914 to 1915. Subsequently he began a long service commanding destroyers in the Harwich Force. Between 1915 and 1916 he was in the *Moorsom* and in the *Taurus* from 1917 to 1918. He was appointed to the *Strenuous*, home waters, in 1921, to the *Queen Elizabeth*, home waters, 1922 to 1924 and in 1925 to the Royal Yacht, *Victoria and Albert*, becoming a commander in 1926. He next served in the destroyers *Wanderer* and *Wild Swan*, Mediterranean and China, 1927 to 1928, returned to the Mediterranean for a short period in 1929 and was at the Admiralty from 1931 to 1932. He was promoted to captain in 1932, commanded the *Norfolk*, flagship on the East Indies Station, 1935 to 1937, and was Captain of the Royal Naval College, Greenwich, 1938 to 1939. Promoted to rear-admiral in 1941, he commanded the First Cruiser Squadron, Home Fleet, from 1940 to 1942, during which he was ordered to abandon the Arctic convoy PQ17. He was Flag Officer, Malta, 1943 to 1945, and then went to Australia as First Member of the Commonwealth Naval Board, 1945 to 1948. He was made an admiral in 1947 and retired in 1948.

The papers were presented by Hamilton's sister, Miss Jean Hamilton, in 1957. The diaries cover most of his career and all periods afloat from 1908 to 1928. There are also diaries for journeys in the merchant ships *Lagos*, 1915, and in the *Usaramo* to Lisbon in 1924. In addition there are official reports and signals for the time when Hamilton commanded the First Cruiser Squadron and a very full collection of letters written by him to his family, 1906 to 1956. Those from 1939 are not available for inspection until 1985. There are also photograph albums of Osborne and Dartmouth, 1903 to 1907,

of the Durbar, 1911, and of other periods in Hamilton's life.
Finally, there are lecture notes and memoranda from Dartmouth,
1922 to 1924, and papers relating to Australia, 1947.
(13ft; 390cm)

123 HAMILTON, *Sir* Richard Vesey, *Admiral*, 1829-1912

Hamilton entered the Navy in 1843 and served in the *Virago* on
the Mediterranean Station. From 1850 to 1851 he served in the
Assistance and from 1852 to 1854 in the *Resolute* in the Arctic
expeditions searching for Sir John Franklin (*q.v.*). He was
made a lieutenant in 1851. During the Crimean War he served in
the Baltic in the *Desperate*, 1855 to 1856. After this he took
part in the Second Chinese War in command of the *Haughty*, and
was promoted to commander in 1857 for his services. In 1858
he commissioned the *Hydra* for service off the African coast
but was sent instead to Halifax, serving on the North American
and West Indies Station until 1868. During this time he was
promoted to captain, 1862, and commanded the *Vesuvius* until
1864 and the *Sphinx* from 1865 to 1868. Hamilton then served in
home waters. In 1875 he was appointed Superintendent of
Pembroke Dockyard, became a rear-admiral in 1877 and in 1878
was made Director of Naval Ordnance. From 1880 to 1883 he was
in command off the Irish coast. He became vice-admiral in
1884 and was Commander-in-Chief, China Station, from 1885 to
1888. He became an admiral in 1887. Hamilton was appointed
Second, later First, Sea Lord, 1889 to 1891. From 1891 to
1894 he was President of the Royal Naval College, Greenwich.
He retired in 1895 and wrote works on naval administration
and historical subjects.

The papers were purchased by Sir Eric Miller and presented to
the Museum in 1956. Hamilton's letterbooks, 1865 to 1868 and
1885 to 1887, official papers and correspondence, cover his
career in outline and provide detailed information for some
periods, notably his time as Commander-in-Chief on the China
Station. Among the Arctic papers there are some orders from
Sir Edward Belcher (*q.v.*), Captain Henry Kellett (1806-1875)
and Captain Horatio T. Austin (*ca.*1800-1865). The letters
which he received also include some references to his Arctic
service but the majority relate to his work at the Admiralty
and there are several from Lord George Hamilton (1845-1927),
who was instrumental in the passing of the Naval Defence Act
of 1889. There is a series of photograph albums and notes
made by Hamilton for his articles on naval and historical
subjects, as well as some service memoranda. (3ft; 91cm)

124 HAMILTON, *Sir* William (diplomat), 1730-1803

Hamilton spent some years in the army before marrying an
heiress. From 1764 to 1800 he was Envoy Extraordinary to
the Court of Naples. His first wife died in 1782 and in 1791
he married Emma Hart, formerly his nephew's mistress, who had
been living with him since 1786. The Hamiltons enjoyed
considerable influence with the Neapolitan royal family and
succeeded in persuading them to ally Naples with Britain
against the French, although this led to the flight of the
government to Sicily in 1798 and 1799. In 1800 Hamilton was
recalled. He travelled home across Europe with Lady Hamilton
and Nelson and eventually settled with them at Merton, where
he died.

The papers were acquired on two occasions in 1939. A series
of one hundred and fifty-five letters received by Hamilton
between 1791 and 1800 was purchased from a dealer, M. Breslauer,
and a series of sixty letters from Hamilton to Sir John Acton
(1736-1811), Prime Minister of Naples, written between 1795
and 1800, was bought from Maggs Bros. Hamilton's correspondents include Earl St. Vincent (*q.v.*), Viscount Hood (*q.v.*),
John Hampden-Trevor (1749-1824), British Minister at Turin,
Lord Macartney (1737-1806) and the Marquis di Gallo, Secretary
of State at Naples. There are also drafts of some of
Hamilton's replies. (2 boxes)

125 HAMMILL, Tynte Ford, *Captain*, 1851-1894

Hammill entered the Navy in 1865, was made a lieutenant in
1871 and a commander in 1881. At the bombardment of
Alexandria, 1882, he commanded the *Monarch* and then the
Naval Brigade. He later served with the Naval Brigade at
Port Said. Hammill again served with a Naval Brigade during
the Sudan Campaign of 1884 to 1885, when he accompanied the
Nile Expedition despatched for the relief of General Gordon.
He commanded the naval force south of Wadi Halfa during the
passage of the steamers through the Second Cataract and served
with the Nile Flotilla in surveying the Upper Nile. For
these services he was promoted to captain in 1885. Hammill
held various posts at the Admiralty between 1886 and 1892.
He then returned to service afloat until his early death.

The papers were presented to the Museum in 1960 by Captain C.
Ford Hammill, son of Captain Hammill. They cover the bombardment of Alexandria and the landing at Port Said, for which

there are some orders received and a report of proceedings;
for the Nile Expedition there is a record of telegrams sent
and received, orders received and printed reports on the
navigation of the river. There is also a volume of press
cuttings on the courts martial following the stranding of the
Howe in 1892 at which Hammill gave evidence. (1ft; 31cm)

126 HAMOND, *Sir* Graham Eden, 2nd Bt., *Admiral of the Fleet*, 1799-1862

Hamond was the son of Captain Sir Andrew Snape Hamond (1738-
1828), Comptroller of the Navy. He entered the Navy in 1785,
was promoted to lieutenant in 1795 and commander in 1798. He
served during the French wars but was invalided in 1814. His
next appointment was in 1824 to the *Wellesley* and in 1825 he
conveyed the British ambassador, Sir Charles Stuart (1779-
1845), later Lord Stuart de Rothesay, to Brazil. While there
Hamond was promoted to rear-admiral. He was ordered home in
the *Spartiate* and on the way he delivered the Treaty of
Separation between Brazil and Portugal to the King of Portugal.
From 1834 to 1838 he was Commander-in-Chief on the South
American Station; this was his last employment. Hamond became
a vice-admiral in 1837, an admiral in 1847 and Admiral of the
Fleet in 1862.

The papers were purchased by Sir James Caird in 1937. There
are three diaries, 1834 to 1838, and about one hundred letters,
most of which are letters received by Hamond and copies or
drafts of his replies during his period on the South American
Station. There are a few earlier and later letters but all
are from the year 1819 onwards, except for copies of two
letters written by his father. His correspondents included
Sir John Barrow (1764-1848) and Robert Dundas, 2nd Viscount
Melville (*q.v.*). (1ft; 31cm)

127 HAMPSHIRE, Cyril Beaumont, *Commander*, *ca.*1875-1963

Hampshire entered the Navy in 1888. He served from 1890 to
1892 in the *Benbow* and *Immortalité*, Mediterranean Station and
from late 1892 in the *Cleopatra*, North America and West Indies
Station. He became a lieutenant in 1896 and retired in 1910
as a commander, although he served again during the First World
War. He was present at the Dardanelles landing and later
commanded the *St. George*, base ship at Mudros.

The papers were presented by Miss J.M. Hampshire in 1964.
There are two logs, 1890 to 1894, but no papers survive for
Hampshire's subsequent peacetime service. The loose papers
and charts relate to the Aegean, 1915 to 1919. (2ft; 61cm)

128 HARVEY, *Sir* Thomas, *Vice-Admiral*, 1775-1841

Harvey entered the Navy in 1787. He was present at the battle
of the First of June 1794 and became a lieutenant four months
later. In 1796 he was promoted to commander and to post rank
in the next year. He was appointed to the *Standard* in 1805
under Vice-Admiral Collingwood (*q.v.*), in the Mediterranean and
in 1807 took part in the action of Sir John Duckworth (*q.v.*) in
the Dardanelles. Returning to England in 1808, he was appointed
to the *Majestic* in the Baltic until 1810 and then served until
1815 in the North Sea. Between 1815 and 1839 he had no employment. He was made rear-admiral in 1821, vice-admiral in 1837
and in 1839 was appointed Commander-in-Chief, North America and
West Indies Station; he died during this command.

The papers are part of the Rainier collection, presented in
1948 by Captain J.W. Rainier. Harvey was connected with the
Rainier family through his daughter, Sarah Harvey, who
married the Reverend George Rainier and was the mother of
Admiral John Harvey Rainier (*q.v.*). The papers consist of a
journal, 1805 to 1807, loose papers containing letters and
orders, 1807 to 1809, and a few miscellaneous memoranda.
(1 vol, 1 file)

129 HAWKE, Edward, *Admiral of the Fleet, 1st Baron Hawke*, 1705-1781

Hawke entered the Navy in 1720 and was promoted to lieutenant in
1729. He served in the Mediterranean, West Indies and off the
West African coast between periods on half pay and became a
captain in 1734. At the outbreak of war in 1739 he blockaded
Barbados for four years until his appointment to the *Berwick*, in
which he took a noteworthy part in the battle of Toulon and
remained in the Mediterranean for the next eighteen months.
After a brief period at home he was appointed, in 1747, vice-
admiral and second-in-command of the Channel Fleet under Sir
Peter Warren (1703-1752), and he succeeded to the command when
Warren fell ill. His decisive victory off Finisterre in 1747
won him a knighthood and, in December of that year, he was
elected a Member of Parliament for Portsmouth, a seat he held

for thirty years. When peace came he commanded the Channel
Fleet until 1752. In 1755 he again hoisted his flag, in the
St. George, and was appointed to the Western Squadron. He was
sent to the Mediterranean in June 1756 but was too late to
prevent Minorca falling to the French. Having been promoted
to admiral in 1757 and appointed to command the Channel Fleet,
he took part in the Rochefort expedition. He held this command
again in 1759 in the *Royal George*, enforced the blockade of
Brest and won a decisive victory at Quiberon Bay. From 1766
to 1771 Hawke was First Lord of the Admiralty and was raised
to the peerage in 1776.

See Montagu Burrows, *The Life of Edward, Lord Hawke* (London,
1883) and Ruddock F. Mackay, *Admiral Hawke* (Oxford, 1965).

The papers were purchased by Treasury grant in 1970 from Lord
Oxmantown. They contain a virtually unbroken series of letter
and order books relating to Hawke's career afloat from June
1743 onwards. The only gap appears in the in-letters between
November 1759 and April 1762; otherwise chronological omissions
correspond with Hawke's periods ashore. There is nothing
relating to his service as First Lord of the Admiralty.
(3ft; 91cm)

130 HAWKER, Edward, *Admiral*, 1782-1860

Hawker, son of Captain James Hawker (*ca.* 1731-1787), went to
sea in 1793. He joined the *Swiftsure*, home waters, in 1794,
commanded by his brother-in-law, Captain Charles Boyles (*q.v.*),
and was also with him in the West Indies when he was promoted
to lieutenant in the *Raisonnable*. Again in the West Indies,
1803, Hawker commanded the prize brig, *La Mignonne*, and in
1804, having been promoted to captain, was appointed to the
Theseus, flagship of the station. He then commanded the *Tartar*,
1805 to 1806, and the *Melampus*, 1806 to 1811, on the North
America and West Indies Stations, engaged against the enemy's
privateers. From 1813 to 1815, in the *Bellerophon* and then in
the *Salisbury*, he was Flag-Captain to Sir Richard Goodwin
Keats (*q.v.*), Commander-in-Chief, Newfoundland. His last
appointments were to the *Britannia*, 1828 to 1829, and *St.
Vincent*, 1829 to 1830, flagships at Plymouth to the Earl of
Northesk (1758-1831). He became rear-admiral in 1837, vice-
admiral in 1847 and admiral in 1853.

The papers were purchased at Sotheby's in 1955 with those of
Admiral Sir Erasmus Gower (*q.v.*). They consist of logs
covering Hawker's service afloat, two order books for the
Bellerophon and *Britannia* and a notebook of vessels captured

1805 to 1806. There is also a letterbook of his father, Captain James Hawker, kept during his command of the *Iris*, 1779 to 1781, on the North America and West Indies Station. (1ft; 30cm)

131 HEALD, *Doctor* Charles Brehmer (Temporary Surgeon), 1882-1974

After qualifying at Cambridge, Heald served in the Navy as a Temporary Surgeon, 1914 to 1915. He was in the *Rohilla*, hospital ship, which was wrecked in 1914, and then the *Conqueror*. He was subsequently Principal Medical Officer, R.A.F., Middle East, and Medical Adviser, Department of Civil Aviation, Air Ministry. Dr Heald was Consulting Physician to the Royal Free Hospital and Consulting Physician, Rheumatic Diseases at the Middlesex Hospital.

The papers were presented by Dr Heald in 1957. They consist of two diaries, 1914 to 1915, memoranda on medical procedure in the First World War and letters written to him while at sea from his family. (1 box)

132 HENDERSON, *Sir* William Hannam, *Vice-Admiral*, 1845-1931

Henderson entered the Navy in 1859, served on the North America and West Indies Station, 1860 to 1864, in the *Nile* and the *Styx* and then joined the Channel Squadron in the *Prince Consort*. He became a lieutenant in 1866 and was at Portsmouth in the *Crocodile* from 1867 until he took part in the voyage round the world of the Flying Squadron in the *Liverpool*, flagship of Sir Geoffrey Phipps Hornby (*q.v.*). From 1872 to 1875 he was in the *Peterel*, Pacific Station, in the *Eclipse* in 1877 on the North America and West Indies Station, and was on 'particular service' in the *Hydra*, 1878. He was promoted to commander in 1879 and to captain in 1886, after having been in Australia for four years, 1881 to 1885. Going to the East Indies in command of the *Conquest*, 1889 to 1892, Henderson was in the Naval Brigade under Sir Edmund Fremantle (*q.v.*) in the punitive expedition against the Sultan of Vitu, 1890. He then went out to the Mediterranean and later to China in the *Edgar*, 1894 to 1896, when he returned to Devonport to command the Fleet Reserve. From 1898 to 1900 he was Commodore and Naval Officer in command at Jamaica and was Admiral Superintendent of Devonport Dockyard, 1902 to 1906. At the end of this appointment he retired and occupied himself with voluntary work such as his service for the Metropolitan Asylums Board, 1909 to 1921. Always much interested in the professional education of naval officers, in 1913 he was one of those who founded the *Naval Review*, which he edited for several years.

The papers were arranged by Admiral Henderson himself and were presented by his daughter, Mrs L.C. Dunne, in two instalments in 1951 and 1955. They consist of official service documents; a log, 1860 to 1866; a personal notebook, 1867 to 1869; an order book, 1873 to 1878; five out-letterbooks, 1889 to 1896, and accounts, estimates, memoranda, plans, personnel lists and proposed social reforms for Devonport Dockyard; also for this period, 1902 to 1905, are two out-letterbooks to the Admiralty. Among Henderson's letters received, dating from his schooldays to his death, are copies of those from Lloyd George, written during the First World War. Finally there are scrapbooks, photograph albums and news cuttings, 1847 to 1931, and proofs of his articles, including those published in the *Naval Review* between 1917 and 1924 entitled 'Admiralty and Command of the Sea'. In the Royal United Service Institution collection, now in this Museum, are some of Henderson's watch bills, a notebook, 1870 to 1880, and an order book for the *Conquest*, 1889 to 1891. (12ft; 372cm)

133 HENSLOW, *Sir* John (Surveyor of the Navy), 1730-1815

Henslow entered the dockyard service as a shipwright apprentice to Sir Thomas Slade (d.1771). After a period at the Navy Office as a draughtsman, he moved quickly up the service as Master Boat Builder at Woolwich, 1762 to 1764, Purveyor of Chatham Yard, 1764 to 1765, and Master Caulker of Portsmouth, 1765 to 1767. In 1767 he was Second Assistant to the Master Shipwright at Portsmouth and in 1771 was the Assistant to the Surveyor of the Navy. He was Master Shipwright at Plymouth, 1775 to 1784. In 1785 he was appointed Surveyor of the Navy, which post he held until 1806.

The papers were presented by the family in 1957 and include several examples of Henslow's drawings as a young man when he was draughtsman to Sir Thomas Slade. There is a list of the ships built under his supervision in Plymouth yard and family photographs, notes and other papers until 1878. In 1975 some of Henslow's drawings of ships' figureheads were purchased from Mrs V. Bloomfield. (1 box; 1 file)

134 HERSCHEL, *Sir* John Frederick William, 1st Bt. (astronomer),
 1792-1871

Sir John was the son of Sir William Herschel (*q.v.*). He was
Senior Wrangler at Cambridge and was elected a Fellow of the
Royal Society in 1813 for his contributions to chemistry and
mathematics. Through assisting his father he came to adopt
astronomy as his career and went to live at the Cape of Good
Hope from 1833 to 1838, making a star survey of the southern
sky. The results of this work were published in 1847. On his
return to England, Herschel became an active member of
several scientific societies. He was employed as Master of
the Mint from 1850 to 1855 and wrote many articles for the
Encyclopaedia Britannica and other general works of reference.

There is a translation of Günther Buthman's *The shadow of the
telescope. A biography of John Herschel* by B.E. Pagel (New
York, 1970).

The papers, for the most part, were presented in 1958 by Mrs
Shorland, great-great-niece of Sir John, and consist of notes,
news cuttings and Lady Herschel's housekeeping accounts for
1832 to 1838 and for 1852 to 1886. Maggs Bros. also presented
some notes and correspondence in 1958 concerning the family's
Molyneux chronometer together with a description of Sir John's
barometer, 1832 to 1833. (1 box)

135 HERSCHEL, *Sir* William Frederick (astronomer), 1738-1822

William Herschel was a self-taught astronomer who began life
as an army musician in Hanover and came to England in 1758
as a refugee during the Seven Years War. In 1781 he discovered
the planet Uranus and was made a Fellow of the Royal Society.
George III appointed him Court Astronomer. He settled at
Slough in 1786 and built a telescope which was the largest in
the world until it was dismantled in 1839. In 1788 he
married Mary Pitt (née Baldwin).

Among a number of biographies is Angus Armitage, *William
Herschel* (London, 1962).

The papers were presented by Mrs Shorland, great-great-great-
niece of Sir William, together with the papers of his son,
Sir John Herschel (*q.v.*). There are three volumes of cash
accounts kept by Lady Herschel between 1795 and 1825. The
first gives details of Sir William's salary as Court Astronomer
and of the proceeds from selling telescopes; the other two are
housekeeping accounts. There are also letters, proofs and

notes about the publication of Herschel's catalogues of the brightness of stars and pamphlets about him and his sister, Caroline, who assisted him with his observations. (3 vols; 1 file)

The main body of the Herschel papers is in the University of Texas Library and the Linda Hall Library, Kansas City.

136 HOLBURNE, Francis, *Admiral*, 1704-1771

Holburne entered the Navy in 1720 and was promoted to lieutenant in 1727 and to captain in 1739. Between 1740 and 1745 he served in the Channel and the North Sea, between 1745 and 1746 in the West Indies and between 1748 and 1752 was Commander-in-Chief on the Leeward Islands Station. In 1755 he was promoted to rear-admiral, sailed in 1756 to reinforce Admiral Boscawen (1711-1761) at Louisbourg and returned to the Channel to maintain the blockade off Brest. He then was a member of the court at Byng's court martial. In 1757 he was promoted to vice-admiral and again sailed to North America, in order to attack Louisbourg, but he soon returned to England. He was then immediately appointed Commander-in-Chief, Portsmouth, a post he occupied for eight years apart from a break, 1760 to 1762, when Sir Francis Geary (*q.v.*) held the post. Holburne became an admiral in 1767 and after a brief period as a Lord of the Admiralty, he accepted the post of Governor of Greenwich Hospital, 1771, but died later that year.

The papers form part of the collection transferred from the Royal United Service Institution in 1968. They are in two parts. The first, presented by Commander Sir Thomas Holburne, consists of letters and orders received by Admiral Holburne between March 1755 and October 1766 and includes letters from Admirals Anson (1697-1762) and Boscawen (1711-1761). The second consists of Holburne's letterbooks, 1759 to 1764. There is also an Admiralty Warrant to him of 1765, presented separately. (1 ft; 30cm)

137 HOOD, Alexander, *Admiral*, *1st Viscount Bridport*, 1726-1814

Alexander Hood, younger brother of Samuel, Viscount Hood (*q.v.*), entered the Navy in 1741 and was made lieutenant in 1746. During the Seven Year War he served in the Mediterranean and under Hawke (*q.v.*) in the Channel. He was made captain in 1756 and, after further service in the Channel and

in the Mediterranean, was promoted to rear-admiral in
1780. From 1784 to 1790 he was a Member of Parliament for
Bridgwater, after which he sat for Buckingham until 1796. In
1787 he was promoted to vice-admiral and in 1794 to admiral.
In that year he was appointed second-in-command of the Channel
Fleet, under Lord Howe (q.v.), and took part in the battle of
the First of June, after which he was given an Irish peerage.
In the following year when Howe was ashore because of ill-
health, he won a partial victory over the French Fleet. For
this action, he was raised to the peerage of Great Britain.
When Howe finally retired in 1797, Hood was made Commander-in-
Chief of the Channel Fleet. In 1800 he was relieved by St.
Vincent and accepted no further active command. He was
created a viscount in the same year.

The papers form a small part of the collection presented by
a descendant, Commander Mackinnon, in 1952. They consist of
letters from Bridport to his first and second wives, 1761 to
1799. There are also a number of other letters, including
two from Lord Howe, 1787. (1 box)

138 HOOD, Alexander, *Captain*, 1758-1798

Alexander Hood, elder brother of Sir Samuel Hood (q.v.) and
cousin of Viscount Bridport (q.v.) and Viscount Hood (q.v.),
entered the Navy in 1767. In 1772 he joined the *Resolution*
for Cook's second voyage. He became a lieutenant in 1777 and
a commander in 1781. In the same year he was made Flag-
Captain to Rear-Admiral Samuel (later Viscount) Hood (q.v.)
in the *Barfleur* in the West Indies, and was later given
command of the *Aimable*, a French prize, which he took to
England in 1783. In 1793 he commanded the *Hebe* and in 1794
the *Audacious* but was compelled in the same year to retire
from active service through ill-health until 1797. In this
year he was appointed to the *Mars* and was put ashore at the
mutiny at Spithead. He was killed soon afterwards in action.

The papers form part of the collection presented by a descendant, Commander Mackinnon, in 1952. There was a further
addition in 1954. In 1968 Mrs Mackinnon presented some
letters, a log and some printed material. Hood's papers
consist of a log, January to September 1772, and some signal
books for the *Barfleur* and the *Aimable*. There are also a
number of private letters, 1772 and 1793 to 1794, a muster
book for the *Audacious*, 1794, official correspondence, 1793
to 1797, and three signal books for the *Hebe*. In addition,
there are some official service documents and a small collection
of documents relating to the mutinies of 1797. (1ft; 30cm)

139 HOOD, Samuel, *Admiral, 1st Viscount Hood*, 1724-1816

Samuel Hood, elder brother of Viscount Bridport (*q.v.*) entered
the Navy in 1741 and was made a lieutenant in 1746. His first
command was in the Mediterranean in 1754. In 1757 he was at
the blockade of Brest and was successful in a noteworthy
single-ship action. Between 1760 and 1763 he served in the
Mediterranean. He was employed during the peace and in 1767
was appointed Commander-in-Chief, North America, in the *Romney*.
From 1771 to 1776 he commanded the *Royal William*, guardship
at Portsmouth, and in 1778 was appointed Resident Commissioner
at Portsmouth Dockyard. In the following year he was created
a baronet and in 1780 promoted to rear-admiral, when he went
in the *Barfleur*, with reinforcements to Rodney in the West
Indies. Here he too part in the taking of St. Eustatius and
the manoeuvering off Martinique. When Rodney sailed for England,
Hood went to North America to reinforce Admiral Graves (*q.v.*)
and commanded the rear squadron at the battle of Chesapeake in
1781. Early in 1782 Hood worsted De Grasse at Frigate Bay at
St. Kitts, and soon afterwards took an important part in the
battle of the Saints, the *Ville de Paris* surrendering to the
Barfleur. As a result in 1782 Hood was raised to the Irish
Peerage and was Member of Parliament for Westminster, 1785 to
1788 and 1790 to 1796 and for Reigate, 1789 to 1790. Between
1787 and 1788 he was Commander-in-Chief, Portsmouth, having
been promoted to vice-admiral, and from 1788 to 1795 he served
at the Board of Admiralty. At the beginning of the Revolutionary
Wars, he was appointed Commander-in-Chief, Mediterranean,
where he commanded the forces which took Toulon in August 1793.
However, he had to withdraw to Corsica in December. In late
1794 he returned to England. He was promoted to admiral and
in 1796 was appointed Governor of Greenwich Hospital, which
post he held until his death. He was raised to the British
peerage in 1796.

See David Hannay *ed.*, *Letters of Lord Hood, 1781-82* (Navy
Records Society, 1895).

The papers were deposited on loan by Viscount Hood in 1950 and
were supplemented by a smaller group in 1954. They consist of
twenty-one official letterbooks, 1767 to 1794, and some five
hundred loose letters, 1771 to 1815. Among Hood's correspondents were George III, 1778, 1782; Sir George Rodney (1719-
1792), 1781 to 1782; Prince William Henry, 1786 to 1787; Lord
Howe (*q.v.*), 1787; Henry Dundas, Viscount Melville (*q.v.*),
1794; and Lord Nelson (*q.v.*), 1794. There are also a collection
of charts of the Mediterranean, drawn between 1760 and 1761,
and some papers relating to diplomatic affairs, 1793 to 1794,
and to Hood's appointment as Governor of Greenwich Hospital.

In the collection of Hood family papers presented by Commander
Mackinnon in 1952 and Mrs Mackinnon in 1968, there are some
private letters from Hood to Lord Bridport (*q.v.*), 1779 to
1802, and one from Hood to his sister after the battle of the
Saints. (4ft; 122cm)

140 HOOD, *Sir* Samuel, 1st Bt., *Vice-Admiral*, 1762-1814

Samuel Hood, younger brother of Captain Alexander Hood (*q.v.*),
entered the Navy in 1776 and was promoted to lieutenant in
1780. For most of the American War he served in the West Indies
and afterwards was employed in North America. He was promoted
to captain in 1788. In 1793 he went in the *Juno* to the
Mediterranean where he was present at the occupation of Toulon.
In 1798 he commanded the *Zealous*, and after the battle of the
Nile was left by Nelson to command the force blockading the
French army in Egypt. The next year he was at the defence of
Salerno and in 1800 in the Atlantic in the *Courageux*. In 1801
he was again in the Mediterranean, and during the peace was
sent out as a Commissioner for the government of Trinidad. On
the death of the Commander-in-Chief, Leeward Islands, he
succeeded to the position in the *Centaur*. Returning to England
in 1805, he served in the Channel and lost an arm in a
successful squadron action off Rochefort. From 1806 to 1807
he was Member of Parliament for Westminster and from 1807 to
1812 for Bridport. He was promoted to rear-admiral in 1807,
and in the same year was at Copenhagen, still in the *Centaur*;
he was then second-in-command to Admiral Saumarez (1757-1836)
in the Baltic when he played an important part in assisting
the Swedes against the Russians. He next covered the re-
embarkation of the army at Corunna in 1809, after which he
returned to the Mediterranean. He was appointed vice-admiral
and Commander-in-Chief, East Indies, in 1811, and after a
comparatively uneventful command died of fever in Madras.

The papers form the major part of the collection presented by
Commander Mackinnon in 1952. There was a further donation in
1957. They consist of letter and order books, 1794 to 1795,
1806, 1808 to 1809; signals and instructions, 1790 to 1791;
and logs, 1806 to 1814. The large section of papers relating
to the East Indian command includes letters from the Admiralty,
Victualling and Transport Boards, as well as copies of
correspondence with Sir Stamford Raffles (1781-1826). In
addition there are extracts from logs of ships on the East
Indies Station during Hood's command, including the *Modeste*,
1810; *Hesper*, 1810; *Cornelia*, 1811; *Doris*, 1811; *Phaeton*,
1812; *Hecate*, 1813; *Salsette*, 1813 to 1814. Finally, there
are a number of Hood family papers, 1745 to 1817. (5ft; 152cm)

141 HORNBY, *Sir* Geoffrey Thomas Phipps, *Admiral of the Fleet*, 1825-1895

Geoffrey Phipps Hornby, son of Sir Phipps Hornby (*q.v.*), entered the Navy in 1837 and became a lieutenant in 1844. In 1852 he was promoted to captain but remained on half-pay until 1858, after which he commanded the *Tribune*, China, 1858 to 1860, *Neptune*, flagship, Mediterranean, 1861 to 1862, and *Edgar*, flagship, Channel, 1863 to 1865. In 1865 he was appointed Commander-in-Chief on the west coast of Africa. He was promoted to rear-admiral in 1869 and commanded the Flying Squadron in the *Liverpool* on its voyage round the world, 1869 to 1871, and then the Channel Squadron from 1871 to 1874. Hornby was one of the Lords of the Admiralty from 1875 to 1877. He was promoted to vice-admiral in 1875. From 1877 to 1880 he was Commander-in-Chief, Mediterranean. He played an important part in the Balkan crisis of 1878, for which he was knighted and was promoted to admiral in 1879. He was President of the Royal Naval College, Greenwich, 1881 to 1882, and Commander-in-Chief, Portsmouth, 1882 to 1885. In 1885 he commanded an Evolutionary Squadron and became Admiral of the Fleet in 1888.

See Mrs Frederick Egerton, *Admiral of the Fleet Sir Geoffrey Phipps Hornby, G.C.B., a biography* (London, 1896).

The papers were presented by Admiral R.S. Phipps Hornby in 1945, by his daughter-in-law, Mrs R.M. Phipps Hornby, in 1956 and by Commander W.M. Phipps Hornby in 1954, 1964 and 1971. Except for a few service papers and a letterbook, 1858 to 1870, the entire collection dates from 1865 onwards. The most important part of the collection is Hornby's official, semi-official and private correspondence, 1873 to 1894, in which many leading naval officers and other figures of the day are represented. There are also some letters written by Hornby and some correspondence of his wife and of his daughter, Mrs Egerton. Relating to Hornby's commands, there are official letterbooks for the years 1870 to 1874 and 1877 to 1880, memoranda and orders, 1865 to 1874 and 1877 to 1880, private letterbooks, 1865 to 1874, 1877 to 1878 and 1885 to 1891, and registers of telegrams received and despatched, 1877 to 1880. There are printed memoranda and papers relating to his time at the Admiralty, including the work of the Construction and Torpedo Committees. (12ft; 360cm)

142 HORNBY, *Sir* Phipps, *Admiral*, 1785-1867

Hornby entered the Navy in 1797, was promoted to lieutenant in 1804 and to captain in 1810. He was in command of the

Volage in the Mediterranean, 1810 to 1811, and took part in the action off Lissa in March 1811. From 1812 to 1814 he commanded the *Stag* at the Cape of Good Hope and from 1814 to 1816 the *Spartan* in the Mediterranean. Between 1816 and 1832 he was on half-pay. He then held several posts ashore until his promotion to rear-admiral in 1846. From 1847 to 1850 he was Commander-in-Chief, Pacific Station. On his return he served briefly as a Lord of the Admiralty. He became a vice-admiral in 1854 and an admiral in 1858.

The papers were presented by Commander W.M. Phipps Hornby in 1958 and 1971. There is a copy of a letter written in the *Volage* and a letterbook, 1812 to 1816. Most of the papers are from the Pacific Command and include an admiral's journal, 1847 to 1849, and three official letter and order books, 1847 to 1851, together with correspondence on particular aspects of the Squadron's duties. There are also some probate documents concerning members of the Hornby family. (2ft; 62cm)

143 HORNBY, Robert Stewart Phipps, *Admiral*, 1866-1956

R.S. Phipps Hornby, son of Sir Geoffrey Phipps Hornby (*q.v.*), entered the Navy in 1879. He became a lieutenant in 1886. From 1901 to 1903 he commanded the *Pylades* on the Australian Station and was promoted to captain in 1903. While commanding the *Diana* in the Mediterranean, 1904 to 1906, he was involved in the Akbar boundary dispute. After commanding the *Glory* in home waters from 1907 to 1908, he was appointed Captain of the *Vernon* (the naval torpedo school) where he remained until 1911. He then commanded the *Swiftsure*, *Inflexible* and *Monarch* before being promoted to rear-admiral in 1913. He was Commander-in-Chief, North America and West Indies Station, 1914 to 1915, when he went in the *Glory* to reinforce the Allied Fleet at the Dardanelles. He was invalided during this voyage for the rest of the war and was engaged in torpedo work. He was involved between 1917 and 1920 in the work of several Admiralty committees, including the Submarine Committee, the Armament Personnel Committee and the Post-War Reconstruction Committee. He was promoted to admiral in 1922 on the retired list.

The papers were deposited on indefinite loan in 1958 and 1959 by Commander W.M. Phipps Hornby, apart from a few items presented earlier by Admiral Hornby himself. From 1900 to 1913 there are official letterbooks, memoranda and other papers. There are a diary, a rough journal and papers for his second command from 1914 to 1915. Finally, there are papers relating to his work on torpedoes and reports from the various Admiralty committees on which he served. (2ft; 61cm)

144 HORNBY, Windham Mark Phipps, *Commander*, 1896-

Son of Admiral R.S. Phipps Hornby (*q.v.*), W.M. Phipps Hornby entered the Navy in 1909. After his time at the Royal Naval Colleges at Osborne and Dartmouth and in the training ship *Cumberland*, he was appointed midshipman in 1914 in the *Hampshire*, moving to the *Warspite* in 1915. He was promoted to sub-lieutenant in 1916, joined the *Ramillies* in 1917, was promoted to lieutenant in 1918, to lieutenant-commander in 1925 and retired in 1932.

The papers were presented by Commander Phipps Hornby in 1955 and 1958. Some of them relate to his cadet days, and are mostly printed magazines and programmes; there are also two gunnery notebooks, 1914, and a report on the organization of the *Ramillies*. The collection contains some items relating to other members of the family. (1ft; 30cm)

145 HORTON-SMITH, Lionel Graham Horton (naval propagandist), 1871-1953

Horton-Smith was a barrister and joint founder and Secretary of the Imperial Maritime League, which was active between 1908 and 1913. It was founded as a protest against the British Navy League, which fully supported the actions of Lord Fisher. The Imperial Maritime League felt that the Navy League did not go far enough in its demands for the strengthening of British naval power. Horton-Smith was the author of numerous pamphlets on naval affairs.

The papers were presented in 1954 by Mr I.A.G. Horton-Smith, his son. They consist of twenty-eight volumes of pamphlets and newspaper cuttings, put together by Horton-Smith himself, on naval policy and the activities of the Imperial Maritime League, 1895 to 1913. (5ft; 153cm)

146 HOWE, Richard, *Admiral of the Fleet, 1st Earl Howe*, 1726-1799

Howe entered the Navy in 1740, was made a lieutenant in 1744 and a captain in 1746. After service on the Guinea coast, the West Indies, the Mediterranean and on the North American Station, he served in the Channel during the Seven Years War. He was elected Member of Parliament for Dartmouth in 1757, and succeeded his brother to the Irish peerage in the following year. He held his parliamentary seat until raised to the British peerage in 1782. In 1763 he was a Lord of the Admiralty and from 1765 to 1770 was Treasurer of the Navy. He was promoted to rear-admiral in 1770 and to vice-admiral in 1775. He was then appointed Commander-in-Chief, North America, but came home in 1778 and did not serve again until 1782. Howe became First Lord of the Admiraly in 1783, which position, apart from the period between April and December 1783, he held until 1788. He was created Earl Howe in this year. In 1790 he took command of the Channel Fleet during the Nootka Sound mobilization as he did later at the outbreak of war in 1793. During this time Howe continued reforms in signalling. In 1794 he commanded the fleet which brought the French to action at the battle of the First of June. He finally gave up the command after a long period of ill-health, in 1797.

See George Mason, *The life of Richard Earl Howe* (London, 1803) and Sir John Barrow, *The life of Richard Earl Howe K.G. Admiral of the Fleet and General of Marines* (London, 1838).

The papers were purchased at Christie's in 1958 and come from the Marquess of Sligo's papers, inherited through Howe's daughter. They include signal books, undated, a notebook on signals, letters from George III, 1785 to 1794, Admiral John Blankett (d. 1801), 1786, and family letters of the 1790s. There is also an annotated copy of the Naval Instructions of 1772. (1 box, 1 vol)

147 HULBERT, George Redmond (naval agent), 1774-1825

Hulbert acted as an admiral's secretary and prize agent early in the nineteenth century. He served on the North American Station in 1804 as secretary to Sir John Borlase Warren (1753-1852) and between 1808 and 1809 exchanged with the secretary of Admiral Rowley (1765-1842) on the Jamaica Station. He served again with Warren, 1810 to 1814, on the North American Station, 1813 to 1814, when a large number of prizes were taken.

The papers were presented in 1956 by a descendant of Hulbert's, Mrs W.B. Jackson. They consist of his correspondence, 1807 to 1823, with the Navy Pay Office, Navy Prize Office, Treasury, Greenwich Hospital, Doctors' Commons and naval officers. There are also accounts and lists of prizes, including some printed papers, 1793 to 1798. The collection provides detailed information on the procedure followed in the collection and distribution of prize money. (5ft; 152cm)

148 INVERNAIRN, *Lady* Elspeth, *fl.*1902-1952

Lady Invernairn, née Elspeth Tullis, married William (later Sir William) Beardmore (1856-1936), Chairman and Managing Director of William Beardmore & Co., Engineers and Shipbuilders, in 1902. He was created Baron Invernairn of Strathnairn in 1921. They both met Ernest (later Sir Ernest) Shackleton (1874-1922) in Edinburgh in 1905, not long after the latter's return from the Antarctic where he had taken part as a junior officer in the British National Antarctic Expedition, 1901 to 1904. In 1906 Shackleton entered Beardmore's employment at Parkhead, Glasgow. With Mrs Beardmore's encouragement, he planned his own British Antarctic Expedition in the *Nimrod* in 1907. Shackleton went south again in the *Endurance* as leader of the Imperial Trans-Antarctic Expedition, 1914 to 1917.

See H.R. Mill, *The life of Sir Ernest Shackleton* (London, 1923) and Margery and James Fisher, *Shackleton* (London, 1957).

The papers were presented in accordance with the wishes of Lady Invernairn by Miss V. Blackhall in 1958. They consist of letters from Shackleton to Lady Invernairn and other papers about the *Nimrod* and *Endurance* expeditions. Some of the letters are unavailable to readers until the year 2000. Lady Invernairn had already between 1938 and 1939 presented to the Museum Shackleton's volume of Browning's poems, as well as presentation copies of the *Aurora Australis* and the *Heart of the Antarctic* (1909). (1 box, 4 vols)

149 ISMAY, Margaret, *fl.* 1859-1907

Margaret Bruce married Thomas Henry Ismay (1837-1899) in 1859. At this time Ismay was running a fleet of sailing ships to the west coast of South America. In 1864 he became director of a

steamship line trading between Liverpool and New York and in
1867 purchased the White Star Line, which ran fast sailing
ships to Australia and New Zealand and which found itself in
difficulties through lack of capital. Soon afterwards he set
up the firm of Ismay, Imrie and Company and the partners and
he established the Oceanic Steam Navigation Company (generally
known as the White Star Line). In 1902 the Company was taken
over by the new American Combine, the International Mercantile
Marine Co., but their ships still sailed under the British flag.

The papers were presented in 1972 by Commander Charles Drage.
They consist of twenty-seven diaries kept by Mrs Ismay, 1881
to 1907. There are also a number of items deposited on loan
in 1965 by Mrs Ismay's daughter-in-law, Mrs Julia Ismay. They
consist of four diaries kept on a voyage to South America in
1856 by T.H. Ismay and also diaries kept by his son, Joseph
Bruce Ismay (1862-1937), on a journey round the world, 1887 to
1888. (1ft; 30cm)

150 JENKINSON, Henry, *Rear-Admiral*, 1790-1865

Jenkinson entered the Navy in 1806. In 1808 he was appointed
to the *Decade* and was in the *Venerable* in 1809 during the
Walcheren expedition. In 1810 he was promoted to lieutenant.
He next served in the *Clyde* in the Channel and then in the
Inconstant, 1811 to 1812, at Vera Cruz and in the Channel.
He was promoted to commander in 1812 and from this time until
1814 commanded the *Jasper* in home waters. He was promoted
to captain in 1814. Between 1816 and 1817 he was in Russia,
apparently on a private visit. He was promoted to rear-
admiral in 1850.

The papers were presented by Mrs A.G. Bayley in 1950. They
consist of fifty letters written by Jenkinson to his parents,
1808 to 1817, and a letter written by a sister-in-law, 1828.
(1 box)

151 JERRAM, *Sir* Thomas Henry Martyn, *Admiral*, 1858-1933

Martyn Jerram entered the Navy as a navigating cadet in 1871.
He served in home waters in the *Valorous*, 1873, and the
Hercules, 1873 to 1874, and was then in the *Monarch*, 1874 to
1877, Mediterranean, with two short periods spent in the
Cruiser in 1876 and the *Swiftsure* in 1877. In 1881 he became

a lieutenant and was on the China Station from 1882 to 1883 in the *Iron Duke*. He took out the new torpedo boat *Childers*, built for the government of Victoria, Australia, in 1884 and was then appointed to the *Reindeer*, East Indies Station, and in 1889 to the *Conquest*. In 1891 Jerram was called upon to act as vice-consul in Mpanda, Tanganyka, until the British South Africa Company's expedition to Mashonaland had disembarked. He became a commander in 1894, a captain in 1899, a rear-admiral in 1908 and was appointed second-in-command in the Mediterranean, 1910 to 1912. From 1913 to 1915 he was Commander-in-Chief, China, and had to counter Von Spee's powerful squadron. To make best use of his ships, Jerram shifted his flag on shore at Singapore. From 1915 to 1916 he commanded the Second Battle Squadron, Grand Fleet, and led the line at Jutland, handing over his command when Beatty became Commander-in-Chief. When the Naval Welfare Committee was established, Jerram became its President.

The papers were presented by Admiral Jerram's son, Brigadier R.M. Jerram, in 1967. The collection includes official service documents; logs, 1872 to 1877, 1884 to 1888; a diary, 1882; official and private letters and memoranda, relating mainly to the China command, 1913 to 1915. There are some papers for the Vitu expedition, 1890, and for Jerram's time in the Grand Fleet, 1915 to 1916, and a few post-Jutland reports, and some photograph albums. (3ft; 91cm)

152 JERVIS, John, *Admiral of the Fleet, 1st Earl St. Vincent*, 1735-1823

Jervis, son of Swynfen Jervis, Counsel to the Admiralty between 1747 and 1757, entered the Navy against his father's wishes in 1749. He was promoted to lieutenant in 1755, served with distinction in the Seven Years War and reached captain's rank in 1760. He served in the Channel during the American War of Independence. After the war he became a Member of Parliament, representing Launceston, Yarmouth and Wycombe successively. In 1787 Jervis became a rear-admiral and in 1793 a vice-admiral. He was Commander-in-Chief of the West Indies Expedition, 1793 to 1794, capturing Martinique and Guadeloupe. He returned home in 1795 and in the same year was promoted to admiral and appointed Commander-in-Chief, Mediterranean. In February 1797 he defeated the Spanish fleet off Cape St. Vincent, for which victory he was created an earl. He gave up his command in 1799. After a brief period in command of the Channel Fleet he served as First Lord of the Admiralty, 1801 to 1804. His term of office aroused considerable controversy and he refused further service afloat until after the death of Pitt, but took the Channel command in 1806. He resigned after a further change of ministry in 1807. In 1821 he was made Admiral of the Fleet.

Among a number of biographies is Jedediah Tucker, *Memoirs of Admiral the Rt. Hon. the Earl of St. Vincent, G.C.B.* (London, 1844), while some correspondence has been published by David Bonner-Smith, *ed., Letters of Admiral of the Fleet the Earl of St. Vincent whilst First Lord of the Admiralty, 1801 to 1804* (Navy Records Society, 1922, 1927, 2 vols).

The papers were purchased from a dealer in 1941. They consist of letters and copies of letters received from Lord Nelson (*q.v.*), 1794 to 1804. They had been inherited through St. Vincent's nephew, Admiral of the Fleet Sir William Parker (*q.v.*), in whose collection there are further papers of St. Vincent. (5 vols) His lieutenant's promotion book, 1801, was loaned to the Museum by Mr H.R. Reade, in 1962. There is also his letterbook, 1806 to 1807, in the section of volumes acquired singly by the Museum.

153 JOHNSTONE, Charles, *Vice-Admiral*, 1843-1927

Johnstone entered the Navy in 1858 and served on the Mediterranean Station and then in the *St George* between 1860 and 1864. He was promoted to lieutenant in 1865. From this time until 1873 he served on the China Station in the *Serpent*, *Perseus* and *Juno*, was then appointed to the command of the training brig *Liberty*. He was made a commander in 1877. Afterwards he commanded the *Egeria* in China and the *Dryad* in the East Indies; in both ships he was involved in diplomatic affairs in Borneo and then in Madagascar, for which service he was promoted to captain in 1883. He attended the Royal Naval College, Greenwich, and subsequently served on a committee inquiring into the education of naval officers. From 1885 to 1889 he commanded the *Volage* in the Training Squadron. In 1891 he took command of the *Agamemnon* and turned over with his crew to the *Camperdown* the following year; he was still in command when the *Camperdown* collided with the *Victoria*, for which incident he was held partly to blame by the Admiralty. His only service after this was as Flag-Captain to the Commander-in-Chief, Devonport, 1896 to 1898. He retired as rear-admiral in 1899 and became a vice-admiral in 1903.

The papers came to the Museum in its early days. They consist
of eighteen diaries, 1880 to 1897, 1890 and 1895 excepted,
which describe all the major events of Johnstone's life in
detail. His logs cover the years 1858 to 1864, 1866 to 1867
and 1871 to 1873. There are official letters among the loose
papers as well as letterbooks, 1883, 1892 to 1894, 1896 to
1898, and many of these refer to Madagascar and to the *Victoria*
and *Camperdown* collision; for the latter affair there is
Johnstone's own vindication of his conduct. The printed papers,
including news cuttings, refer to Borneo and Madagascar and
to the education of naval officers. (3½ft; 105cm)

154 JONES, Jenkin, *Captain*, *ca*.1793-1843

Jones became a lieutenant in 1813 and a commander in 1816,
being appointed to the *Julia*. She was wrecked on the island
of Tristan da Cunha in 1817 but Jones was acquitted at the
subsequent court martial. From 1822 to 1824 he commanded the
Sappho on the Cork Station and in 1828 the *Gloucester*.
Soon after, however, he was promoted captain into the *Royal
Adelaide* but remained on half-pay until he took command of the
Curacoa in 1839, on the South American Station, remaining there
until 1842.

The papers were presented by Mr Charles Jones. They consist
of official service documents, logs, 1822 to 1839, 1841 to
1842, and a letterbook, 1822 to 1824 and 1839 to 1842. There
are also a number of personal letters and papers relating to
Jones's court martial. (6 vols; 1 file)

155 JONES-BYROM, William Henry, *Commander*, 1829-1867

Jones, son of Captain Jenkin Jones (*q.v.*), took the name of
Byrom under terms of inheritance which stipulated that his
wife's name should be added to his own. He entered the Navy
in 1844 in the *Collingwood*, which was stationed at Portsmouth,
became a lieutenant in 1850 and was in the Baltic and Black
Sea during the Crimean War. In 1857 he sailed to China in a
fleet of fifteen gunboats under Captain Sherard Osborn (1822-
1875), sent to reinforce the China Squadron. The *Lee*,
commanded by Jones, accompanied the *Furious* in 1858, when
Lord Elgin was escorted up the Yangtse river to Hankow. In
1859 Jones was promoted to commander. The *Lee* was lost in the
attack on the Taku forts and the consequent courts martial
ended in honourable acquittal for Jones. On his return home

the early symptoms of tuberculosis were beginning to appear
and he only served at sea again for one year, 1861 to 1862.

The papers were presented by Mr Charles Jones, a descendant,
in 1944. They contain one log, 1844 to 1848, letters to his
mother, 1859, appointments, 1844 to 1860, and Captain Osborn's
report on the mission of the *Furious* in China. (1 file; 1 vol)

156 KEATS, *Sir* Richard Goodwin, *Admiral*, 1757-1834

Keats entered the Navy in 1770 and was promoted to lieutenant
in 1777. He was made a captain in 1789. After service in the
Southampton and *Niger*, he was appointed in 1794 to the *Galatea*
and during his service in her was put ashore by the mutineers
of 1797. He was appointed to the *Superb* in 1801 under Sir
James, later Lord, Saumarez (1757-1836). After the resumption
of hostilities with France, he served in the Mediterranean
under Nelson, and took part in the chase to the West Indies;
the *Superb*, however, was refitting when Trafalgar was fought.
Until 1807 Keats took part in the blockade of Brest, being
promoted to rear-admiral also in that year. He was with
Saumarez again during the blockade of the Baltic. In 1811
Keats became a vice-admiral and in 1812 was forced to resign
his command through ill-health. He was appointed Governor and
Commander-in-Chief, Newfoundland, in 1813, returning to England
at the peace in 1815. In 1821 he was appointed Governor of
Greenwich Hospital and given the rank of admiral in 1825.

The papers were purchased by Sir James Caird in 1946. They
consist of letters received from naval officers, 1788 to 1828.
The main section comprises those from Prince William Henry for
the above dates. Other correspondents include Lord Nelson (*q.v.*),
1803, Earl St. Vincent (*q.v.*), 1800 to 1809, Sir James Saumarez
(1757-1836), 1807-1809, Sir Edward Pellew (*q.v.*), 1811 to 1812,
and Sir Richard Strachan (1760-1828), 1809. There are also
official service documents and some relating to Greenwich
Hospital and the Chatham Chest; some of these are retrospective,
dating back as far as 1696. (1ft; 30cm)

157 KELLY, *Sir* John Donald, *Admiral of the Fleet*, 1871-1936

John (known as 'Joe') Kelly, brother of Sir (William) Howard
Kelly (*q.v.*), entered the Navy in 1884, became a lieutenant
in 1893, commander in 1904 and captain in 1911, serving on the

Australian, Cape and China Stations. In 1914 he was captain
of the light cruiser *Dublin* in the Mediterranean and attempted
to locate and attack the *Goeben*. The *Dublin* later went to the
Dardanelles and was for a short time in the Adriatic. Subsequently Kelly commanded the *Devonshire* and *Weymouth* on the
South American Station and the *Princess Royal* in the Grand Fleet.
After the war he became Director of the Operations Division in
the Admiralty and was made rear-admiral in 1921. As such he
commanded a force in the Dardanelles and the Sea of Marmora
before going back to the Admiralty as Fourth Sea Lord. Two
years as second-in-command, Mediterranean, followed this
appointment and then a similar period as Admiral Commanding
Reserves. After this Kelly expected to retire but in 1932 he
was called upon to take over the command of the Atlantic Fleet
(which was renamed the Home Fleet during this time) after the
mutiny at Invergordon. His final command was as Commander-in-
Chief, Portsmouth, from 1934 to 1936.

The papers were deposited on permanent loan by the Hon. David
St. Clair Erskine in 1967. They consist of reports on the
unsuccessful attack on the *Goeben*; on the Dardanelles,
February to May 1915, and on a German raider in West Indian
and South American waters, December 1916 to March 1917.
There are orders relating to the Dardanelles, 1915, to the
surrender of the German High Seas Fleet, 1918, to the Chanak
incident of 1922, to the Invergordon mutiny in 1931 and to
Kelly's final commands. The letters are mainly official but
the private correspondents include Prince Louis of Battenburg
(1854-1921), 1903, Earl Beatty (1871-1936), 1918 and 1932,
Lord Louis Mountbatten (1900-   ), 1929, Sir Roger Keyes
(1872-1945), 1930 to 1931, and Lord Chatfield (*q.v.*), 1932 to
1936. In addition, a small collection of fifteen letters,
1831 to 1847, relate to Captain, later Vice-Admiral, William
Kelly (*ca.* 1795-1874), and are mostly concerned with the
attack on the forts of Tamatave, Madagascar, in 1845.
William Kelly is believed to have been a relative of Sir John
Kelly. (1ft; 30cm)

158 KELLY, *Sir* William Archibald Howard, *Admiral*, 1873-1952

Howard Kelly, brother of Sir John Kelly (*q.v.*), served in the
Téméraire and *Cruiser* in the Mediterranean between 1889 and
1892 and was promoted to lieutenant in 1894. From 1902 to
1904 he served in Somaliland, returning from the East Indies
Station in 1906. He was in naval intelligence from 1907,
promoted to captain in 1911 and was then naval attaché in
Paris for three years. In 1914 he was given command of the
Gloucester and won distinction by his determined chase of

the *Goeben*. He was Commodore of the Light Cruiser Squadron, 1917, and, in 1918, of the British Adriatic Force. Between 1919 and 1921 he was head of the Naval Mission to Greece and was promoted to rear-admiral in 1922. In the next year he commanded the First Battle Squadron and in 1925 the Second Cruiser Squadron. He was promoted to vice-admiral in 1927 and for the next two years he commanded the First Battle Squadron. After this he was second-in-command, Mediterranean Fleet, until 1930. In 1931 he became an admiral and went out to China until 1933, as Commander-in-Chief of the station. Kelly retired in 1936. He visited Australia in 1938 and then went to lecture in Canada in 1940. From that year until 1944 he was naval representative in Turkey.

The papers were presented in 1953 by Captain Charles Ford Hamill after Admiral Kelly had, to a large extent, arranged them. They consist of a draft of his memoirs which is very detailed until 1933; after this period it has only a few notes and observations on Turkey. The diaries for 1899, 1901, 1903, 1905 to 1907, 1910, 1914 to 1916, 1919 to 1921, 1923 to 1929 and 1931 to 1933 are also detailed. The correspondence forms two groups; the first, 1914 to 1917, includes letters from Earl Beatty (1871-1936), Admiral Tyrwhitt (1870-1951) and Lord Jellicoe (1859-1935); the second group, 1940 to 1944, includes those from Admirals Cunningham (*q.v.*), Harwood (1888-1950) and Willis (1889-1976). Some notebooks, news cuttings and articles complete the collection. (6ft; 180cm)

159 KENNEDY, James Branch (Master Mariner), 1816-*ca.*1891

Kennedy was first mate of the *Tigris* from 1845 to 1849 on three voyages from England to India and was also first mate of the *Medway* from 1849 to 1852 during three voyages to Australia, taking emigrants to Port Phillip. He commanded the *Aries*, going again to Australia, 1853 to 1854, the *Racer*, 1862 to 1863, London to Melbourne, to Calcutta and back and then home, the *Canopus* from England to India, 1864 to 1866 and the *Hornet*, 1866 to 1867 to India, Trinidad, home and back to India. The *Hornet* was burnt in 1868. Between 1868 and 1870 Kennedy carried mules and horses for the Abyssinian campaign in the *Tynemouth* and from 1871 to 1873 made five voyages to India in the *Yorkshire*. He gained his master's certificate in 1849 and an endorsement in steam in 1870.

The papers were presented by Mrs Jean Stead in 1952. They consist of logs, 1845 to 1854, 1862 to 1870, letterbooks, 1853 to 1870, and account books, 1848, 1857 to 1873. There is also a notebook with newspaper cuttings and official forms which relate to the *Hornet*, when burned in 1868. In addition there is a midshipman's log of Lieutenant James Robert Branch Kennedy (d. 1913), kept in the *Commonwealth*, 1908 to 1909, *Adventure*, 1909 to 1910, and *Collingwood*, 1910, all in home waters. (1¼ft; 38cm)

160 KEPPEL, Augustus, *Admiral, 1st Viscount Keppel*, 1725-1786

Keppel entered the Navy in 1735 and served off the coast of Guinea and then in the Mediterranean. In 1740 he accompanied Anson on his voyage round the world. Anson promoted him to acting lieutenant, which rank was confirmed on Keppel's return to England in 1744. In 1745 his ship ran aground off Belle Isle and he and his crew were taken prisoner by the French; later Keppel was released on parole. After peace was made, in 1748, he was made a captain and sent out in the *Centurion* to the Mediterranean as Commander-in-Chief and Ambassador to the States of Barbary to treat with the Dey of Algiers. In 1754 he was appointed to take command of the North American Station and returned home when Boscawen relieved him. In 1755 he was Member of Parliament for Chichester and represented two other constituencies until 1782. He sat as a member of the court martial on Admiral John Byng (1704-1757). In 1758 he was put in command of a squadron which captured Gorée, and in 1759 joined Hawke's squadron and fought at Quiberon Bay. He was the naval commander of the force which reduced Belle Isle in 1761 and in 1762 went as second-in-command of the naval forces in the Havana Expedition. When the Commander-in-Chief, Sir George Pocock (1706-1792), returned to England, Keppel was left in command, appointed rear-admiral and remained for a time at Jamaica until the peace. In 1765 and 1766 he was on the Admiralty Board, was promoted to vice-admiral in 1770 and to admiral in 1778. He was appointed Commander-in-Chief of the Channel Fleet in 1778, when the French entered the American War of Independence. After the inconclusive battle off Ushant, Keppel and his deputy, Palliser (1723-1796), blamed each other. At the subsequent court martial requested by Keppel, he was acquitted but soon afterwards struck his flag; this ended his active service. He was briefly First Lord of the Admiralty, for two short periods in 1782 and 1783, and was created Viscount Keppel in 1782.

See Thomas Robert Keppel, *The life of Augustus Viscount Keppel* (London, 1842).

The papers consist of two groups. The first, deposited on permanent loan in 1944 by Lord Albemarle, is a collection of letters, 1778, from the Admiralty and Keppel's replies. There are also court martial resolutions on Admiral Byng, 1757. In 1946 the Museum purchased through the Caird Fund, from Lord Albemarle, a series of order books, 1748 to 1778, and two Quarter Deck order books, 1761 to 1762, 1778. (1ft; 30cm)

The Ipswich and East Suffolk Record Office holds most of the Albemarle family papers.

161 KEPPEL, *the Hon. Sir* Henry, *Admiral of the Fleet*, 1809-1904

Keppel entered the Navy in 1822 and was promoted to lieutenant in 1828, when he was appointed to the *Galatea* in home waters and later in the West Indies. He then went to the East Indies in the *Magicienne*. In 1833 he was promoted to commander and the following year commanded the *Childers* off Spain during the Carlist War. In 1837 he was promoted to captain and in 1841 commanded the *Dido* during the China War. After this he remained in the East Indies, helping Sir James Brooke (1803-1868) to suppress pirates off Borneo. He commanded, after two years on half-pay, the *Meander* on the same station, returning to England in 1851. In 1853 he was appointed to the *St Jean d'Acre* in the Baltic and then, in 1855, went to the *Rodney* in the Black Sea, serving with distinction in the Crimea. In 1856 he went again to China where he lost his ship the *Raleigh*; Keppel was acquitted in the subsequent court martial. He commandeered the *Hong Kong*, a river steamer, and at the battle of Fatshan Creek, on the Canton River, destroyed a powerful force of pirates in 1857, the year he was promoted to rear-admiral. In 1860 he was appointed Commander-in-Chief of the Cape and Brazil Station. He became a vice-admiral in 1864 and from 1866 to 1869 commanded the China Squadron. Between 1872 and 1875 he was Commander-in-Chief at Devonport and in 1877 was promoted to Admiral of the Fleet.

Keppel published his memoirs, *A sailor's life under four sovereigns* (London, 1899). See also Sir Algernon Edward West, *Memoir of Sir Henry Keppel G.C.B. Admiral of the Fleet* (London, 1945) and V.E. Stuart, *The beloved little admiral* (London, 1967).

The papers are part of the Hamilton collection, Keppel's daughter having married Sir Frederick Tower Hamilton (*q.v.*). They were presented in 1957 and 1958 by Miss Jean Hamilton and consist of logs, 1824 to 1825, 1830 to 1831, 1834 to 1835, 1842 to 1845, 1847 to 1851, 1853 to 1857, 1860 to 1861; private journals, 1867 to 1869; annual diaries, 1834 to 1838, 1842 to 1844, 1855 to 1857, 1867 to 1869; private letterbooks, 1867 to 1869, 1874 to 1875 and loose papers. These are mainly letters received, 1841 to 1900, the bulk of which date from 1870.

Of the two groups of Keppel's letters to his family, one covers the Crimean War and the other his tour of the Far East, 1897 to 1900. (6½ft; 195cm)

162 KINGSMILL, *Sir* Robert Brice, *Admiral*, 1730-1805

Brice was made lieutenant in 1756, commander in 1761, captain in 1762 and served in the West Indies until 1764. In 1766 he changed his name to Kingsmill when his wife received an inheritance. In 1778 he took part in the action off Ushant but declined to serve again until the fall of Lord Sandwich's administration at the Admiralty. He sat for Yarmouth, Isle of Wight, 1779 to 1780. He was appointed in 1783 to the *Elizabeth*, which served as a guardship until 1786. From 1784 until 1790 he was Member of Parliament for Tregony, Cornwall. Kingsmill was promoted to rear-admiral in 1793 and was appointed Commander-in-Chief on the Cork Station in the *Swiftsure* and *Polyphemus*, during which time he had to contend with the French invasion of Ireland, 1797. He held this post until 1800 and was promoted to admiral in 1799.

The papers were purchased in 1932 by Sir James Caird. Apart from the log of the *Elizabeth*, 1783 to 1786, the collection consists of ten letter and order books, 1793 to 1800. (11 vols)

163 LARKING, Dennis Augustus Hugo, *Captain*, 1876-1970

Larking entered the Navy in 1889, served on the Mediterranean, West Indian and China Stations and became a lieutenant in 1898. He retired from active service in 1906. On the retired list he was promoted to commander in 1916 and to captain in 1918. He was Naval Attaché in Rome from 1915 to 1919 and in the Balkans from 1939 to 1941. He was then recalled to the Admiralty until 1945.

The papers were purchased from Messrs. Francis Edwards in 1974 and consist of private letters to Captain Larking from Admiral of the Fleet Earl Beatty (1871-1936) and Lady Beatty (d. 1932). Lady Beatty's letters, 1914 to 1918, were mostly written from Aberdour House, Fife. The letters from Earl Beatty, 1914 to 1928, date mostly from the war, when the Admiral commanded the First Battle Cruiser Squadron, later the Battle Cruiser Force, and then the Grand Fleet. (1 box)

164 LEE, *Sir* George (Lord of the Admiralty), 1700-1758

Lee was a civil lawyer, and admitted as an advocate in
Doctor's Commons in 1729. He was Member of Parliament for
Brackley, 1733 to 1742, and afterwards represented Devizes,
1742 to 1747, Liskeard, 1747 to 1754, and Launceston, 1754
to 1758. In 1742 he was on the Board of Admiralty but in
1744 followed Lord Carteret (1690-1763) out of office. His
connection with the Navy ceased from this time.

The papers, part of the Hartwell collection, were acquired
in two sections. The first was bought at Sotheby's in 1939
and a further instalment, from Hartwell, was acquired through
the British Records Association in 1941. The collection
consists of notes on Admiralty prize cases, 1720 to 1745, on
courts martial, 1742 to 1744, on the case of *Nuestra Señora
de Cabadonga*, 1744, and on the impressment of seamen. There
are some letters, 1712 to 1758, which include those from
Thomas Pelham-Holles, Duke of Newcastle (1693-1768), written
in 1744. (2 boxes)

There are further papers relating to Lee in the Hartwell
Collection in the Buckinghamshire Record Office.

165 LEE, *Doctor* John (lawyer and scientist), 1783-1866

Born John Fiott, brother of William Edward Fiott (*q.v.*), Lee
changed his name on inheriting property from his mother's
family. In 1827 he also inherited the estate of Hartwell in
Buckinghamshire. Lee was keenly interested in science and
antiquities and was an active member of the Temperance
Movement.

The collection was used by E.S. Dodge, *The Polar Rosses*
(London, 1973).

The papers were purchased by Sir James Caird at Sotheby's
in 1939 and form part of the Hartwell papers sold by Mrs
Benedict Eyre. They consist of forty-three letters written
to Lee by Rear-Admiral Sir John Ross (1777-1856) and some
papers, mainly printed, relating to the organization of the
Felix expedition of 1850 to 1851 in search of Sir John
Franklin (*q.v.*). The earlier letters refer to this voyage,
which was unsuccessful in finding Franklin. The later letters
contain many references to Ross's participation in scientific
societies, and in particular to the British Association for
the Advancement of Science. There are critical comments on
the official expeditions searching for Franklin. The letters

also deal with the translation and publication in 1856 of a
Memoir of the Russian circumnavigator Admiral Krusenstern
(1770-1846). There are many references to events in and
around Ross's home town of Stranraer. (1 box)

There are further papers relating to Lee in the Hartwell
Collection in the Buckinghamshire Record Office.

166 LEGGE, George, *Admiral of the Fleet, 1st Baron Dartmouth,*
1648-1691

Legge served with his cousin, Sir Edward Spragge (d. 1673),
in the Second Dutch War, 1665 to 1667. During the Third
Dutch War, 1672 to 1674, he was Captain of the *Fairfax*,
under Sir Robert Holmes (1622-1692) and took part in the
battle of Solebay, 1672. In 1673, he commanded the *Royal
Katherine*, under Prince Rupert (1619-1682). He held
various posts in the household of the Duke of York and was
Lieutenant-Governor, then Governor, of Portsmouth from
1670 to 1682, when he was appointed Master-General of the
Ordnance; he was created Baron Dartmouth in the same year.
In 1683 he was sent to Tangier to supervise the evacuation.
After the accession of James II in 1685, he was appointed
Admiral of the Fleet in 1688, in the hope that he would be
able to use the fleet to prevent the invasion of the Prince
of Orange. This he was unable to do and he took the oath
of allegiance to William and Mary in 1689. In 1691 he was
accused of plotting on behalf of the exiled James and died
while imprisoned in the Tower of London.

The papers were deposited on loan by the Earl of Dartmouth
in 1936. They consist of twenty-seven volumes, partly
of Dartmouth's own papers and partly of journals by his
contemporaries. In the first category is the log of the
Royal Katherine, 1673; the letter and order book of the
Sub-Commissioners of Prizes at Portsmouth, 1672 to 1674;
papers relating to Tangier, which include three letterbooks,
two order books and a journal of the proceedings of Samuel
Pepys and others, enquiring into the properties of the
inhabitants, letterbooks and an order book, 1688 to 1689.
The papers not directly relating to Dartmouth include a
commonplace book, 1666; two logs, 1671 to 1672, 1672 to
1673, of Sir Edward Spragge; a log of the *Resolution*,
Captain Sir Thomas Allin (1612-1685), 1669 to 1670,
Mediterranean; the log of the *Assistance*, Captain Sir
Richard Munden (1640-1680), during the expedition to St
Helena in 1673; a log of the *Saudadoes*, Captain James
Jenefer, 1672 to 1673, on a voyage to Lisbon; a log of the

Centurion, Captain Charles Wyld on a voyage conveying Sir John
Finch (1626-1682), as ambassador to Constantinople, 1673 to
1674, and a log of Captain Grenvile Collins (fl.1679-1693),
surveying in home waters, 1688 to 1689. There is a letterbook,
1666, of Prince Rupert and George Monck, Duke of Albemarle
(1608-1670), joint Commanders-in-Chief. This was published
as *The Rupert and Monck Letterbook, 1666*, ed. J.R. Powell and
E.K. Timings (Navy Records Society, 1969). There are copies
of the Duke of York's Sailing and Fighting Instructions, 1672
and 1673, accounts of the battle of Solebay, an account of
the battle of Texel by Sir John Narbrough (1640-1688) and
notes on seventeenth-century naval affairs. The papers are
described in the Historical manuscripts Commission's *Eleventh
Report* (appendix, part v, 1887) and *Fifteenth Report* (appendix,
part i, 1896). A further volume, a 'Discourse on the state
of the Navy', 1660 to 1661, by Sir Robert Slingsby (1611-1661),
was presented by Mr J. Ehrman in 1951. (3ft; 91cm)

167 LEVESON-GOWER, Osbert Charles Gresham, *Commander*, 1888-1968

Leveson-Gower entered the Navy as a cadet in the *Britannia*
from 1903 until 1905, when he joined the *Isis*; in August of
the same year he went to the *Commonwealth* and, apart from a
short period in the *Mars* in 1907, stayed in her until 1908,
when he joined the *Africa*; all these ships were based in
home waters. As a sub-lieutenant he was on the Mediterranean
Station in the *Diana*, 1909 to 1910, becoming a lieutenant in
1911. During the First World War he served again in the
Mediterranean in the *Racoon*, 1913 to 1915, the *Sappho*, 1916
to 1917, and the *Minerva*, 1918 to 1919, when he became a
lieutenant-commander. Between 1920 and 1921 he was in the
Dauntless and from 1922 to 1924 was in the *Colombo*, both in
home waters. He went out to Hong Kong in 1926 and served in
the dockyard there until 1928, retiring as a commander in
1929.

The papers were presented by Commander Leveson-Gower's sister,
Miss Victoria Leveson-Gower, in 1969. They include letters
home, circulars and telegrams bound into five volumes, 1893
to 1908, and loose letters to Miss Leveson-Gower, 1919 to
1928. There are also two logs, 1905 to 1908. (2½ft; 75cm)

168 LEWIS, Thomas, *Captain*, 1742-1795

Lewis was made a lieutenant in 1761 and, unusually, went to
Germany on a diplomatic mission as a private secretary between

1776 and 1778. He was then recommended to Lord Carlisle
(1748-1825) as a secretary and in April 1778 sailed in the
Trident, Captain John Elliot (*q.v.*), with the unsuccessful
Peace Commission to America. In 1781 Lewis was First
Lieutenant of the *Sampson* and then Commander of the *Pluto*
in 1782. He was promoted to captain in the same year when
he commanded the *Romney* but had no naval service after
1783. In 1779 his brother died and he succeeded to the
family property of Gellidywyll, Cenarth, Carmarthen.

The papers were presented by Admiral H.W.W. Hope, a
descendant, in 1955. They consist of correspondence with
Lord Sandwich (*q.v.*) concerning Lewis's attempts to obtain
promotion, 1779 to 1782, orders relating to ships' administration, 1780, and orders relating to the *Romney*, 1782.
There are also notes and an account of the Carlisle
Commission. (1 box)

169 LIDDON, Matthew, *Captain*, *ca.*1792-1869

Liddon entered the Navy in 1804 and after service in the
West Indies, South America and the Mediterranean, was
promoted to lieutenant in 1811. In January 1819 he
commanded the *Griper*, which accompanied an expedition to
the Arctic under Lieutenant (later Rear-Admiral Sir
William Edward) Parry (1790-1855), the object of which was
to discover the North-West Passage. He paid off the
Griper in December 1820 and saw no further active service,
although he was promoted to captain on the retired list.

The papers were presented by Mr D. Dawson in 1953. They
consist of a collection of letters and orders received,
mainly from Parry, 1819 to 1821, together with a number
of drafts of letters written by Liddon to Parry. (1 box)

170 LILLICRAP, *Sir* Charles Swift (Director of Naval Construction),
1887-1966

Lillicrap became a shipwright apprentice at Devonport in
1902. After a time at Keyham and Greenwich he was appointed
Assistant Constructor at Devonport in 1910. He then joined
the Director of Naval Construction's department at the
Admiralty, where he was made Acting Constructor in 1917.
Lillicrap was appointed Lecturer in Naval Architecture to

Probationary Assistant Constructors at the Royal Naval College, Greenwich, in 1921 and became Constructor, Director of Naval Construction Department, in 1922. He was Acting Assistant Director of Naval Construction, in charge of submarines from 1936, and Assistant Director of Naval Construction in charge of cruisers from 1938. In 1941 he was appointed Deputy Director, and in 1944, Director, of Naval Construction, a post he held until his retirement in 1951.

The papers were presented in 1970 by Mrs J. Lillicrap. They consist of memoranda and letters relating to the reorganization of the Royal Naval Corps of Constructors, 1945 to 1947, appointment diaries, 1951 and 1952, and many programmes, invitations, photographs and details of honours relating to the latter part of Lillicrap's career. ($\frac{1}{2}$ft; 46cm)

171 LIMPUS, *Sir* Arthur Henry, *Admiral*, 1863-1931

Limpus entered the Navy in 1876. He served in the *Alexandra*, in the Mediterranean, 1878 to 1879, in the *Bacchante*, Detached Squadron, 1880 to 1882, and the *Albacore*, again in the Mediterranean, 1884 to 1885. He was made a lieutenant in 1885 and a commander in 1898. He took a prominent part in the relief of Ladysmith when he was second-in-command of the Naval Brigade during the Boer War. He was specially promoted to captain in 1900 for his efforts. In 1910 he was made rear-admiral, hoisting his flag in the *Jupiter*, Home Fleet. Between 1912 and 1914 he was Naval Adviser to Turkey and was made vice-admiral in the Turkish Navy. Between 1914 and 1916 he was Admiral Superintendent at Malta and was much concerned with the organization of supplies to the Dardanelles. He was President of the Shell Committee at the Admiralty in 1917 and retired in 1919.

The papers were acquired in three parts. The first was presented by Mrs Le Geyt in 1972 and the other two were purchased at Sotheby's in 1975. They include official service documents; logs, 1878 to 1879, 1880 to 1882, 1884 to 1885; notes, photographs and diaries for the Boer War period; an official out-letterbook, 1912 to 1913; a diary kept by Limpus's wife during their stay in Turkey and letters from Limpus to his wife, 1912 to 1916. There are also letters concerning the Dardanelles Campaign from Admirals de Roebeck (1862-1928) and Wemyss (1864-1933) and Field-Marshal Methuen (1845-1932), Governor of Malta. ($4\frac{1}{2}$ft; 137cm)

172 LISTER, Francis Allen, *Captain*, 1902-1972

Lister entered the Navy in 1916. He qualified in engineering
as a lieutenant in 1924, was Commander (E) in the *Newcastle*,
1943 to 1945, and served in the Engineer-in-Chief's department,
1946 to 1949. Lister had become Captain (E) in 1946 and in
1950 joined the Mechanical Training and Repair Establishment
at Portsmouth where he remained until his retirement in 1953.

The papers were presented in 1973 by Captain Lister's widow,
Mrs F.A. Lister. They consist of a large number of files of
engineering and thermodynamic notes. There are also files on
a damage control course, 1943, the Senior Officers' Course,
War College, 1949 to 1950, and intelligence reports about
Nazi Germany, 1947. In addition, there are two physics
notebooks, undated, and official service documents. Finally,
there are a large number of photographs, some of which
relate to the life of Lister's father, Engineer Rear-Admiral
Francis Henry Lister (d. 1918). (3½ft; 107cm)

173 LORAINE, *Sir* Lambton, 11th Bt., *Rear-Admiral*, 1838-1917

Loraine entered the Navy in 1852. He was promoted to lieutenant in 1858 and served in the Mediterranean. In 1864 he was
appointed Flag-Lieutenant to Rear-Admiral the Hon. Joseph
Denman (1810-1875), Commander-in-Chief, Pacific Station. In
1866 he was acting commander of the *Mutine* during the hostilities between Spain and her former colonies, Peru and Chile,
being promoted to commander in 1867. From 1871 to 1874
Loraine commanded the *Niobe* on the North America and West
Indies Station. He spent part of this time engaged in
fishery protection off the Canadian coast and the remainder
in the West Indies. In March 1873 the *Niobe* was sent to
Santo Domingo to support the diplomatic status of the British
representatives there over a case of political asylum. In
June of that year, Loraine was sent to protect British
interests in Omoa, Honduras, against the local military
commander and representative of the provisional government
and in November he was ordered to intervene in the *Virginius*
affair. The *Virginius* was an American ship, owned by Cuban
exiles. She had been captured by Spanish forces and taken
to Santiago de Cuba where the officers and crew were
summarily executed and the lives of the passengers threatened.
Loraine's intervention led to the release of the ship and
passengers. He was promoted to captain in 1874 and saw no
further service. He retired as rear-admiral in 1889.

The papers were presented in 1961, 1963 and 1964 by Lady
Loraine, daughter-in-law of Rear-Admiral Loraine. They
consist of diaries, 1871 to 1913, letterbooks, 1866, 1871
to 1874, and loose papers, 1871 to 1874. There is a volume
of transcripts of the more important documents, with
Loraine's accounts of the various incidents in his career.
There are also some letters to Loraine's son, Sir Percy
Loraine (1880-1961), and some pamphlets in Spanish.
(3½ft; 106cm)

174 LOUIS, *Sir* John, 2nd Bt., *Admiral*, 1785-1863

Louis, son of Rear-Admiral Sir Thomas Louis (*q.v.*), entered
the Navy in 1795, was promoted to lieutenant in 1801, to
commander in 1805 and to captain in 1806. He served during
1810 off the coast of Ireland and off Cadiz, was in the
Mediterranean in 1811 and then went out to the West Indies.
After several years on half-pay, he served again in the West
Indies, 1826 to 1830. In 1837 he was appointed Captain
Superintendent of Woolwich Dockyard and also to the command
of the *William and Mary* yacht. He was Superintendent of
Malta Dockyard, 1838 to 1843, and of Devonport, 1846 to 1850.
Louis became rear-admiral in 1838, vice-admiral in 1849 and
admiral in 1851.

The papers were deposited on loan through the National
Register of Archives in 1958. They consist of personal
letters and official appointments, 1811 to 1848. (1 file)

175 LOUIS, *Sir* Thomas, 1st Bt., *Rear-Admiral*, 1759-1807

Louis entered the Navy in 1770, was promoted to lieutenant
in 1777 and to captain in 1783. In 1794 he took command of
the *Minotaur*, one of the ships in Nelson's squadron during
the battle of the Nile, 1798; he continued under Nelson's
orders in 1799, off the coast of Italy. Promoted to rear-
admiral in 1804, Louis commanded the blockade off Boulogne,
after which he hoisted his flag in the *Canopus*, off Toulon,
in 1805. Still in the *Canopus*, Louis was second-in-command
of the squadron which destroyed the French fleet at the
battle of San Domingo, 1806; for this he was rewarded with
a baronetcy. Later in 1806 he took charge of a small
squadron in the Eastern Mediterranean and remained there
until his death.

See H.B. Louis, *One of Nelson's Band of Brothers: Admiral Sir Thomas Louis, bart* (Malta, 1951).

The papers were deposited on loan through the National Register of Archives in 1958. They consist of thirty-eight items relating to the official honours Louis received for his services between 1796 and 1806. (1 file)

176 McCLINTOCK, *Sir* Francis Leopold, *Admiral*, 1819-1907

McClintock entered the Navy in 1831. He served as a midshipman in the *Samarang*, South America, 1831 to 1835, then in the survey ship *Carron* in the Irish Sea, 1835, and the *Hercules* in the Channel, 1836 to 1837. From 1838 to 1841 he was in the *Crocodile* on the North American Station. Between 1841 and 1842 he took courses in the *Excellent* and at the Royal Naval College, Portsmouth. McClintock next served as mate of the *Gorgon*, on the South American Station, 1843 to 1845. He received his promotion to lieutenant in 1845 and was appointed to the *Frolic*, Pacific Station, where he remained until 1847. For the next twelve years he was almost continually in the Arctic regions, serving on expeditions searching for Sir John Franklin (*q.v.*) and his men. During 1848 and 1849 McClintock was in the *Enterprise*. From 1850 to 1851 he was Lieutenant of the *Assistance* on the expedition led by Captain Horatio T. Austin (1801-1865). During the expedition of 1852 to 1854 he commanded the *Intrepid*, steam tender to the *Resolute*, Captain Henry Kellett (1806-1875). On his return he was promoted to captain. Lady Franklin chose McClintock to command her private search expedition in the yacht *Fox*, from 1857 to 1859. This effort was at last successful in solving the mystery and many relics of the lost expedition and Franklin's final message were recovered from King William Island. McClintock was knighted on his return. He published an account of his expedition, *The voyage of the Fox* in 1859. In 1860 McClintock commanded the *Bulldog* making soundings between Britain, Iceland, Greenland and Labrador, over the route of a proposed submarine telegraph cable. From 1861 to 1862 he commanded the *Doris* in the Mediterranean, acting as escort to the Prince of Wales on his tour of the Near East, and from 1863 to 1865 commanded the *Aurora*, in the Channel and the North Sea during the Prusso-Danish War and later in the West Indies. He was Commodore-in-Charge at Jamaica from 1865 to 1868, was promoted to rear-admiral in 1871 and from 1872 to 1879 was Admiral Superintendent of Portsmouth Dockyard, being appointed to vice-admiral in 1877. He sat on the organizing committee for the British Arctic Expedition of 1875 to 1876 led by Captain G.S. Nares (*q.v.*). From 1879 to 1883 he was Commander-in-Chief on the North American and West Indies Station. He was promoted to admiral and retired in 1884.

See Sir Clements Markham, *Life of Admiral Sir Leopold McClintock* (London, 1909).

The papers were deposited on permanent loan in 1958 by Major H.F. McClintock, McClintock's eldest son. They cover most of his service career and in particular the Arctic voyages. There are official service documents; logs, 1831 to 1848, 1857 to 1859; diaries, 1848 to 1854, 1860 to 1862, 1879 to 1882, and a letterbook, 1865. The papers relating to the Franklin search expeditions include orders issued by Austin, 1850 to 1851; a letterbook of Kellett's, 1853; papers on the expedition led by Lieutenant F. Schwatka, United States Army, 1878 to 1880, and several notebooks, including those kept during the courses McClintock took between 1841 and 1842. Finally there is private correspondence which includes letters from Lady Jane Franklin (1792-1875), from many other people involved in arctic and maritime exploration and from McClintock to members of his family. (3½ft; 106cm)

177 McCLURE, *Sir* Robert John Le Mesurier, *Vice-Admiral*, 1807-1873

McClure entered the Navy in 1824. He was made a lieutenant in 1837 and had already taken part in two Arctic expeditions when, in 1850, he was appointed to command the *Investigator* in the search expedition for Sir John Franklin (*q.v.*) via the Bering Strait, led by Captain Richard Collinson (*q.v.*). McClure and the men of the *Investigator* were the first to make the traverse of the North-West Passage, though they were forced to abandon their ship which was beset in the ice off Banks Island, arriving back home in 1854. They were awarded £10,000 by Parliament in 1855 and McClure was knighted. In 1856 he was appointed to command the *Esk* on the Pacific Station and the following year was ordered to China. In December 1857 he commanded a battalion of the Naval Brigade at the capture of Canton. He was then appointed Senior Officer in the Straits of Malacca. He returned home in 1861 and had no further service, being promoted to rear-admiral in 1867 and vice-admiral in 1873 on the retired list.

The papers were presented in 1962 by a descendant of McClure's, Lieutenant-Commander H.R.W. Higgins, RNVR, and are mostly commemorative of the voyage of the *Investigator*, although there are a few papers relating to the Chinese War, two letters from the King of Siam and a record of service. (1 box)

178 MACGREGOR, John (canoeist), 1825-1892

As an infant, MacGregor was saved from the Indiaman, *Kent*, which caught fire in the Bay of Biscay in 1825. He was well known as Rob Roy MacGregor because of his pioneering zeal while travelling in his canoe, the *Rob Roy*. This was first launched in 1865 and he navigated a network of rivers, canals and lakes, including the Rhine, Danube and Seine and Lakes Constance, Zurich and Lucerne. His most demanding voyage was in 1868 when he went through the Suez Canal down to the Red Sea and from thence to Palestine, navigating the Jordan and Lake Gennesareth.

He published *A Thousand Miles in the Rob Roy Canoe* (London, 1866), *A voyage alone in the Yawl Rob Roy* (London, 1867), *The Rob Roy on the Baltic* (London, 1867) and *The Rob Roy on the Jordan, Red Sea and Gennesareth* (London, 1869). See also Edwin Hodder, *John MacGregor ('Rob Roy')* (London, 1894).

The papers were presented by MacGregor's son, Professor MacGregor-Morris, in 1958. They consist of a letter from MacGregor's father, one in verse from Hannah More (1745-1833) and a letterbook concerning the loss of the *Kent* which is closed to readers until 1983. Some later items, 1869 to 1883, relate to canoeing. There is also a copy of a letter from MacGregor's father-in-law, Admiral Sir James Crawford Caffin (1812-1883), written to his parents in 1827 after the battle of Navarino. (1 box)

179 MACKAY, *Doctor* Andrew (astronomer), *ca.*1760-1809

Mackay was in charge of the astronomical observatory at Aberdeen from 1781 to 1795. In 1793 he published *The theory and practice of finding the longitude at sea or land* (London, 2 vols). When the chair of Natural Philosophy at Aberdeen fell vacant in 1800, MacKay was proposed but the election was contested. In 1802, Nevil Maskelyne (1730-1811), the Astronomer Royal, suggested that he should go to Australia to join the expedition led by Matthew Flinders (*q.v.*), as their astronomer had returned home early in the voyage. Mackay, however, still hoped that he might win the Aberdeen election and, in addition, felt the pay offered by the Board of Longitude was too small. In 1804, his hopes having failed, he came to London. He was appointed mathematical examiner to Trinity House in 1805 and to similar posts with the East India Company and Christ's Hospital during the year following. As well as teaching and examining, he published further works on astronomy, navigation and mathematics.

The papers were presented in 1941 by A.L. Mackay, on behalf of his aunt, Andrew Mackay's grand-daughter, and in 1961 by Mrs M. Thresher, Mackay's great-great-grand-daughter. They consist of letters received including several from Maskelyne, 1787 to 1805, and a series, written between 1794 and 1806, by Francis Maseres (1731-1824), the mathematician. In addition, there are several papers relating to his career, a manuscript copy of *The theory and practice of finding the longitude* and several of his printed works. (1ft; 30cm)

180 McKINLEY, George, *Vice-Admiral*, *ca.*1760-1852

McKinley entered the Navy in 1773, served in the West Indies during the campaign of 1778 and was promoted to lieutenant in 1782. He took part in the battle of the Saints and continued to serve during much of the peace. In 1798 he was promoted commander into the *Otter* fireship, in which vessel he was present at the North Holland landing of 1799, when Enkhuisen was taken, and was also present at the battle of Copenhagen in 1801, the year he became a captain. He then commanded a succession of ships in the West Indies, including the *Ganges*, 1802 to 1803, in which he returned home. As Senior Officer at Lisbon in 1806, he was given command of the *Lively* until her wreck in 1810, off Malta. During this time she took part in the capture of Vigo Bay and Santiago, 1809, and in the evacuation of part of Sir John Moore's army. From 1811 to 1815 McKinley served in the Mediterranean and then in the North Sea. In 1818 he was appointed Third Captain of the Royal Hospital at Greenwich and in 1821 Governor of the Royal Naval Asylum; this appointment was combined with that of Captain Superintendent of Greenwich Hospital School in 1828. He was made rear-admiral in 1830 and vice-admiral in 1841.

The papers. In 1947 the Reverend Keatinge-Clay, McKinley's grandson, presented one group of papers to the Museum and in 1958 loaned another group, which in 1975 became the property of Mrs Kit Cooper, Keatinge-Clay's daughter. She subsequently deposited them on loan in 1975. They consist of official papers for the Dutch expedition of 1799 and for the period of the Peninsular War; minutes and other documents relating to the Royal Naval Asylum, 1821 to 1830; a log of the *Ganges*, 1803; a draft account of the wreck of the *Lively* and many personal letters, 1789 to 1841. (1 box; 1 file)

181 MACLEAR, John Fiot Lee Pearse, *Admiral*, 1838-1907

Maclear entered the Navy in 1851, became a lieutenant in 1859
and a commander in 1868. He sailed with Captain G.S. Nares
(*q.v.*) in 1872 during the *Challenger* expedition. When Nares
left the ship at Hong Kong, Maclear was the most senior officer to complete the voyage which lasted until 1876, the year
he was promoted to captain. In 1879 he succeeded Nares in
command of the *Alert* and completed his survey of the Magellan
Straits before moving to the Indian Ocean and Australian
waters. From 1883 to 1887 he commanded the survey ship
Flying Fish charting the Korean and China coasts. In 1891
he became a rear-admiral and retired. He was promoted to
vice-admiral in 1897, to admiral in 1903 and continued working
at the Hydrographic Department compiling Admiralty sailing
directions.

See Sir Archibald Day, *The Admiralty Hydrographic Service*
(London, 1967).

The papers were presented by Maclear's nephew, the Reverend
Sir John Herschel, in 1948. They consist of Maclear's
journal of magnetic observations kept in the *Challenger*, 1872
to 1876; two logs for the *Alert*, 1879 to 1881, and one for
the *Flying Fish*, 1885 to 1887; captain's out-letterbooks from
Maclear to the Hydrographer of the Navy, 1878 to 1882, 1884
to 1887; work books, 1879 to 1882, 1885 to 1886, and two
remark books kept by Captain Alfred Carpenter of the *Magpie*,
1881 to 1882, annotated by Maclear. (11 vols)

182 MADDEN, *Sir* Charles Edward, 1st Bt., *Admiral of the Fleet*,
1862-1935

Madden entered the Navy in 1875 and served as a midshipman on
the Mediterranean Station from 1877 to 1880. He then went to
the East Indies, being promoted to a sub-lieutenant in 1881.
After becoming a lieutenant in 1884 he specialized in torpedoes.
He was made a commander in 1896 and a captain in 1901, after
which he was senior officer in destroyers in the Mediterranean
and then in a cruiser on the Cape Station. From 1904 to 1905
Madden served at the Admiralty under Fisher and was Naval
Secretary to the First Lord of the Admiralty, 1906 to 1910.
In 1911 he became a rear-admiral. He was Chief-of-Staff to
his brother-in-law, Admiral Jellicoe, 1914 to 1916, and was
promoted to vice-admiral immediately after the battle of
Jutland. From 1916 to 1919 he was second-in-command of the
Grand Fleet, with the acting rank of admiral. He was promoted

to admiral and created a baronet in 1919. From 1919 to 1922 he commanded the newly-constituted Atlantic Fleet. He became Admiral of the Fleet in 1924 and succeeded Earl Beatty as First Sea Lord in 1927. He retired in 1930.

The papers were presented by his son, Admiral Sir Charles Madden, 2nd Bt., in 1952 and 1975. They consist of the War Diaries of Admiral Sir Charles Madden, 1st Bt., August to December 1914, and his Grand Fleet Diaries, kept in his official roles, 1914 to 1918, and official service documents, 1877 to 1900. Sir Charles Madden, 2nd Bt., also presented his own service documents, 1924 to 1946, in 1975. (2ft; 61cm)

183 MADDEN, Humphrey Page, *Commander*, 1905-

Madden entered the Navy in 1919 and after training at Osborne and at Dartmouth served in the *Thunderer* training ship in 1923, then in the *Warwick*, Fifth Destroyer Flotilla, in the Atlantic, and in the *Repulse* in the Atlantic Fleet. He served in the *Victoria and Albert* in 1927, after which he trained as a pilot in the Fleet Air Arm. In 1934 he qualified at the Navigation School, *H.M.S. Dryad*, serving subsequently as navigator for a short period in the *Malaya*, Atlantic Fleet, in the *Sandwich*, on the China Station, 1934 to 1936, and the *Orion* in North America, 1939. During the Second World War he served in Naval Intelligence and with the Fleet Air Arm. He retired in 1950.

The papers were presented by Commander Madden in 1971. They consist of official service documents; logs, 1923 to 1925, and photograph albums, 1919 to 1923, 1925 to 1927, 1929, 1930 to 1932 and 1934 to 1941. (2½ft; 76cm)

184 MALCOLM, *Sir* Charles, *Vice-Admiral*, 1782-1851

Charles Malcolm, younger brother of Admiral Sir Pulteney Malcolm (*q.v.*), entered the Navy in 1795 and served under his brother's command in the East Indies, being promoted to lieutenant in 1799. In 1801 he was appointed acting commander of the *Albatross*. This promotion was confirmed in 1802 and in the same year he was sent to command the *Eurydice*, in which ship he sailed home in 1803. He was promoted to captain in the same year. In 1804 Malcolm was in command of the *Raisonnable* in the North Sea and two years later was

appointed to the *Narcissus* serving off the coasts of France
and Portugal. Early in 1809 he was ordered to the West Indies
where to took part in the capture of the Îles des Saintes.
Later in 1809 he was appointed to the *Rhin* and from 1810 to
1812 was engaged in supporting Spanish guerrillas on the north
coast of Spain. From 1812 to 1814 he was in the West Indies.
Following his return and during the 'Hundred Days' he carried
out a raid on the coast of Brittany in July 1815. After two
years without employment Malcolm was appointed Flag-Captain
to Sir Home Popham (1762-1820) in the *Sybille* on the West
Indies Station in 1817. He was invalided home in 1819. His
next commission, 1822 to 1827, was the command of the Royal
Yachts *William and Mary* and *Royal Charlotte*, which were at
the disposal of the Lord Lieutenant of Ireland. He was
appointed Commissioner of Dublin Harbour in 1823. In 1827
Malcolm became Superintendent of the Bombay Marine, renamed
the Indian Navy in 1830. He built up the surveying side of
the work of the service and introduced steamships to the
Red Sea. In 1837 he was promoted to rear-admiral and
retired from his post the following year. He became a vice-
admiral in 1847.

The papers were purchased from several sources in 1960. They
consist of nine volumes of official letterbooks, 1801 to
1838, most of which relate to Malcolm's years in the Indian
Navy. (1ft; 30cm)

There are further papers relating to Malcolm in the National
Library of Scotland.

185 MALCOLM, *Sir* Pulteney, *Admiral*, 1768-1838

Pulteney Malcolm, elder brother of Charles Malcolm (*q.v.*),
entered the Navy in 1778, became a lieutenant in 1783, a
commander in 1794 and a captain later in the same year.
From 1795 to 1803 he was in the East Indies. In 1804 he
went out to the Mediterranean in the *Royal Sovereign* and,
after brief commands in the *Kent* and *Renown*, was appointed
to the *Donegal* in 1805. In this ship he sailed with Nelson
(*q.v.*) during the pursuit of the French Fleet to the West
Indies and then joined the blockade of Cadiz. The *Donegal*
was at Gibraltar when the battle of Trafalgar was fought
and Malcolm hastened to the scene, arriving in time to
capture the Spanish ship *Rayo* and assist with the prizes.
He then went to the West Indies with Sir John Duckworth (*q.v.*)
and took part in the battle of San Domingo, 1806. The
Donegal was subsequently attached to the Channel Fleet and
in 1808 convoyed troops to Portugal. In 1811 Malcolm was

appointed to the *Royal Oak*, off Cherbourg. From 1812 to 1814 he was Captain of the Fleet   Lord Keith (*q.v.*), his uncle by marriage, being promoted to rear-admiral in 1813. In 1814 he took a squadron to America and served under Sir Alexander Cochrane (1758-1832) during the operations in the Chesapeake and New Orleans. During the 'Hundred Days' in 1815 he commanded a squadron in the North Sea and was then Commander-in-Chief at St. Helena from 1816 to 1817. He became a vice-admiral in 1821 and later held commands in the Mediterranean and the North Sea. He was promoted to admiral in 1838.

The papers were purchased in several instalments in 1961. They consist of official letterbooks, 1804 to 1810 and 1812 to 1817; a log, 1810 to 1813, which contains entries for the *Donegal*, the *Royal Oak* and Malcolm's log as Captain of the Fleet; a book of memoranda relating to actions in America, 1806, 1814 to 1815; a 'journal of events', May 1814 to May 1815, and a signal book. (6 vols)

There are further papers relating to Malcolm in the National Library of Scotland.

186 MARKHAM, *Sir* Albert Hastings, *Admiral*, 1841-1918

Markham entered the Navy in 1856 and served for eight years on the China Station in the *Camilla*, *Niger*, *Retribution*, *Impérieuse*, *Coromandel* and *Centaur*. He was promoted to lieutenant in 1862 and served in the *Victoria* in the Mediterranean from 1864 to 1867 and in the *Blanche* on the Australian Station from 1868 to 1871. He was then acting commander of the *Rosario*, 1871 to 1872, during a voyage to the New Hebrides in connection with the suppression of the South Seas labour trade. He became a commander in 1872 and, while on leave in 1873, sailed in the whaler *Arctic* to Davis Strait and Baffin Bay. From 1873 to 1874 he served in the *Sultan*, Channel Squadron. Markham was commander of the *Alert* under Sir George Nares (*q.v.*) during the British Arctic expedition of 1875 to 1876. His sledging party reached Latitude 83° 20' 26" N. in May 1876, which remained a record until 1895. He was promoted to captain for his services. In 1879 he accompanied Sir Henry Gore-Booth (1800-1881) on a cruise to Novaya Zemlya. He was Captain of the *Triumph*, flagship on the Pacific Station, 1879 to 1882, and Captain of *Vernon*, 1883 to 1886. In 1885 he was senior officer on board the *Hecla* torpedo depot ship, when she collided with the schooner *Cheerful*. Whilst on leave in 1886 Markham made a survey of Hudson Bay and Strait for the proposed Hudson Bay Railway Company. From 1886 to 1889 he was

Commodore of the Training Squadron. He was promoted to rear-
admiral in 1891 and from 1892 to 1894 was second-in-command
in the Mediterranean. In 1893, off the Syrian coast, Markham's
flagship the *Camperdown* collided with the fleet flagship, the
Victoria, which sank with great loss of life. The courts-
martial exonerated Markham but he was later censured in an
Admiralty minute. He became vice-admiral in 1897 and served
on the Joint Antarctic Committee and on the Executive Committee
for Scott's first Antarctic expedition of 1901 to 1904 in
the *Discovery*. He was Commander-in-Chief at the Nore, 1901
to 1904, knighted in 1903 and retired in 1906. Markham
combined his naval career with a considerable literary output,
which included *The cruise of the Rosario* (London, 1873), *The
great frozen sea* (London, 1878)(on the British Arctic expedition), a *Life of Sir John Franklin* (London, 1889) and a
Life of Sir Clements R. Markham (London, 1917).

See M.E. and F.A. Markham, *The life of Sir Albert Hastings
Markham* (Cambridge, 1927).

The papers were purchased in 1960 and 1963. The volumes
include a log, 1856 to 1874; a diary, 1875 to 1876, and an
admiral's journal, 1892 to 1894. For the *Triumph*, 1879 to
1882, there is a night order book, a captain's information
book, a remark book and a letterbook. There is a night order
book for the *Hecla*, 1879 to 1885, a remark book for the *Active*,
Training Squadron, 1888, a telegram book and reports for the
Mediterranean, 1892 to 1894, and press cuttings and photograph
albums. The papers include correspondence on the voyage
of the *Rosario*; official correspondence, 1886 to 1889, 1892
to 1893; papers relating to the collisions in which Markham
was involved; letters and papers on Antarctic exploration and
on Markham's literary work. Finally, there is Markham's
semi-official and private correspondence throughout his
career. This includes letters from his cousin Sir Clements
Markham (1830-1916). (7ft; 213cm)

187 MARRYAT, Frederick, *Captain*, 1792-1848

Marryat entered the Navy in 1806 and served under Lord
Cochrane (1775-1860), whose career was the model for many
of Marryat's heroes in his novels. In 1810 he served in the
Centaur under Sir Samuel Hood (*q.v.*) in the West Indies and
North America, was made a lieutenant in 1812 and went again
to the West Indies in the *Espiègle*; he was forced to return
in 1815 because of ill-health. He was appointed commander
into the *Beaver* in 1820, at St. Helena, and remained there
until the death of Napoleon. He then went in the *Larne* to the

East Indies, 1823, where he played a distinguished part in the First Burmese War, 1824. In 1825 he was promoted to Captain of the *Tees* and returned to England in 1826. He resigned from the service in 1830. He was elected a Fellow of the Royal Society in 1819 for his work on Sir Home Popham's system of signalling.

Biographies of Marryat include Florence Marryat, *The life and letters of Captain Marryat* (London, 1872), C.C. Lloyd, *Captain Marryat and the old navy* (London, 1939), and Maurice-Paul Gautier, *Captain Frederick Marryat l'homme et l'oeuvre* (Paris, 1972).

The papers were presented in 1952 by Marryat's grand-daughter, Mrs Ethel Barry. They consist of sketches, a diary, 1808 to 1821, his signal book and an album of official letters and press cuttings, 1808 to 1841. There is also his prayer book and other personal relics. (1ft; 30cm)

188 MARTIN, Henry John, *Commander*, 1841-1876

Martin served in the Mediterranean in the steam frigate *Curacoa* from 1854 to 1857 and on the west coast of Africa in the *Spitfire* from the end of 1857 to 1860, when he became acting mate. He was promoted to lieutenant in 1861 and appointed to the *Surprise*, gun vessel, in the Mediterranean, until 1866. In 1869 he became a commander.

The papers were presented by Commander Martin's daughter-in-law, Mrs E.M.V. Martin, in 1955. They cover Martin's service career, 1854 to 1870, and consist of logs, 1854 to 1866, private letters to his family (which include references to the Crimean War), 1855 to 1861, and details of ship administration between 1860 and 1870. There are also papers relating to the appointments and promotions of Admiral Sir George Martin (1764-1827), Commander Martin's grandfather, between 1811 and 1848. (4 vols; 1 box)

189 MASON, Henry Browne, *Commander*, 1791-*ca.*1871

Mason entered the Navy in 1803 and served on the Channel Station and then in the *Amphion*, Mediterranean. He was captured by the French in 1809, escaped the following year and was made a lieutenant in 1811. His subsequent service was off Lisbon and in the Mediterranean. He was promoted to commander in 1815, after which he saw no further active service.

The papers were presented by Dr. A.B. Clark in 1970. They consist of a typewritten transcript of Mason's autobiography from 1791 to 1831; four logs which he kept in the *Amphion* between 1805 and 1808, a watch bill for the *Warspite*, undated; a signal book, undated, and copies of five letters written between 1805 and 1812 concerning Daniel Finch (1647-1730), second Earl of Nottingham and an ancestor of Mason's. (7 vols)

190 MASSIE, Thomas Leeke, *Admiral*, 1802-1898

Massie entered the Navy in 1818 and was in the *Asia*, flagship of Sir Edward Codrington (*q.v.*), at Navarino in 1827, the year he was promoted to lieutenant. Between 1831 and 1832 he was First Lieutenant of the *Carysfort* in the Mediterranean and was then in the *Satellite*, 1833 to 1836, on the South American Station. In 1838 he was made commander and the next year was sent to assist in organizing the Turkish Navy. He was appointed to the *Thunderer* in 1840, took part in the capture of Acre and was promoted to captain in 1841. In 1849 he was given the command of the *Cleopatra*, East Indies and China Station, and took part in the Second Burma War (1852-1853). He commissioned in 1854 the *Powerful*, which was on the North American and West Indies Station in the latter part of 1855 and during 1856. Massie saw no further service, was promoted to rear-admiral in 1860 and was placed on the retired list in 1866 as a vice-admiral, becoming an admiral in 1872.

The papers were presented by Admiral Massie's great-grandson, Lieutenant-Colonel Massie, in 1957. They include copies of his official letterbooks, 1842 to 1861, logs, 1831, 1833 to 1836 and 1850 to 1854, and diaries, 1847 to 1849 and 1862 to 1880. There are also official service documents and twenty-one letters written to his family, 1826 to 1828 and 1840 to 1841. (2ft; 75cm)

191 MAY, *Sir* William Henry, *Admiral of the Fleet*, 1849-1930

May joined the Navy in 1863 and in the following year went to the *Victoria*, flagship in the Mediterranean, until 1867. From that year until 1870 he served in the *Liffey* in the Pacific, being promoted to sub-lieutenant in 1869. He then joined the

Hercules in the Channel between 1873 and 1874, after which he took the course at the gunnery school in *H.M.S. Excellent*. He next served during the British Arctic Expedition, 1875 to 1876, under Sir George Nares (*q.v.*) in the *Alert*. Becoming a captain in 1888, he held a series of important posts, including Flag-Captain in the *Impérieuse* on the China Station; Naval Attaché in Europe; Assistant Director, Torpedoes; Chief of Staff, Mediterranean and then at Portsmouth; Captain of *Excellent* and finally Director of Naval Ordnance and Torpedoes. Having reached flag-rank, he spent four years as Third Sea Lord from 1901 to 1905. This was followed by a period as Commander-in-Chief, Atlantic Fleet, 1905 to 1907, Second Sea Lord, 1907 to 1909, Commander-in-Chief, Home Fleet, 1909 to 1911 and finally at Devonport, 1911 to 1913. In retirement, he was appointed to the Dardanelles Commission, 1916 to 1917.

He wrote his autobiography, *Life of a sailor* (London, 1934).

The papers were presented by May's son, General Reginald May, in 1948. They consist of logs, 1864 to 1873 and, for the Nares Expedition, there is a detailed weather log, a personal journal, a sledging journal and some bills of plays performed in the *Alert* during the Arctic winter. There are also reports on torpedoes, 1884; the international situation, 1908 to 1909 and 1914; naval manoeuvres, 1912 to 1913; the Dardanelles Commission, 1916 to 1917 and on Reconstruction and other post-war problems, 1919. (1½ft; 46cm)

192 MELLERSH, Arthur, *Admiral*, 1812-1894

Mellersh entered the Navy in 1825, was promoted to lieutenant in 1837 and to commander in 1849. He was appointed to the *Rattler* in 1851 and served in her during the Burmese War, 1852. He pursued and destroyed a large force of pirate junks off Ping-hoey on the Fukien Coast, for which he received his promotion to captain. His last service was on the South American Station from 1862 to 1864. Mellersh eventually became an admiral on the retired list.

The papers were presented in 1963 by Mr J.M. Long. They contain papers concerning the Chinese pirates, some from Chinese officials and letters and printed material relating to the dismissal of Rear-Admiral Sir Fleetwood Pellew (1789-1861) from the East Indies and China Station in 1853. There are also official service documents. (2 boxes)

193 MEYNELL, Francis, *Lieutenant*, 1821-1870

In 1834 Meynell entered Henry Burney's Academy at Gosport
and in 1836 joined the *Partridge*, home waters. From 1837
to 1839 he was in Australian waters in the *Alligator* and then
took part in the China War, 1840 to 1843, in the *Calliope*.
Between 1844 and 1845 he was a mate in the *Penelope* during
the anti-slavery operations off the west coast of Africa. In
1846 he was presented with a commission and re-appointed as
additional lieutenant to the *Penelope*. He was unemployed
from 1847 until 1853, when he joined the *Royal George* in the
Baltic during the Crimean War. After 1855 he saw no further
service.

The papers were presented by Mrs Meynell, Lieutenant Meynell's
daughter-in-law, in 1957. There is an illustrated log, 1853
to 1854, kept while Meynell was in the *Royal George*. His
letters cover his whole career, 1833 to 1854, and have been
organized by his mother, together with newspaper cuttings
relating mainly to the China War. In addition, there is a
sketch book which includes several ships' portraits and
places Meynell visited, from China to the South Atlantic.
(2 vols; 1 box)

194 MICHELL, *Sir* Frederick Thomas, *Admiral*, *ca.*1785-1873

Michell attended the Royal Naval Academy at Portsmouth
between 1800 and 1803. He served in various ships in the
Mediterranean from 1803 to 1809, becoming a lieutenant in
1807. He spent six years in the *Rhin*, 1809 to 1815, in
home waters, off Brazil and in the West Indies. In 1816 he
was made a commander and led the battering flotilla
attached to the squadron of Admiral Edward Pellew (*q.v.*) at
the battle of Algiers. He subsequently commanded the
Rifleman in the Mediterranean, 1826 to 1830, when he was
promoted to captain; and the *Magicienne* and the *Inconstant*,
also in the Mediterranean, 1840 to 1843. In the *Magicienne*
he was engaged in the Syrian operations of 1840. His last
service, 1852 to 1855, was the command of the *Queen*, flagship
in the Mediterranean; in her he distinguished himself at the
bombardment of Sebastopol and was Senior Officer when Lord
Lyons (1790-1858) took his force to Kerch, 1855. He was
promoted to rear-admiral in July of the same year, finally
becoming an admiral in 1866.

The papers were acquired through the British Records Association in 1964. They are a collection of commissions,

appointments and letters which cover Michell's whole career, although the Crimean papers are the most numerous; these include landing orders, 1854, and orders for the bombardment of Sebastopol. (1 vol)

195 MIDDLETON, Charles, *Admiral*, *1st Baron Barham*, 1726-1813

Middleton entered the Navy in 1738, was made a lieutenant in 1745 and captain in 1758. In 1778 he was appointed Comptroller of the Navy and both during and after the American war carried through many reforms in the dockyards. In 1787 he was made rear-admiral and a vice-admiral in 1793. He resigned from the Navy Board in 1790, was briefly a member of the Admiralty Board, 1794 to 1795, and retired until brought back to be First Lord of the Admiralty between May 1805 and January 1806. He was given a peerage in 1805.

The papers were purchased from Maggs Bros. in 1966. They consist of notes and plans of projects for the six home dockyards and Hawlbowline, 1783 to 1792. There are also drafts and memoranda relating to the Commission to examine Fees, 1786 to 1788. (1 box)

196 MILLER, Charles Blois, *Vice-Admiral*, 1867-1926

Miller entered the Navy in 1880 and after service during the Egyptian campaign of 1882 went to the *Audacious* on the China Station until 1884. He was promoted to lieutenant in 1890 and then served successively in the *Partridge* in the West Indies, 1890 to 1892, the *Speedwell* in the Channel, 1892, and the *Howe* in the Mediterranean, 1893 to 1894. From 1894 until 1897 he was in the East Indies in the *Bonaventure*, from 1897 to 1900 on the North America and West Indies Station in the *Pearl* and from 1901 to 1903 on the China Station in the *Talbot*. He was promoted to commander in 1903 and to captain in 1908, serving subsequently on the Australian Station and in home waters. During the First World War he commanded ships in the Grand Fleet. He became a rear-admiral in 1920 and vice-admiral in 1922. He retired the same year and died in a motoring accident four years later.

The papers were presented by Mr J. Patrick Stevenson in 1950. They consist of a continuous series of logs, 1882 and 1903, and a diary, 1887 to 1890. (1ft; 30cm)

197 MILNE, *Sir* Alexander, 1st Bt., *Admiral of the Fleet*, 1806-1896

Milne, son of Admiral Sir David Milne (*q.v.*), was entered on
the books of the *Leander* in 1817 but probably did not go to
sea until 1820, when he joined the *Conway* on the South
American Station. Again on this station between 1824 and
1830, he served in the *Albion*, 1824 to 1825, the *Ganges*, 1825
to 1827, and the *Cadmus*, 1827 to 1830. He became a lieutenant in 1827. In 1837 he was promoted to commander into the
Snake, North America and West Indies Station, where he operated
against slavers, and in 1839 was appointed Captain of the
Crocodile on the same station. He transferred to the *Cleopatra*
for a brief period in 1841 and then returned home. Milne was
Flag-Captain to his father from 1842 to 1845 in the *Caledonia*,
Devonport, and from 1845 to 1847 was in the *St. Vincent* at
Portsmouth. He was on the Board of Admiralty until 1859,
having become a rear-admiral in 1858. During the American
Civil War Milne was Commander-in-Chief, North America and West
Indies. On his return, he again joined the Board of Admiralty
until 1869 when he commanded the Mediterranean Station for
a year. In 1872 he was appointed Senior Naval Lord and after
his retirement in 1876 he continued to be called upon for
important tasks, including membership of the Carnarvon
Commission on Colonial Defence, 1879 to 1882.

The papers were presented by Captain A.J.F. Milne Home, R.N.,
in 1949 and 1965. They consist of logs, 1817 to 1827 and
1837 to 1839, letterbooks, 1827 to 1839, and letters and
papers, 1838 to 1847. There are also a number of ship's
books relating to the *Snake* and the *Crocodile*. For the North
American command there are official out-letterbooks, letters
received and memoranda to squadrons, 1860 to 1864, as well
as private letters from the Duke of Somerset (1804-1885),
First Lord of the Admiralty, and to and from Sir Frederick
Grey (1805-1878), First Naval Lord, between 1861 and 1862.
There are also notebooks and sailing orders for this period.
For the Mediterranean Command there are letterbooks, general
and squadron memoranda and sailing orders, 1869 to 1870.
For his period at the Admiralty there are copies of private
and semi-official letters, 1854 to 1855, 1869 and 1873 to
1876, and letters to his brother, David Milne Home, 1820 to
1847. There are a considerable number of official papers
relating to the loss of the *Megaera* and the *Captain* and the
first, second and third *Reports of the Royal Commissioners
appointed to enquire into the Defence of British Possessions
and Commerce Abroad*, 1882. Finally there are diaries for
1825, 1833 to 1835, 1837, 1840 to 1841, 1843 to 1845, 1849
and 1870. (22ft; 671cm)

198 MILNE, *Sir* Archibald Berkeley, 2nd Bt., *Admiral*, 1855-1938

Milne, son of Sir Alexander Milne (*q.v.*) entered the Navy in
1869 and served in the Channel and the Mediterranean in the
Trafalgar and then in the *Royal Alfred*, flagship in the North
America and West Indies Station. He went to the *Sirius*,
Newfoundland Division of the Station, in 1873 and afterwards
to the *Raleigh* in the Channel, West Indies and at the Cape of
Good Hope. In 1875 he became a sub-lieutenant and a lieuten-
ant in the following year. He next joined the *Tourmaline*,
Cape Station, transferring later to the *Active* and the *Boadicea*.
During the Zulu War of 1879 he served with the Naval Brigade.
Between 1879 and 1882 he was in the *Minotaur* in the Channel,
going then to the Mediterranean, and once again serving on
shore during the Egyptian operation. Having been promoted to
commander in 1884, Milne served in the Royal Yacht before
going again to the Channel Squadron in the *Minotaur*, 1886.
He turned over to the *Northumberland*, also in the Channel
Squadron, 1887 to 1889. From 1889 to 1893 he commanded the
Royal Yacht *Osborne*, being promoted to captain in 1891. After
service in the Mediterranean and the Channel, he became a
rear-admiral in 1904 and second-in-command, Atlantic Fleet,
in 1905. He commanded the Second Division of the Home Fleet
until 1910. In 1912 he was appointed Commander-in-Chief,
Mediterranean, his term of office expiring soon after the
outbreak of war in 1914; short as his period of office was
during the hostilities, it included the escape of the *Goeben*
and the *Breslau* into Turkish waters. Consequently, Milne
was not employed again, his appointment to the Nore being
cancelled. Despite his vigorous efforts to justify his
conduct, Milne was unable to reverse this decision. He wrote
a book defending his actions, *The flight of the Goeben and
Breslau* (London, 1914). Some of these papers are reproduced
in E.W.R. Lumby *ed.*, *Policy and Operations in the Mediterranean,
1912-1914* (Navy Records Society, 1970).

The papers were presented in 1949 and 1965 by Captain A.J.F.
Milne Home, R.N. They consist of logs, 1870 to 1875, 1879
to 1881 and 1889 to 1893, and a notebook of events in
Egypt in 1882. A section of papers is devoted to the Zulu
War. For Milne's later career there are copies of correspondence with Lord Charles Beresford, 1910, and letters and
papers relating to the Mediterranean command, 1913 to 1914.
There is a detailed section on the escape of the *Goeben* and
the *Breslau*, including signal logs, telegrams received from
the Admiralty, diaries, official correspondence and press
cuttings. There are also a number of uncompleted private
diaries, 1870, 1879, 1886, 1913 to 1919, and personal letters,
1879 to 1936. (2ft; 61cm)

199 MILNE, *Sir* David, *Admiral*, 1763-1845

Milne entered the Navy in 1779 and served in the *Canada* until
the end of the American War in the Channel and the West Indies.
During the peace he was employed in merchant ships, among them
the East Indiaman, *General Eliott*, 1788 to 1790. At the outbreak of war, 1793, he went in the *Boyne* to the West Indies
and subsequently joined the *Blanche*, in which ship he earned
promotion to lieutenant for capturing *La Pique* in 1794. He
became commander and captain in 1795 and was appointed to
the command of *La Pique* in 1796. After two years service in
the West Indies and the Channel, Milne, whilst taking *La Seine*,
lost *La Pique* in action off Brittany and returned to the West
Indies in *La Seine*. On renewal of the war in 1803, he was
Commander-in-Chief at Leith until 1808, after which he had
a period ashore in command of the Sea Fencibles. He was then
appointed to the Channel Fleet in the *Impétueux*, 1811 to 1812,
and to the *Venerable*, 1812 to 1813. From 1813 to 1814, when
he became a rear-admiral, he was in North America in the
Bulwark. Milne was Commander-in-Chief of the Halifax Station,
1816 to 1819, but before he departed, served as second-in-
command to Lord Exmouth (*q.v.*) at the battle of Algiers, 1816.
He was made a vice-admiral in 1825 and an admiral in 1841.
His only further service was as Commander-in-Chief, Plymouth,
1842 to 1845, and he died during his journey home to
Scotland.

The papers were presented in 1949 and 1965 by Captain A.J.F.
Milne Home, R.N. They consist of logs, 1779 to 1780, 1788
to 1790, 1793 to 1796, 1799 to 1802 and 1814. There is a
collection of ship's books for *La Seine*, which includes a
surgeon's journal kept by John Martin, 1799 to 1800. There
are also letterbooks, 1804 to 1807 and 1808 to 1815. For
the period of the North American command there is an out
letterbook and order book, 1816 to 1819, and as Commander-in-
Chief, Plymouth, a standing order book, 1842 to 1843. In
addition, there are a large number of letters concerning
prizes, 1799, letters received, 1819 to 1842, and drafts of
letters to Lord Melville (*q.v.*), 1819, and Lord Dalhousie
(1770-1838), 1818 to 1819. A number of documents with no
immediate connection with Milne are also in the collection.
They include the log of the *Prince George*, Captain Nathaniel
Portlock, 1785 to 1787, on a voyage to the North Pacific;
the log of the *Africa*, Alexander Purvis, 1793 to 1796, and
the log of the United States privateer, *Harlequin*, 1814.
(3ft; 91cm)

200 MONTAGU, John, *4th Earl of Sandwich* (First Lord of the Admiralty), 1718-1792

Montagu took his seat in the House of Lords in 1739 and in 1744 was appointed one of the Lords of the Admiralty. He represented the United Kingdom at the negotiations leading to the conclusion of peace in 1748. He then became First Lord of the Admiralty, 1748 to 1761, for a brief period in 1763 and again from 1771 to 1782, after which he held no further public office.

A selection of his papers were published by Sir George Barnes and Commander J.H. Owen, *The private papers of John, Earl of Sandwich, 1771-1782* (Navy Records Society, 1932-1938, 4 vols). There is a biography by George Martelli, *Jemmy Twitcher, a life of the Fourth Earl of Sandwich* (London, 1962).

The papers consist of five volumes of Sandwich's appointment books, 1771 to 1782. These were purchased from the Montagu family in 1957. The remainder of the collection consists of transcripts. In 1956 and 1960 the Secretary of the Navy Records Society deposited on loan transcripts of Sandwich's papers, 1771 to 1782, not included in the Society's publication. (1ft; 30cm)

201 MONTGOMERIE, Alexander, *Commander* (H.E.I.C.), 1744-1802

Montgomerie was a brother of Hugh Montgomerie, 12th Earl of Eglinton. The family intermarried with the Hamiltons of Rozelle, Ayrshire. The two families managed and commanded East India Company ships for nearly fifty years. Montgomerie was commander of the *Besborough* for three voyages, 1777 to 1788, and commander and managing owner of the *Bombay Castle* on her first voyage, 1793 to 1794. He was managing owner of the ship for her next three voyages, between 1795 and 1801, which were made under the command of his cousin, John Hamilton (*q.v.*).

The papers are part of the Hamilton (East India) Company collection, presented between 1965 and 1968 by Lieutenant-Commander John Hamilton of Rozelle. There are account books for the *Besborough*, 1777 to 1781; a letterbook, 1786 to 1788, and a log book of the *Bombay Castle*, 1793 to 1794. (5 vols)

202 MURRAY, Charles Wadsworth, *Sub-Lieutenant*, 1894-1945

Murray served as Base Intelligence Officer in the *Iolaire*,
Stornoway, from 1914 to 1918, when he was given the rank of
temporary sub-lieutenant in the Royal Naval Volunteer Reserve.

The papers were presented by Mrs Elizabeth Murray, Murray's
widow, in 1956. They include notebooks dealing with his time
at Stornoway and contain information about German submarine
warfare. There are lists of ships lost and of those that
engaged enemy submarines and accounts of the loss or
surrender of submarines. There are also three manuscripts
unrelated to the main collection, consisting of an order book
of Captain Richard Grindall, 1801 to 1805; a Navy Prize
Office register, 1803 to 1820, and a log of the *Revenge*,
Captain Sir John Gore, Mediterranean, 1812 to 1813. (1½ft;
46cm)

203 NAPIER, *Sir* Charles, *Admiral*, 1786-1860

Entering the Navy in 1799, Napier became a lieutenant in 1805,
commander in 1807 and captain in 1809. Between 1811 and 1812
he served on the West coast of Italy and later in American
waters. In 1833 he took service in the Portuguese navy and
was victorious over the forces of Dom Miguel, who had seized
the throne of Portugal from his niece, Maria, in 1828. As
he had not sought permission to enter foreign service, Napier's
name was removed from the Navy List but was restored in 1836.
In 1837 he was appointed second-in-command of the Mediterranean
Fleet, taking a leading part in the Syrian campaign, 1839 to
1841, particularly at the bombardment of Acre and in the
subsequent negotiations with Mehemet Ali. In 1846 he was
promoted to rear-admiral and he took command of the Channel
Squadron until 1849. He was promoted to vice-admiral in 1853
and commanded the Baltic Fleet in the 1854 campaign. In
1858 he was advanced to admiral. Napier was Member of
Parliament for Marylebone, 1841 to 1847, and for Southwark,
1855 to 1860.

There are two biographies: Major-General E. Napier, *Memoirs
and correspondence of Admiral Sir Charles Napier, K.C.B.*
(London, 1862) and H. Noel Williams, *The life and letters of
Admiral Sir Charles Napier, K.C.B. (1786-1860)* (London, 1917).

The papers were presented by Mrs Madelene Tharp, the Admiral's
grand-daughter, in 1930. They consist of private letters
received by Napier, 1813 and 1860, and a few written and

received by Napier's daughter, Mrs Fanny Jodrell, 1847 to 1862. (4 boxes)

Much of Napier's official correspondence is in the British Library.

204 NARES, George, *Lieutenant*, d.1905

George Nares, son of Sir George Strong Nares (*q.v.*), was a midshipman in the *Curacoa* on the Australian Station from 1892 to 1893. He specialized in surveying and became a lieutenant in 1896.

The papers were presented by the Hydrographic Department in 1969 and consist of a log, 1892 to 1893. (1 vol)

205 NARES, *Sir* George Strong, *Vice-Admiral*, 1831-1915

G.S. Nares entered the Navy in 1845 and served as a midshipman in the *Havannah*, flagship on the Australian Station, and in her tender, the *Bramble*. He specialized in surveying, becoming a lieutenant in 1854 and a captain in 1869. In 1872 he was chosen to command the *Challenger* on her voyage round the world, the first major oceanographic expedition. He then led the Arctic Expedition of 1875 to 1876. He became a rear-admiral in 1887 and a vice-admiral in 1892.

See M.B. Deacon, Ann Savours and Geoffrey Hattersley-Smith, *Sir George Strong Nares, 1831-1915* (Scott Polar Research Institute, Cambridge, 1976).

The papers, consisting of a log, 1848 to 1851, were presented by the Hydrographic Department in 1969. (1 vol)

206 NARES, John Dodd, *Vice-Admiral*, 1877-1957

J.D. Nares, son of Sir George Strong Nares (*q.v.*), was a midshipman in the *Crescent*, *Rapid* and *Orlando*, Australian Station, between 1894 and 1897. He became a lieutenant in 1900, commander in 1913 and captain in 1919, serving in numerous survey ships including the *Iroquois*, which he commanded in 1928 on the China Station. From 1924 to 1928,

1930 to 1931 and 1940 to 1945, he was Assistant Hydrographer and Naval Assistant to the Hydrographer. In 1952 he was made Director of the International Hydrographic Bureau at Monaco.

The papers were presented by the Hydrographic Department in 1969. They consist of two logs, 1894 to 1897. and one work book, 1928 to 1932. (3 vols)

207 NELSON, Horatio, *Vice-Admiral, 1st Viscount Nelson*, 1758-1805

Nelson entered the Navy in 1770. His early service included a period in the East Indies and an expedition to the Arctic. He was made a lieutenant in 1777, received his first command in 1778 in the West Indies and was made post captain in the following year. After a year's illness in 1780 he served in the North Sea, America and the West Indies. Following a period on half-pay he was appointed in 1784 to the *Boreas* and served in the West Indies until 1787; in this year he married Frances Herbert Nesbit. In 1793 Nelson was appointed to the *Agamemnon* and took part in the reduction of Toulon and in the next year he lost the sight of his right eye in Corsica. Under Sir John Jervis (later Earl St. Vincent, *q.v.*) he played a decisive part in the Battle of Cape St. Vincent, 1797, and was promoted to rear-admiral. Later in the year he lost his right arm in an unsuccessful attack on Santa Cruz. After a period of recuperation in England he was given the command of a powerful squadron ordered to find the French Mediterranean and expeditionary force which he pursued to Egypt and finally destroyed at Aboukir Bay, generally known as the battle of the Nile. For this victory Nelson was created Baron Nelson of the Nile and Burnham Thorpe. During the next year and a half Nelson was involved in the defence of the Kingdom of Naples and preoccupied with his relationship with Emma Hamilton (1761-1815), wife of Sir William Hamilton (*q.v.*), British Minister to Naples. He was created Duke of Bronte in 1799, returned to England the following year and was appointed vice-admiral. In April, he went with the Baltic Fleet under Sir Hyde Parker and led the attacking squadron at Copenhagen in the *Elephant*. He was made Viscount for his services during this campaign. On the resumption of war in 1803 Nelson was appointed Commander-in-Chief, Mediterranean, and for the next two years with his flag in the *Victory* he blockaded the French fleet. In January 1805, Napoleon ordered the various French fleets to rendezvous at Martinique as part of his scheme for the invasion of England. The French Mediterranean fleet escaped and was chased by Nelson to the West Indies but he failed to bring it to action.

After a brief respite in England, news came that the combined French and Spanish fleets were at Cadiz. Nelson blockaded them there and, when they came out, met them off Cape Trafalgar on 21 October 1805. He was killed as victory was assured.

The papers are contained in the twelve natural and artificial collections described below. Included here are the papers of Lady Hamilton, Lady Nelson, other members of the Nelson family as well as the large amount of 'Nelsoniana' collected by the Museum, but only those artificial collections which are devoted entirely to Nelson are described in this volume; those in which material relating to Nelson forms only a part are described in Volume II of this *Guide*, as are volumes or documents acquired singly by the Museum. Collections in other institutions include those at the Nelson Museum, Monmouth, Lloyd's of London and the McCarthy Collection at the Portsmouth Royal Naval Museum, while the bulk of his letter-books are in the British Library.

Large number of Nelson letters have been printed and can be traced in Sir Nicholas Harris Nicolas, *The dispatches and letters of Vice-Admiral Lord Viscount Nelson*, (7 vols, London, 1844-1846); Thomas Joseph Pettigrew, *Memoirs of the life of Vice-Admiral Lord Viscount Nelson*, (2 vols, London,1849); Alfred Morrison, *The collection of autograph letters and historical documents formed by Alfred Morrison*, (2 vols, privately printed, 1893-1894) and G.P.B. Naish, *Nelson's letters to his wife and other documents, 1785-1831* (London, 1958). Notes on the provenance of some of the collections in the Museum are provided by Miss K.F. Lindsay-MacDougall, 'Nelson manuscripts at the National Maritime Museum', *The Mariner's Mirror*, vol. 41, 1955, pp. 227-232. The most comprehensive of many biographies is Carola Oman, *Nelson* (London, 1947)

The Bridport Collection was deposited on loan in 1948 by Lord Bridport. It consists principally of correspondence between Nelson's brother, William Nelson, (later first Earl Nelson), his wife and his children between 1783 and 1794, but there are seventeen letters from Nelson to his brother, 1783 to 1804, as well as a copy of his will and draft codicils. There are letters from Lady Hamilton to William Nelson, 1801 to 1814, and receipts by Lady Hamilton for the pension left to her under Nelson's will. The rest of the papers are concerned with domestic matters, 1797 to 1805, and honours conferred upon Nelson. (2 boxes, 1 vol)

The Croker Collection is part of the Phillipps collection purchased by Sir James Caird in 1946. This was bought by John Wilson Croker (1780-1857) in 1817 and purchased by Sir Thomas Phillipps in 1858 following Croker's death. The first

part consists of over two thousand letters received by
Nelson between 1796 and 1805. This is the main collection
of letters to Nelson and his correspondents include most of
the important political, naval and social figures of the time.
Among the most frequent were Sir John Acton (1736-1811)
Prime Minister of Naples, Captain (later Rear-Admiral) Sir
Alexander Ball (1757-1809), Alexander Davison (*q.v.*),
Admiral Sir Richard Strachan (1760-1828) and Admiral Sir
Thomas Troubridge (?1758-1807). There are also letters from
Admiral Viscount Hood (*q.v.*) to Sir William Hamilton (*q.v.*),
1793 to 1794. The second part consists of five boxes of
drafts by Nelson, Admiralty letters to him, mostly for 1801,
letters from Nelson to other commanders, 1794 to 1805, and
some relating to lands granted to him in Sicily. There is
also a log, 1793 to 1794. In the third section there are
letters from Nelson to Lady Hamilton, 1798 to 1804, and
letters received by Sir William and Lady Hamilton, 1787 to
1810. Among these are over a hundred letters from the Queen
of Naples to Lady Hamilton, 1794 to 1803. (6ft; 183cm)

The Girdlestone Collection was purchased from Miss Girdlestone
in 1935 and 1939 by Sir James Caird. It was originally
collected by Nelson's elder sister, Susanna Bolton, and was
handed down through the family to Miss Girdlestone. It
consists of letters, 1789 to 1805, written by Nelson to his
brother-in-law, Thomas Bolton. There are also a number of
memoranda and instructions, 1796 to 1805, as well as family
papers, 1731 to 1846. (1 box)

The Haslewood Collection was deposited on loan by a firm of
London solicitors in 1955. Written permission must be
gained before it can be used. It consists of papers and
legal documents of Nelson's lawyer, William Haslewood,
concerning Nelson family affairs, 1806 to 1843. (1½ft; 46cm)

The Matcham Collection was deposited on loan in 1962 by Mr
George Jeffreys, a descendant of the Matcham family. Nelson's
sister Catherine married George Matcham. It consists of
thirty-three letters written by Nelson to the Matchams,
1792 to 1802, by Lady Hamilton to the Matchams, 1802 to 1808,
and by Francis Oliver, Nelson's cousin, to George Matcham,
1803. (1 box)

The Monsarrat Collection was purchased from Mr Nicholas
Monsarrat through Messrs Charles Sawyer in 1960. It consists
of fifty-two letters written by Nelson between 1786 and 1805,
including some to Sir John Duckworth (*q.v.*), 1799, Sir
Andrew Snape Hamond (1738-1828), 1797, Lady Hamilton, 1798
and 1801, and Captain (later Admiral) Frank Sotheron (1765-
1839), 1804 to 1805. There is also a French account of the
battle of Trafalgar and items of domestic interest. (3 vols)

The Nelson-Ward Collection was presented in 1939 by the Reverend Hugh Herbert Edward Nelson-Ward and Mrs Nelson-Ward, widow of Admiral Philip Nelson-Ward. The Nelson-Ward family is descended from Horatia Nelson and this collection contains papers inherited by Horatia from Lady Hamilton. However, a third of the collection was acquired by the Reverend Hugh Nelson-Ward, largely from the collection once owned by the Victorian collector, Alfred Morrison. It consists of Emma Hamilton's letters from other members of the Nelson family, 1791 to 1815, and a small number of letters from Nelson to Horatia and Lady Hamilton, 1803 to 1805. There are four letters received and lists and inventories of Lady Hamilton's possessions. (1½ft; 46cm)

In addition, there are notes and letters written by the Reverend Hugh Nelson-Ward on the authenticity of Nelson relics and the personal records of Admiral Philip Nelson-Ward (1866-1937). He served as a midshipman in the *Minotaur*, 1881, saw service in the Egyptian campaign of 1882 and the Boxer Rebellion of 1900. He navigated the *Ophir* in 1901 during the Prince and Princess of Wales' colonial tour. From 1913 to 1916 he was Director of Navigation at the Admiralty. He retired in 1916. This part of the collection consists of logs, 1881 to 1886, and diaries, 1892 to 1901 and 1906 to 1935. (3ft; 91cm)

The Stewart Collection was purchased by Sir Malcolm Stewart at the Bridport Sale of manuscripts at Sotheby's in 1933 and presented by him to the Museum in that year. It consists of a letter from Nelson to his father, 1782, a memorandum of his services up to his time in the *Agamemnon*, a copy of the codicil made to Nelson's will, 1803, and other items of domestic interest. (1 box)

The Sutcliffe-Smith Collection was purchased from Mr A.E. Sutcliffe-Smith in 1976. It consists of fourteen letters to Sir John Duckworth (*q.v.*), 1799, thirteen to Captain (later Admiral) Ross Donelly (?1760-1840), 1803 to 1804, as well as a number of engravings of Nelson and Lady Hamilton. (2 vols)

The Trafalgar House Collection was purchased from Earl Nelson in 1947. It consists of Nelson's weather log, 1804 to 1805, a number of letters from Nelson of diplomatic interest, 1792 to 1805, including three to Henry Addington (1757-1844), 1803. The rest of the collection consists of grants of honours made to Nelson, 1798 to 1802, and family papers 1783 to 1840. (1½ft; 45cm)

The Walter Collection was placed on loan in 1935 but was purchased through the Caird Fund in 1960. The documents consist mainly of letters from Nelson to his agents and others of domestic interest; it also includes a book of sketches made at Merton by Thomas Baxter (1782-1821). (1 box, 1 vol)

The Western Collection was deposited on loan in 1965 by Messrs Western Sons and Neave, Solicitors. It consists of letters from Lady Nelson to her lawyer, James Western, between 1806 and 1807 and other legal papers relating to Nelson's will, 1806. (1 box)

208 NEPEAN, *Sir* Evan, 1st Bt. (Secretary to the Admiralty), 1751-1822

Nepean entered the Navy as a clerk and, after serving in several ships, became secretary to Sir John Jervis (later Earl St. Vincent, *q.v.*) in 1780. He then turned to politics and held various government appointments, becoming Secretary to the Admiralty in 1795. He was created a baronet in 1802. In 1804 he was Chief Secretary for Ireland for some months before joining the Board of Admiralty. He went out of office in 1806. Nepean was Member of Parliament for Queenborough 1796 to 1802, and Bridport, 1802 to 1812. Between 1812 and 1819 he was Governor of Bombay.

The papers were purchased from Sotheby's in 1931, 1959, 1960 and 1972. The first two sections consists of letters from Earl St. Vincent, 1793 to 1803. There are also two series from agents, one of fifty-four letters, 1796 to 1801, which include some from Sir Sidney Smith (*q.v.*) and the second of seventy-one letters from William May, 1797 to 1798. There is also a secret account book kept by Charles Wright, Chief Clerk to the Admiralty, between 1795 and 1804. This was purchased from Maggs Bros. in 1969. (3 vols, 2 boxes)

In the Gosse collection of papers relating to piracy (Section 5) there are letters received by Nepean, 1817 to 1819.

209 NIAS, *Sir* Joseph, *Admiral*, 1793-1879

Nias entered the Navy in 1807 and served during the remaining years of the Napoleonic wars. During the next few years he took part in three Arctic expeditions, being promoted to lieutenant in 1820. In 1826 he was appointed to the *Asia*, flagship of Sir Edward Codrington (*q.v.*). Following the battle of Navarino in 1827 he was promoted to commander and appointed to the *Alacrity*, remaining in the Aegean until 1830. Nias was promoted to captain in 1835 and in 1840 commissioned the *Herald* for service in the East Indies. After a period in New Zealand, he took part in the First Chinese War,

1839 to 1842, and was involved in operations leading to the
capture of Canton. After his return home in 1843, he was on
half-pay until 1850 when he was appointed to the *Agincourt*
and then to the *St. George*, guardship of the reserve at
Devonport. From 1854 to 1856 he was Superintendent of the
Victualling Yard and Hospital at Plymouth. He saw no further
service. He was promoted to rear-admiral in 1857, to vice-
admiral in 1863 and admiral in 1867, being knighted in the
same year. He was placed on the retired list in 1866.

The papers are part of the Baynes collection, presented in
1936 by Mrs H.C.A. Baynes and Miss Nias. They consist of
letters and orders received, 1815 to 1867, and service papers,
and there are eighteen letters from Sir William Parker (*q.v.*)
to Nias while he was Senior Officer at Hong Kong, 1841 to
1842. (1 box)

210 NOEL, *Sir* Gerard Henry Uctred, *Admiral of the Fleet*, 1845-
1918

Noel entered the Navy in 1859. He served as a midshipman in
the *Hannibal*, Mediterranean, from 1859 to 1861 and in the
Shannon in the Mediterranean and West Indies from 1862 to
1865. He was promoted to lieutenant in 1866 and served in
the *Rattler*, on the China Station, until 1869. Following
this he took courses in the *Excellent* and at the Royal Naval
College, Portsmouth. He was appointed Gunnery Lieutenant
of the *Minotaur*, Channel Squadron, in 1871. In 1873 he went
in the *Active* to the West Coast of Africa, where he commanded
the seamen landed with the force under Sir Garnet Wolseley
(1833-1913). He was promoted to commander in 1874 and
appointed to the *Immortalité*, Detached Squadron. From 1878
to 1881 he served in the Royal Yacht, *Victoria and Albert*,
and was promoted to captain in 1881, but then had several
years on half-pay. In 1884 he served on the Admiralty
Torpedo Committee and in 1885 was appointed Captain of the
Rover, Training Squadron, until 1888. The following year
he became Captain of the *Téméraire*, on the Mediterranean
Station. In 1891, on the same station, he commissioned the
Nile, which ship was the next astern when the *Victoria* and
Camperdown collided. He was appointed a junior Sea Lord in
1893 and was promoted to rear-admiral in 1896. In 1898 he
was appointed second-in-command, Mediterranean, and was
involved in settling the disturbances in Crete. Noel was
made Superintendent of Naval Reserves and commanded the Home
Fleet from 1900 to 1903. He was promoted to vice-admiral
in 1901 and was Commander-in-Chief, China, 1904 to 1906, and
at the Nore from 1907 to 1908. He was promoted to admiral in
1905 and Admiral of the Fleet in 1908, retiring in 1915.

The papers were presented by Noel's son, Lieutenant-Colonel Francis Noel, in 1938 and 1943. They consist of some volumes and a large collection of correspondence, papers and printed material. The volumes include Noel's midshipman's log, 1861 to 1865; the captain's letterbook of the *Immortalité*, 1877; for the *Téméraire* and *Nile*, a night order book, 1889 to 1893; Noel's admiral's journal, 1898 to 1900, and three letter-books, 1904 to 1906. There are papers for Noel's service on the torpedo committee, 1884, for his time at the Admiralty; his command in the Mediterranean, in particular for Crete, 1898; and for his commands at home, 1901 to 1903; in China, including reports on the Russo-Japanese War, 1904 to 1906; and at the Nore. There are papers and printed reports for the National Service League, of which Noel was an active member, and many printed pamphlets, some by Noel himself who wrote on education and various other naval topics. His personal papers include diaries, 1880 to 1918, student's notebooks, personal notebooks, press cuttings and a large amount of private and semi-official correspondence, for all his career. There are also letters by Noel to his wife and letters written by his son, Francis Noel, to Admiral Noel's wife during the 1914-1918 war. (21ft; 650cm)

211 NORRIS, David Thomas, *Admiral*, 1875-1937

Norris entered the Navy in 1889. In 1893 as a midshipman in the *Nile*, Mediterranean, he was an eye-witness of the collision between the *Victoria* and *Camperdown*. He was promoted to lieutenant in 1896, commander in 1907 and captain in 1914. During the First World War he commanded the *Arlanza*, 1915, and then served at the Admiralty. In 1918 he was appointed Commodore of the Persian Gulf Squadron. He subsequently commanded British naval forces in the Caspian Sea and, in May 1919, with six armed merchant vessels, some coastal motor boats and an air unit, attacked thirty Bolshevik ships, fourteen of which were destroyed. He headed a naval mission to Persia, 1920 to 1921. During the next eight years Norris held several appointments afloat and ashore. He was promoted to rear-admiral in 1924 and retired on his promotion to vice-admiral in 1929. He was promoted to admiral on the retired list in 1933.

The papers were deposited on loan by Miss A.E. Norris and Mr J. Norris in 1967. They contain official letters and memoranda for 1915, papers relating to Norris's commands in the Caspian Sea and in Persia, as well as photograph albums, 1892 to 1926. (3ft; 92cm)

212 NORTH, Frederick, *Paymaster-in-Chief*, 1839-1927

North entered the Navy as an assistant clerk in 1854 and served in the Crimean War. He was promoted to assistant paymaster in 1860 and paymaster in 1870. In 1878 he was appointed to the survey ship *Alert*, under Captain Sir George Nares (*q.v.*). The first season was spent surveying in the Magellan Strait and the surrounding area. In the spring of 1879 Nares was recalled and succeeded by Captain J.F.L.P. Maclear (*q.v.*). The *Alert* carried out survey work in the Pacific, the Torres Strait (Prince of Wales Channel) and the Indian Ocean (Amirante Islands) before arriving home in 1882. North was promoted to Fleet Paymaster in 1886 and he retired in 1895 as Paymaster-in-Chief.

The papers were presented in 1959 by North's great-niece, Miss C.N. Brown. The collection consists of his diaries in the *Alert*, 1878 to 1882. (3 vols)

There are also photograph albums relating to North in the Department of Pictures.

213 OLIVER, Algernon Hardy, *Commander*, *ca.*1855-1934

Oliver entered the Navy in 1869. He served in the *Bristol*, 1870 to 1871, and was rated midshipman in 1871. He was in the Mediterranean from 1871 to 1874, in the *Ariadne* and then for two years in the flagship *Lord Warden*. From 1874 to 1876 he served in the *Audacious*, flagship on the China Station. He was promoted to sub-lieutenant in 1876 and served in the *Shannon*, 1877 to 1880, on the same station. In 1880 he was promoted to lieutenant and appointed to the *Pelican*, Pacific Station, 1880 to 1882. From 1882 to 1884 he was in the Indian troopship *Jumna* and served in operations in the Sudan in 1884. Between 1885 and 1887, Oliver served in three Coast Guard ships based at Southampton, the *Hector*, *Northampton* and *Invincible*. He returned to China in the *Wanderer* between 1888 and 1891. During the 1890s Oliver served in various posts, in a training ship, in the dockyard reserve and the coastguard. He retired with the rank of commander in 1900.

The papers are part of the Oliver-Bellasis collection, on permanent loan to the Museum since 1936. They comprise a series of logs, some watch, station and quarter bills, a sights book, 1872 to 1876, three diaries, 1879 to 1881, and a notebook, 1888. (1½ft; 46cm)

214 OLIVER, *Sir* Henry Francis, *Admiral of the Fleet*, 1865-1965

Oliver entered the Navy in 1878 and passed for lieutenant in 1884. In 1903 he was promoted to captain and founded the navigation school in the *Mercury*. This school was later given the name *H.M.S. Dryad*. Oliver became Naval Assistant to the First Sea Lord in 1908, and after a seagoing appointment became Director of Naval Intelligence in 1913. He was promoted to rear-admiral in the same year. In 1914 Oliver became Naval Secretary to the First Sea Lord. At the end of the war he commanded the First Battle Cruiser Squadron in the Grand Fleet, hoisting his flag in the *Repulse*. In 1919 he was promoted to vice-admiral and in 1921 he was appointed Second Sea Lord. In 1923 he was made admiral. His last active employment was as Commander-in-Chief, Atlantic Fleet, in which post he remained until 1927. He was made Admiral of the Fleet in 1928 and retired in the same year.

See Sir William James, *A great seaman. The life of Admiral of the Fleet Sir Henry F. Oliver* (London, 1956).

The papers were deposited on loan by *H.M.S. Dryad*, the Navigation School, in 1967. They include papers relating to the establishment of the Navigation School, and to the Dardanelles Operations, 1915 to 1917; included in the latter are minutes and notes by Churchill. There is also a Report of the Grand Fleet Committee on Officers' Pay and Prospects, 1919. Other letters and papers span Oliver's career, 1914 to 1965, although thinly. There is a diary, 1925 to 1927, a draft autobiography and official service documents. (1ft; 30cm)

215 OLIVER, Richard Aldworth, *Admiral*, 1811-1889

Oliver was the son of Admiral Robert Oliver (*q.v.*). He entered the Navy in 1825 and became a lieutenant in 1838. He was in the *Queen* in the Mediterranean from 1842 to 1844 and was promoted to commander in 1844. In 1847 he was appointed to command the *Fly* in Australian and New Zealand waters. Following his return home in 1851 he served during the Crimean War and was promoted to captain in 1854 but from then had no further service. He retired in 1864 and rose to the rank of admiral on the retired list.

The papers are part of the Oliver-Bellasis collection, placed on permanent loan to the Museum in 1936 by Captain Oliver-Bellasis. They consist of a notebook kept in the

Queen; a general order and memoranda book, 1840 to 1850; a letterbook, 1847 to 1851, and a diary, 1848 to 1850, kept in the *Fly*, describing Oliver's time in New Zealand and a voyage to the New Hebrides. (4 vols)

216 OLIVER, Robert Dudley, *Admiral*, 1766-1850

Oliver entered the Navy in 1779. He served in the West Indies and was promoted to lieutenant in 1790, commander in 1794 and captain in 1796. After the battle of Trafalgar he was appointed to the *Mars*, whose captain, George Duff, had been killed. He continued to serve until 1814 and was promoted to rear-admiral in 1819, vice-admiral in 1830 and admiral in 1841.

The papers are part of the Oliver-Bellasis collection placed on permanent loan to the Museum by the late Captain Oliver-Bellasis in 1936. There are three standing order books, one for Plymouth and Spithead, 1798 to 1799, probably when Oliver was Captain of the *Nemesis*, and two for the *Mars*, 1804, 1805 to 1806. There are also two letters written by Nelson to Oliver's father-in-law, Sir Charles Saxton (*q.v.*). (3 vols, 1 file)

217 OLIVER, Thomas William, *Commander*, *fl.*1848-1872

Oliver was midshipman in the *Asia* in 1848 when she was flag-ship of the Pacific Squadron. He then served in the *Rapid* on the China Station. In 1854 he was promoted to lieutenant while in the *Spartan* at Hong Kong. Between 1855 and 1856 he served in the *St. George* off Lisbon and in 1857 in the *Exmouth* in the Mediterranean. He commanded the *Louisa*, gun boat tender to the *Edinburgh*, in home waters in 1858, and served in the *Colossus* and *Frederick William* in the Channel, 1864 to 1865, and in the *Aboukir*, West Indies, in 1866. From 1866 he appears to have had no further active post and he retired with the rank of commander in 1872.

The papers are part of the Royal United Service Institution Collection, transferred to the Museum in 1968. They had been presented to the Royal United Service Institution by Captain F.M.L. Oliver, R.N. They consist of logs, 1848 to 1849, 1851 to 1859 and 1863 to 1866. (8 vols)

218 OLIVER-BELLASIS, Richard, *Captain*, 1900-1964

Oliver-Bellasis entered the Navy in 1918. He became a
lieutenant in 1920 and specialized in torpedoes. He was
promoted to lieutenant-commander in 1928 and commander in
1933. From 1932 to 1934 he served in the *Renown*, Home Fleet,
and, after a spell at the Admiralty, was in the *Eagle*, China
Station, 1937 to 1939. During the Second World War, Oliver-
Bellasis held both posts ashore and at sea, being promoted to
captain in 1941. He was Director of Underwater Weapons from
1947 to 1950 and retired in 1953.

The papers were deposited on loan by Captain Oliver-Bellasis
in 1953. They consist of standing orders and routines for
some of the ships in which he served. There are also papers
for a course at the Royal Naval College in 1936 and for a
damage control course in 1943. (2 boxes)

219 OMMANEY, Erasmus Denison St. Andrew, *Rear-Admiral*, *ca.*1853-
1936

As a sub-lieutenant Ommaney served in the *Topaze*, 1873 to
1874, in home waters, and in the *Barracouta*, 1874 to 1877, on
the Australian Station. In 1877 he became a lieutenant and
from 1878 to 1881 was in the *Penguin* in the Pacific. He
then served in the *Algerine* between 1881 and 1886 on the Cape
and West Africa Station and in the *Cruiser*, 1886 to 1889, in
the Mediterranean. In 1890 he was promoted to commander and
served in the *Aurora*, Channel Squadron, from 1890 to 1891
and in the *Boadicea*, East Indies, from 1891 to 1894. He was
promoted to captain in 1897 and commanded the *Calliope*,
tender to the training ship *Northampton*, from 1901 to 1903,
when he retired. He became a rear-admiral in 1907.

The papers were presented by Mr V.E.J. Strickland in 1972.
They consist of logs, 1873 to 1877 and 1883 to 1894, and
diaries, 1878 to 1881 and 1901 to 1903. (13 vols)

220 ORDE, *Sir* John, 1st Bt., *Admiral*, 1751-1824

Orde entered the Navy in 1766 and served on the Mediterranean,
Newfoundland and West Indies Station until he became a
lieutenant in 1774. Between 1775 and 1781 he served in

American waters, being promoted to both commander and captain in 1778. He became Governor of Dominica in 1783, not returning to the Navy until 1793 when he commanded the *Victorious* in the Channel Fleet and in the following year, the *Venerable*. In 1795 he was promoted to flag-rank. After a short period in the *Prince George* and *Minotaur* maintaining the blockade off Cadiz, he flew his flag in the *Princess Royal*. In 1798, after a dispute with Earl St. Vincent, he was sent home. He was unemployed until 1804 when he commanded the squadron blockading Cadiz in the *Glory*, withdrawing to join the Channel Fleet when the Toulon Fleet escaped. He saw no further active service. From 1807 until 1812 Orde was Member of Parliament for Yarmouth, Isle of Wight.

The papers were deposited on loan by Sir Simon Campbell Orde, Bt., in 1967 and are now owned by Sir John Campbell Orde Bt. They consist of order books and in and out-letterbooks, 1794 to 1798, and 1804 to 1805, as well as a secret order book, 1804 to 1805, and signal books, 1805. There are many letters received, including those from Nelson (*q.v.*), 1786 to 1805, Earl Howe (*q.v.*), 1793 to 1797, Earl St. Vincent (*q.v.*), 1797 to 1798, Lord Gambier (1756-1833), 1797, Spencer Perceval (1762-1812), 1809 to 1811, and others, particularly concerning Orde's quarrel with St. Vincent. Finally there are prize accounts, 1800 to 1813. (3ft; 91cm)

221 OSBORN, Henry, *Admiral*, 1694-1771

Osborn served in the Mediterranean before becoming a lieutenant in 1717. In 1718 He took part in the action off Cape Passaro in the Mediterranean and the following year served in a squadron on the north coast of Africa. His first command was the *Squirrel* in 1728. In 1734 he commanded the *Portland* in the Channel and in 1738 the *Salisbury* in the Mediterranean. He was appointed to the *Prince of Orange* in 1740, returning to England in the *Chichester* in 1741, when he moved to the *Princess Caroline*, Channel, until 1743. Osborn was promoted to rear-admiral in 1747 and in 1748 was appointed Commander-in-Chief, Leeward Islands; in the same year he became a vice-admiral. He was promoted admiral and appointed Commander-in-Chief, Mediterranean, in 1757 but after blockading the French fleet in 1758, he suffered a stroke and saw no more active service. Osborn was Member of Parliament for Bedfordshire, 1758 to 1761.

The papers form part of the Caldwell collection, presented by Mrs C.B.H. Caldwell in 1938 (Sir Benjamin Caldwell (*q.v.*) married Osborn's daughter). They consist of five logs, 1730 to 1742, and an order book, 1747 to 1757. (6 vols)

222 OWEN, *Sir* Edward William Campbell Rich, *Admiral*, 1771-1849

Edward Owen, elder son of Commander William Owen (*q.v.*),
entered the Navy in 1786, was made a lieutenant in 1793 and
a commander in 1796. In 1797 he commanded a division of
gun-brigs at the Nore. He was promoted to captain in 1798,
commanding several ships in home waters during hostilities
with France. In 1809, in the *Clyde*, he commanded the
Brouershaven Squadron during the Walcheren expedition. From
1822, when he was promoted to rear-admiral, to 1825, he
Commander-in-Chief, West Indies. In 1827 he was Surveyor-
General of the Ordnance and from March to September, 1828,
was a Member of the Council of the Lord High Admiral.
Between 1828 and 1832 he was Commander-in-Chief in the East
Indies. He was appointed vice-admiral in 1837. From 1841
to 1845 he was Commander-in-Chief, Mediterranean, and he
became admiral in 1846. Owen was Member of Parliament for
Sandwich from 1826 to 1829.

The papers, part of the Cochrane collection, were presented
by Mrs Cochrane in 1952. They consist of an account, drawn
up in 1825, of the mutiny at Spithead in 1797 and of
documents and narrative towards a history of the Walcheren
expedition of 1809. There is also a letter of Privy Seal
appointing Owen Clerk of the Ordnance, 1834. (2 boxes,
1 file)

223 OWEN, William, *Commander*, d.1778

William Owen, a lieutenant in 1758, lost an arm at the siege
of Pondicherry in 1760. He was on half-pay from 1761
to 1766, when he went to America as Secretary to Lord
William Campbell (d.1778). In 1770 he started a venture to
aid the settlers on Passamaquoddy, an island in the Bay of
Fundy, Nova Scotia; he placed them under his jurisdiction
and renamed the island Campo Bello. Owen became a commander
in 1777. After serving at the second siege of Pondicherry
in 1778, he was killed while on his journey home with
despatches.

The papers, part of the Cochrane collection, were presented
by Mrs Cochrane in 1952. They comprise the second volume of
Owen's autobiographical narrative, 1761 to 1771. (1 vol)

224 OWEN, William Fitzwilliam, *Vice-Admiral*, 1774-1857

Younger son of Commander William Owen (*q.v.*), W.F. Owen
entered the Navy in 1788 and served on the Home and West
Indies Stations. He was in the *Culloden* at the battle of
the First of June 1794 and became a lieutenant in 1797. In
1803 he went to the East Indies where he surveyed the Maldive
Islands and assisted at the capture of Batavia in 1806. He
was a captive of the French in Mauritius from 1808 to 1810
during which time, in 1809, he was promoted to commander.
In 1811 he commanded the *Barracouta* at the capture of Java.
He became a captain and was posted to the *Cornelia*, East
Indies Station, in 1812. From 1815 to 1816 Owen was engaged
in a survey of the Great Lakes and from 1821 to 1826 in the
Leven, with the *Barracouta*, conducted the first survey of the
coasts of Africa. In the *Eden* he founded a colony on
Fernando Po in 1827 and then served on the coast of South
America until 1831. His only other command was the *Columbia*,
North America, in 1847. He returned to England at the end
of the year on his promotion to rear-admiral. Owen became
a vice-admiral in 1854 and retired in 1855.

The papers, part of the Cochrane collection, were presented
by Mrs Cochrane in 1952. They include a narrative of Owen's
naval service, an account of the proceedings in the *Cornelia*
and papers relating to the Africa survey and his work at
Fernando Po. There are also papers concerning the settlement
founded by Commander Owen, Admiral Owen's father, in Nova
Scotia. (1 box)

225 PAKENHAM, Edward Michael, *Captain, 2nd Baron Longford*, 1743-
1792

Pakenham joined the *Dunkirk*, which was attached to the
Western Squadron, in 1758. He took part in the Goree
expedition, remaining in the *Dunkirk* until 1761, when he
joined the *Neptune* at Gibraltar. There he was promoted to
lieutenant, and appointed to the *Terror* but was taken
prisoner by the Spaniards. On his release in 1762 he went
to the *Blenheim*, Mediterranean. From 1763 to 1765 he served
in the *Romney*, Halifax; there, in 1765, he purchased the
command of the *Crown*. He was promoted to captain the
following year but had no further service until 1777, when
he was appointed to command the *America*, 1777 to 1779,
and then the *Alexander*, 1779 to 1783, both in the Channel.

The papers were presented by Sir Eric Miller in 1955. They consist of two logs, 1758 to 1761 (with additional notes up to 1793) and 1779 to 1782, four signal books, 1778 to 1782, and a presentation copy of *Captain Pakenham's invention of a substitute for a lost rudder.* (7 vols)

226 PARKER, *Sir* William, 1st Bt., *Admiral of the Fleet*, 1781-1866

Parker was a nephew of Sir John Jervis (later Earl St. Vincent *q.v.*). He entered the Navy in 1793 as a captain's servant in the *Orion* and, as a midshipman, was present at the battle of the First of June 1794. He was then transferred with Captain (later Admiral) J.T. Duckworth (*q.v.*) to the *Leviathan* and he went out to the West Indies in 1795. From 1796 to 1798 he was acting lieutenant of the *Magicienne* and from 1798 to 1799 of the *Queen*, being promoted to lieutenant in 1799. He was appointed to command the *Volage* and then the *Stork*, in which ship he returned home in 1800 and served for a year in the North Sea. He was promoted to captain in 1801 and during the following year commanded *L'Oiseau*, the *Heldin* and the *Alarm* in home waters. Between 1802 and 1812 Parker was Captain of the *Amazon*. He served in the Mediterranean under Nelson and sailed with him to the West Indies in 1805. From 1806 to 1810 he was employed mainly on the coasts of Spain and Portugal and from 1811 to 1812 in the Channel. Parker was then on half-pay until 1827 when he was sent to the Mediterranean in the *Warspite*, being Senior Officer in the Aegean in 1828. On his return home he was appointed Captain of the Royal Yacht *Prince Regent* until his promotion to rear-admiral in 1830. He was second-in-command, Channel Squadron, in 1831 and commanded a squadron on the coast of Portugal during the Carlist War, 1831 to 1834. He was knighted in 1834 and was a Lord of the Admiralty between August and December of the same year. From 1835 he again had a seat at the Board of the Admiralty until 1841, when he was promoted to vice-admiral and appointed Commander-in-Chief, East Indies, where he brought the First Chinese War to a successful conclusion. In 1845 he was appointed Commander-in-Chief, Mediterranean, a post he held until 1852 and which, from 1846 to 1847, was combined with a command in the Channel during the Portuguese Civil War. In 1851 he was promoted to admiral. He was Commander-in-Chief at Devonport from 1853 to 1857 and was promoted to Admiral of the Fleet in 1863.

See Admiral Sir Augustus Phillimore, *The life of Admiral of the Fleet Sir William Parker* (3 vols, London, 1876-1880).

The papers were acquired in several parts. Some were purchased by the Museum in 1941 and at Sotheby's in 1972. Part of the collection was presented by Sir William Parker in 1956 and a further section was deposited on loan by the family in 1974. The papers form a full collection for all periods of Parker's service. There are official and private logs, 1794 to 1811, 1827 to 1834 and 1841 to 1852; official letterbooks, 1799 to 1834, and order books, 1795 to 1834, 1841 to 1857, and loose papers relating to his commands. Parker's personal papers include official service documents, his letters home, and his correspondence which includes letters from Sir James Graham (1792-1861), 1831-1845, Admiral Sir Thomas Hardy (1769-1839), 1831 to 1834, Gilbert Elliot, 2nd Earl of Minto (*q.v.*), 1841 to 1848, and Admiral Sir Edmund Lyons (1790-1858), 1845 to 1854. There is a log of a Spanish ship captured by Parker in 1794 and a register of lading of *Nuestra Señora de la Esperanza*, captured in 1804. The collection also contains letters written to Dr Andrew Baird (*q.v.*) by Earl St. Vincent (*q.v.*). The final section, loaned in 1974, consists of two series of letters. The first consists of those received by Earl St. Vincent, 1791 to 1821, and includes some from Lord Nelson (*q.v.*), 1796 to 1804, and the second, letters to Parker, including Nelson letters, 1803 to 1805. (16ft; 488cm)

227 PEACHEY, Allan Thomas George Cumberland, *Captain*, 1896-1967

Peachey entered the Navy in 1914. He became a midshipman in the *King George V* in 1915 and was present at Jutland. He joined the *Princess Royal* in 1917 and in 1918 became acting Flag-Lieutenant to Vice-Admiral Sir John de Robeck (1862-1928). He became a lieutenant in 1918 and spent several years in China and the Mediterranean before becoming a lieutenant-commander in 1927. After serving in several ships he was promoted to commander in 1933 and then spent some time at the Admiralty. From 1936 to 1938 he was in the *Royal Oak*, Home Fleet, and on the staff of Rear-Admiral L.D.I. Mackinnon (1882-1948). In 1938 he was appointed Operations Officer, Coast of Scotland. He was promoted to captain in 1940 and commanded the *Delhi*, Mediterranean, from 1941 to 1944. From 1947 to 1948 he was Commodore, Palestine and Levant. He retired in 1950.

The papers were presented in 1966 by Captain Peachey. They contain collections of signals relating to Jutland and to the surrender of the German High Seas Fleet in 1918; a log, 1936 to 1938; signals, 1939 to 1942; papers and signals relating to the *Delhi*, 1942 to 1944, and to the reoccupation of Malaya, 1945, and Peachey's papers as Commodore, 1947 to 1948. (2 ft; 65cm)

228 PELL, *Sir* Watkin Owen, *Admiral*, 1788-1869

Pell entered the Navy in 1799 and was promoted to lieutenant
in 1806. He then served in the *Mercury* on the Newfoundland
and Mediterranean Stations until 1809. He was promoted to
commander in 1810 into the *Thunder* at Cadiz. He was promoted
to captain in 1813 and given command of the *Menai* on the
North American Station until 1816. After a period on half-
pay, Pell was appointed Commodore in command of the Jamaica
Division of the North America and West Indies Station, 1833
to 1837. He commanded the *Howe* in the Mediterranean, 1840
to 1841, and was Superintendent of Pembroke Dockyard, 1842 to
1845. From 1846 to 1863 he was a Commissioner of Greenwich
Hospital. Pell was knighted in 1837 and promoted to rear-
admiral in 1848, vice-admiral in 1855 and admiral in 1861.

The papers were presented in 1935 by Miss Maude, grand-daughter
of Admiral Pell. They consist of his diaries, 1824 to 1863,
and his official, semi-official and private correspondence
from 1809 onwards. This includes a number of letters from
Admiral Sir George Cockburn (*q.v.*), 1834 to 1851, and from
the Spencer family, 1827 to 1856. There are extracts from
logs, notes and drafts for a biography begun by his daughter,
Mrs S.M. Maude, some account books and some items relating
to Greenwich Hospital. There are also a few letters, diaries
and account books of his wife, Lady Pell, and a few diaries
and papers of Lieutenant Edwin Pell, 24th Regiment, dating
mainly from 1809 to 1812 when he was serving in the
Peninsular War. (6ft; 182cm)

229 PELLEW, Edward, *Admiral*, *1st Viscount Exmouth*, 1757-1833

Pellew entered the Navy in 1770. He became a lieutenant in
1778, a commander in 1780, a captain in 1782 and in 1795
commanded a frigate squadron in the *Indefatigable* in the
Channel. From 1802 to 1804 he was Member of Parliament for
Barnstaple. Promoted to rear-admiral in 1804, he was
appointed Commander-in-Chief, East Indies, with his flag
in the *Culloden* and remained there for five years. In 1808
he became a vice-admiral and held the North Sea command from
1810 until 1811, when he was appointed to the Mediterranean
with the *Caledonia* as his flagship. He was promoted to
admiral in 1814 and went again to the Mediterranean in 1815.
In the next year he was ordered to suppress the Moorish

demands.   then combined with a Dutch squadron at
Gibraltar and together they fought the successful battle of
Algiers. His final command was at Devonport from 1817 to 1820.

See Edward Osler, *The life of Admiral Viscount Exmouth* (2 vols, London, 1835, 1841) In 1932 Lord Exmouth lent a collection of loose papers to the Museum, used by C. Northcote Parkinson in *Edward Pellew, Viscount Exmouth, Admiral of the Red* (London, 1934). The papers were returned in 1948.

The papers were deposited on loan in 1931 by Lord Exmouth, with the exception of two volumes which were purchased through the Caird Fund in 1944. They consist of letterbooks, 1804 to 1807, 1815 to 1816, order books, 1810 to 1814, admiral's journals, 1804 to 1807, 1815, and promotion lists, 1804 to 1809. (6ft; 182cm)

230 PENN, *Sir* William, *Admiral*, 1621-1670

Penn served under the Commonwealth in the Irish Fleet. He then went to the Mediterranean in the *Centurion* and *Fairfax*, 1650 to 1651, before becoming First Captain of the *Triumph*. During 1652 and 1653 he was Vice-Admiral of the Fleet under General Robert Blake during the First Dutch War. The following year he was appointed General and Commander-in-Chief of the Fleet, in the *Swiftsure*, for the expedition to capture Hispaniola, returning home in 1655. During the Second Dutch War, Penn was appointed to the *Royal Charles*, the Duke of York's flagship, in a capacity similar to that of 'Captain of the Fleet'. He served at the Navy Board as a Commissioner between 1660 and 1663, influencing the tactical instructions and drawing up the code long-known as the 'Duke of York's Sailing and Fighting Instructions'.

See Granville Penn, *Memorials of the professional life and times of Sir William Penn. From 1644 to 1670* (London, 1833, 2 vols).

The papers, with the Pole papers, were deposited on loan in 1948 by Penn's descendants, the Wynne family of Tempsford Hall, Bedfordshire. They were arranged by Granville Penn. Sir William's life after 1650 is well covered but for the earlier period there are only a few orders, instructions and isolated documents. The collection includes a log, 1650 to 1651, accounts of battles, 1652 to 1653, a log of the *Swiftsure* and sailing and fighting instructions, both to and from Penn, for the expedition to the West Indies. The 1665 campaign is covered by an incomplete log of the *Royal Charles*, a description of the battle of Lowestoft, several sailing and fighting instructions and orders of battle. There are also administrative papers and personal letters covering Penn's tenure of office at the Navy Board. (4 boxes)

231 PHILLIMORE, *Sir* Augustus, *Admiral*, 1822-1897

Phillimore entered the Navy in 1835 and studied at the Royal
Naval College, Portsmouth, until 1837. From 1837 to 1840 he
served as a first-class volunteer and midshipman in the *North
Star* and *Tweed* on the coast of Spain during the Carlist War.
He was in the *Endymion* from 1840 to 1843 on the East Indies
Station and during the First Chinese War, returning home in
1844 in the *Cornwallis*, flagship of Sir William Parker (*q.v.*).
He had been promoted to mate in 1842. In 1845 he was appointed
to the *Hibernia*, Parker's flagship in the Mediterranean, and
promoted to lieutenant in the same year. In 1847 he became
Parker's Flag-Lieutenant. In 1849 he transferred with him to
the *Queen*, on the same station. Phillimore later wrote a
biography of Parker, *The life of Sir William Parker*, (3 vols,
London, 1876-1880). In 1852 he was promoted to commander and
attended a course at the Royal Naval College, before sailing
as Admiralty agent in the first mail steamer to Australia.
From 1853 to 1855 he commanded the *Medea* in the West Indies
and was promoted to captain in 1855. He was appointed to
command the *Curacoa* on the south-east coast of South America
in 1859 and was Senior Officer on the Station. He commanded
the *Defence* in the Channel from 1862 to 1866. Phillimore
was Senior Officer at Jamaica from 1868 to 1869 and at
Gibraltar from 1869 to 1873, becoming a rear-admiral in 1874.
In 1876 he was second-in-command, Channel Squadron, and from
1876 to 1879 Admiral Superintendent of the Royal Naval Reserve.
He was promoted to vice-admiral in 1879 and to admiral in
1884 and was Commander-in-Chief, Devonport, from 1884 to
1887, when he retired.

The papers were deposited on permanent loan in 1967 by a
descendant, Commander Richard Phillimore. They consist
almost entirely of Phillimore's private and semi-official
correspondence from 1835 until the end of his life. These
include many letters from relatives, including Phillimore's
numerous brothers and sisters, and some of his letters to
them. The remainder are mostly from naval officers. Admiral
Sir George Ommaney Willes (1823-1901) was a regular
correspondent from the 1840s onwards. There are official
letterbooks, papers relating to Jamaica and some papers
for the Channel Squadron, a few letters and official
service documents and some biographical notes. (7ft; 214cm)

232 POCOCK, *Sir* George, *Admiral*, 1706-1792

Pocock entered the Navy in 1718, became a lieutenant in 1726,
a commander in 1734, a captain in 1738 and served almost

continuously until the peace in 1748. In 1754 he went to the
East Indies in command of the *Cumberland* and in the following
year was promoted to rear-admiral. In 1757 Pocock became a
vice-admiral and on the death of Rear-Admiral Charles Watson
(1714-1757), succeeded him in command, remaining in the East
Indies until 1760. In 1762 he was promoted to admiral, but
after he commanded the expedition to capture Havana, 1762 to
1763, had no further employment. He was Member of Parliament
for Plymouth from 1760 to 1768.

The papers were purchased in 1939 through the Caird Fund.
They cover only one period of Pocock's career in detail, that
of his time in the East Indies, 1754 to 1760, and include
letters from the Admiralty, the East India Company Secret
Committee at Madras, Company officials and local officials.
The papers relating to the capture of Chandernagore in 1757
include the capitulation, papers signed by General Thomas
Lally (1702-1766) and letters from Robert Clive (1725-1774).
The private correspondence consists of letters received by
Pocock between 1763 and 1789 from the Nabob of the Carnatic,
1766, and other native rulers in India. The collection also
contains some papers of Pocock's son, Sir George Pocock
(1765-1840), and his grandsons, Robert and Edward; this
section is mostly of bills, receipts and accounts for the
years 1792 to 1862. (1ft; 31cm)

A further collection of Pocock's papers is in the Huntingdon
Library, California.

233 POLE, *Sir* Charles Morice, 1st Bt., *Admiral of the Fleet*, 1757-
1830

Pole entered the Royal Naval Academy at Portsmouth in 1770
and joined his first ship in 1772. He went out to the
East Indies, becoming a lieutenant in 1777 and a captain on
his return to England in 1780. In 1788 he became Groom of
the Bedchamber to Prince William Henry. On the outbreak of
war in 1793 he was appointed to the *Colossus*, Mediterranean
Station, and was present at the capture of Toulon. Reaching
flag-rank in 1795 he was appointed, in the *Royal George*,
Captain of the Fleet to Lord Bridport (*q.v.*) and was
involved in the mutinies of 1797. In 1800 he became
Governor and Commander-in-Chief, Newfoundland, and in 1801
succeeded Nelson as Commander-in-Chief in the Baltic.
Between 1803 and 1806 he was chairman of the Commission of
Naval Enquiry. After a short spell at the Admiralty in 1806,
he saw no further service. He was Member of Parliament for
Newark, 1802 to 1806, and for Plymouth, 1806 to 1818. In
1830 he was appointed Master of the Robes, on the accession
of William IV.

The papers, with the Penn papers, are on permanent loan from
the Wynne family of Tempsford Hall, Bedfordshire. They
consist of eight volumes of private letters from a wide
variety of correspondents, 1769 to 1822. Two particularly
large series are those from Admiral Sir William Young (1751-
1821) and Pole's brother, Reginald Pole Carew, while Prince
William Henry also wrote a considerable number of letters to
Pole. The loose papers are mainly administrative and include
accounts, prize papers, orders and memoranda. They also
contain papers concerning Pole's representation of Plymouth
from 1806 to 1818; printed papers and general letters on
naval mutiny, 1795 to 1797, with particular reference to the
mutinies of 1797; reports and surveys on the Sea Fencibles,
1804 to 1806, and other general reports on such matters as
medical experiments, 1791, and experiments with gunpowder,
1796. (3½ft; 100cm)

234 POLLARD, Edwin John, *Rear-Admiral*, 1833-1909

Pollard entered the Navy in 1846 and served in the Black
Sea from 1854 to 1855, when he became a lieutenant. He was
present at the capture of Canton in 1857 and in the later
operations in the north of China, including the attack on the
Peiho forts, 1859, when he commanded the *Staunch*; in the
next year he was in the Gulf of Pechili and was at the
capture of Tientsin. He was promoted to commander into the
Simoom in 1861 and in 1863 was appointed to the *Royalist* on
the North American Station where, during 1864, he was
engaged in the suppression of slaving off the south coast
of Cuba. He was promoted to captain in 1868. From 1878
to 1881 he was in the Mediterranean in command of the *Rupert*
and was then in the *Defence*, coast guard service, between
1882 and 1884. He retired with the rank of rear-admiral in
1855.

The papers, part of the Pollard-Whitshed collection, were
presented by Mr H.H.W. Pollard in 1946. They include
accounts, memoranda and sailing orders for 1858 to 1861,
1863 to 1865 and 1878; a notebook recording the ships in
which Pollard served as a junior officer; a watch bill, 1860
to 1861; a book of technical details on the *Rupert* and the
Defence and newspaper cuttings, 1858 to 1878. (2 files)

235 PORTER, *Sir* James, *Surgeon Vice-Admiral*, 1851-1935

Porter became a surgeon in the Navy in 1877 and after service
abroad joined the *Scout*, Mediterranean Station, from 1889 to
1892. He then served at Bermuda Dockyard. In 1896 he was
Staff Surgeon in the *Britannia* and in 1897 went to the *Doris*,
flagship at the Cape of Good Hope, and was promoted to Fleet
Surgeon there in 1898. Between 1899 and 1900 Porter was
Principal Medical Officer to the Naval Brigade in South
Africa and afterwards received special promotion to the rank
of Deputy Inspector-General of Hospitals and Fleets. In
1902 he was appointed to the Royal Naval Hospital, Chatham
and to Gibraltar in 1905. In the next year he became
Inspector-General. Between 1907 and 1908 he was Principal
Medical Officer at Haslar. In 1908 he became Medical
Director-General of the Navy until his retirement in 1913.
During 1915 he was Principal Hospital Transport Officer for
the Mediterranean Station, being much concerned with the
Dardanelles campaign. He reverted to the retired list in
1917.

The papers were presented by Mr S.G. Beaumont in 1972.
They consist almost entirely of letters to his family, 1889
to 1913, and include accounts of various battles during the
South African War. There are some Gallipoli signals and
letters arranging for hospital trains, 1914 to 1917. Also
included in the collection are about one hundred letters
relating to the family, into which Porter married, of
Inspector-General of Hospitals and Fleets M.W. Cowan (1830-
1903). (7½ft; 232cm)

236 PRIDHAM-WIPPELL, *Sir* Henry Daniel, *Admiral*, 1885-1952

Pridham-Wippell entered the Navy in 1900. He became a
midshipman in 1901, lieutenant in 1907, commander in 1919 and
captain in 1926. Following several commands afloat and two
spells at the Admiralty, he was promoted to rear-admiral in
1938 and vice-admiral in 1941. He was Vice-Admiral
commanding the First Battle Squadron and second-in-command,
Mediterranean Fleet, 1940 to 1941. He was then Flag Officer,
Dover, from 1942 to 1944, in which year he was promoted to
admiral. From 1945 to 1947 he was Commander-in-Chief,
Plymouth, and he retired in 1948.

The papers were presented in 1969 by Admiral Pridham-Wippell's
son, Lieutenant-Commander R. Pridham-Wippell. They consist

of operational orders, signals and letters relating to the
Mediterranean, including fleet narratives and reports on
operations in the Western Desert, 1940 to 1941; and the
Dover Command War Diaries, 1940 to 1944. (1½ft; 46cm)

237 PRYCE-CUMBY, William, *Captain*, 1771-1837

Pryce-Cumby entered the Navy in 1784 and was promoted to
lieutenant in 1792. Between 1795 and 1798 he served in the
Astrea and then in the *Thalia*, being present at the battle of
Cape St. Vincent in 1797. Following three years as Flag-
Lieutenant to Vice-Admiral Alexander Graeme (d.1818) at the
Nore, he was appointed to command the *Swift* in the North Sea
between 1803 and 1804. In 1804 he was appointed to the
Bellerophon and, when the captain was killed at Trafalgar,
took command of the ship. He was promoted to captain in 1806
and in the following year was appointed to the *Dryad* on the
Irish Station. From 1808 to 1811 he was Captain of the
Polyphemus, having command of a squadron at San Domingo in
1809, and from 1811 to 1815 of the *Hyperion*. In 1812 he was
ordered to Davis Strait to protect the whale fishery and in
1813 was on convoy duty in the Atlantic. From 1814 to 1815
he was in the Channel. Pryce-Cumby had no further service
until 1837, when he was appointed Superintendent of Pembroke
Dockyard; he died in the same year.

The papers in this collection were purchased by the Society
for Nautical Research and presented to the Museum in 1938.
They consist of a book containing copies of orders and
memoranda, 1796 to 1798, 1801 and 1804, a watch, station
and quarter bill for the *Thalia*, a private letterbook, 1803
to 1808, night order books, 1807 and 1814, and passwords in
use in Pembroke Dockyard in 1837. (1 box file)

238 PURCELL-BURET, Theobald John Claud (Master Mariner), 1879-1974

Purcell-Buret was at sea for forty-eight years, from 1894 to
1942. From 1894 to 1899 he sailed as apprentice and Third
Mate in the *Pass of Balmaha*. For twenty-six years he
commanded ships of the Royal Mail Steam Packet Company.
During the Second World War, from 1940 to 1942, he commanded
the *Andes* as a troopship on voyages to Africa, the Far East,
New Zealand and America. Following his retirement he lectured
for the Ministry of Information between 1942 and 1945.

The papers were presented in two parts. The first was given
by Captain Purcell-Buret in 1954 and the second was
bequeathed on his death in 1974. There are diaries, 1939 to
1941, and 1958 to 1972; the first volume of these contains an
eye-witness account of the sinking of the *Graf Spee*, when
Purcell-Buret called at Montevideo in the *Highland Chieftain*
in 1939. There are also a scrap book, a volume of articles
and lectures, some of which are partly autobiographical, and
a service record. (3½ft; 100cm)

239 PURVIS, John Child, *Admiral*, 1746-1825

Purvis served as able seaman and midshipman in the *Arrogant*
on the coast of Spain from 1761 to 1763. He was promoted to
lieutenant in 1778, serving in the *Invincible* on the North
American Station. In 1779 he was appointed to the *Britannia*
in the Channel. From 1781 to 1783 he commanded the *Duc de
Chartres* on the North American Station and in 1782 captured
the French ship *L'Aigle*, for which he was promoted to captain.
After being on half-pay during the years of peace, Purvis was
given command in 1793 of the *Amphitrite* and then of the
Princess Royal in the Mediterranean, where he remained until
1796. From 1797 to 1801 he commanded the *London* in the
Channel, followed by the *Royal George*, 1801 to 1802, and the
Dreadnought, 1803 to 1804, on the same station. He was
promoted to rear-admiral in 1804. In 1806 he was sent out to
the blockade of Cadiz and remained in command there until
1810. He was promoted to vice-admiral in 1809 and admiral in
1819.

The papers were purchased in three parts, from Sotheby's in
1955, Weinreb in 1959 and Spink's in 1973. They consist of
logs and admiral's journals for the years 1761 to 1763, 1778
to 1783 and 1793 to 1810, letter and order books, 1781 to 1783
and 1793 to 1810, and correspondence and loose papers,
including some letters with the Spanish authorities, mostly
1806 to 1810. There is also an autobiographical essay. The
letters to Purvis from Collingwood were extracted from the
collection and sold separately in 1955 and were not purchased
by the Museum. There are also some papers relating to
Purvis's son, Lieutenant Richard Fortescue Purvis, 1806 to
1817. (6½ft; 198cm)

240 RAINIER, John Harvey, *Admiral*, 1847-1915

J.H. Rainier was a great-nephew of Captain Peter Rainier (*q.v.*). He joined the Navy in 1862 and served on the Pacific Station from 1862 to 1866 in the *Tribune*, *Topaze*, *Sutlej*, *Leander* and *Alert*. As a sub-lieutenant and from 1869 as a lieutenant, he served in the *Vestal*, *Rattlesnake* and *Plover* on the West African Station, 1867 to 1870, and from 1870 to 1871 was in the *Plover* in the West Indies. From 1872 to 1874 he served in the *Northumberland*, Channel Squadron. He was promoted to commander in 1880 and served in the *Kingfisher* on the East Indies Station from 1884 to 1887. The ship was engaged in anti-slavery patrols off East Africa. He was promoted to captain in 1887 and commanded the *Tourmaline* on the North America and West Indies Station from 1889 to 1891. He was in the *Iris*, home waters, in 1893. Rainier commanded the *Rodney* in the Mediterranean, 1894 to 1897, and was involved in the disturbances in Crete, helping to relieve the town of Kandanos in 1897. He was made a rear-admiral in 1901, a vice-admiral in 1905 and an admiral in 1908.

The papers were presented in 1948 by Captain J.W. Rainier R.N. They consist of a series of logs, 1862 to 1897, with a gap between 1874 and 1884, and loose papers about the relief of Kandanos. There is also a volume of copies of letters relating to the promotion to commander of J.H. Rainier's uncle by marriage, Captain William War Percival Johnson, 1831 to 1835. (9 vols, 2 files)

241 RAINIER, John Sprat, *Rear-Admiral*, 1777-1822

J.S. Rainier served under his uncle Admiral Peter Rainier (*q.v.*) in the East Indies, became a lieutenant in 1794 and a captain in 1796. He commanded the *Swift*, 1795 to 1797, and the *Centurion*, 1797 to 1805, in the East Indies. In 1799 he was in the Red Sea, following the French invasion of Egypt. After a gap in his service between 1805 and 1808, he commanded the *Norge* in the Mediterranean from 1808 to 1812 and then in the North Sea until 1814. He was a Member of Parliament for Sandwich, 1808 to 1812. In 1819 he was promoted to rear-admiral.

The papers were presented by Captain J.W. Rainier, R.N., in 1935. They consist of logs, 1795 to 1800, 1802 to 1805 and 1808 to 1811, and a few loose papers. (6 vols, 1 file)

242 RAINIER, Peter, *Admiral*, *ca.*1741-1808

Peter Rainier entered the Navy in 1756 and served until 1764.
He was then probably with the East India Company for two years.
He was promoted to lieutenant in 1768 but did not return to
sea until 1774. In 1777 he was appointed to command the
Ostrich, in the West Indies, and was promoted to captain in
1778. In 1779 he was appointed to the *Burford*, in the East
Indies, where he was actively engaged during the remainder of
the war. During the peace he was on half-pay but in 1793 was
appointed to the *Suffolk* and from 1794 to 1804 he was Commander-
in-Chief in the East Indies, being promoted to rear-admiral in
1795 and to vice-admiral in 1799. He returned home in 1805
and was promoted to admiral in the Trafalgar promotions. In
1807 he was elected Member of Parliament for Sandwich.

The papers were presented by Captain J.W. Rainier, R.N., in
1948. They consist of his logs, 1778 to 1782, and letter and
order books, 1794 to 1805. (1½ft; 45cm)

243 RAINIER, Peter, *Captain*, 1784-1836

Peter Rainier, son of Admiral Peter Rainier (*q.v.*), entered
the Navy in 1798. He served under his father in the East
Indies and in 1803 to 1804 was a lieutenant in his father's
ship, the *Trident*. He was promoted to captain in 1806 and
commanded the *Caroline* in the East Indies, capturing the *San
Raphael* in 1807. Between 1813 and 1815 he was in command of
the *Niger*, engaged on convoy duties in the Atlantic. From
1831 to 1835 he was Flag-Captain to Sir Pulteney Malcolm
(*q.v.*) in the *Britannia*, off the Dutch coast and in the
Mediterranean.

The papers were presented by Captain J.W. Rainier, R.N., in
1935. They contain a log of the *Caroline*, 1802 to 1803, a
signal book, 1803 to 1804, a letter from Admiral Rainier to
his son, 1805, and loose papers relating to Rainier's service,
1803 to 1814 and 1831 to 1835. (2 files)

244 REES, William Stokes, *Admiral*, 1853-1929

William Stokes Rees entered the Navy in 1866 and served on
the Mediterranean Station in the *Royal Oak* from 1868 to 1870.
In 1872 he was in home waters in the *Pembroke* and the

Bellerophon and then went out to the Pacific in the *Repulse* until 1873. He became a lieutenant in 1877 and specialized in gunnery. Promoted to commander in 1891, he went, in 1894, to the *St George*, flagship at the Cape of Good Hope, and took part in the Brass River, 1895, M'Wele, 1896, Ashanti, 1896, Zanzibar, 1896, and Benin, 1897, expeditions. Having become a captain in 1897, Rees took command of the *Thetis* in the Mediterranean, 1898 to 1900, and then on the Cape Station until 1901. After some short commands followed by two years as senior officer in Australia, 1904 to 1906, he retired as a rear-admiral in 1910 and rose to admiral on the retired list.

The papers were presented in 1962 by Rees' son, Commander Rowland E. Stokes-Rees. They include logs, 1868 to 1870 and 1872 to 1873, two workbooks, 1897, out-letterbooks, 1898 to 1901, and loose papers which relate to the expeditions in Africa, 1895 to 1897. There is also a typescript, 'Yarns from an Admiral's Reminiscences', as retold to Commander Stokes-Rees. (1ft; 30cm)

245 RICE, William McPherson (Master Shipwright), *ca*.1799-1853

Rice entered the School of Naval Architecture in 1813. He held appointments in various dockyards between 1819 and 1822, when he became draughtsman to Sir Robert Seppings (1767-1840). In 1824 he sailed to South America to assist in repairing the *Spartiate*. From 1825 to 1844 he was Foreman of Portsmouth Dockyard. In 1837 he went to Lough Swilly to refloat the *Terror*, Captain George Back (1796-1878), which had returned from the Arctic badly damaged by the ice. He was promoted to Assistant Master Shipwright in 1844 and in 1852 was appointed Master Shipwright at Pembroke Dockyard but held office for less than a year.

The papers were presented in 1953 by Mrs Cantlie, a descendant of Rice. There is a 'Journal kept in passing through the different offices of HM Dockyard, Deptford, 1820', papers relating to the excavation of an ancient vessel found in the River Rother in Kent, in 1822; a log and a diary of Rice's voyage to South America and papers on the *Terror*. There are also service papers, some correspondence, including several letters from Admiral Sir Thomas Byam Martin (1773-1854), and a sketchbook. Three older documents, presumably collected by Rice, also form part of the collection, as do the service papers of Charles Brown, Master, R.N., 1815 to 1850.
(1 box, 4 vols)

246 RICHMOND, *Sir* Herbert William, *Admiral*, 1871-1946

Richmond entered the Navy in 1885 in the *Britannia*. From
1887 to 1890 he served on the Australian Station in the
Nelson, *Calliope* and *Orlando*. He was a midshipman in the
Ruby, Training Squadron, 1890 to 1891, spending some time
in the *Minotaur*, Channel. In 1892 he was promoted to
lieutenant and served in the surveying ship *Stork*,
Mediterranean, until 1893. After a short period in the
Active, Training Squadron, in 1894, he went to the *Vernon*
to specialize in torpedoes and remained on the staff until
1897. He then served as torpedo officer in the *Empress of
India*, *Ramillies* and *Canopus*, Mediterranean, 1897 to 1900,
and in the *Majestic*, Channel Fleet, 1900 to 1903. He was
promoted to commander in 1903. After a brief period at the
Admiralty he served in the *Crescent*, flagship at the Cape
of Good Hope, from 1904 to 1906. He then returned to the
Admiralty for two years, when the Fisher reforms were in
progress, and was promoted to captain in 1908. Richmond
was captain of the *Dreadnought*, flagship of the Atlantic
Fleet, from 1908 to 1911. This was followed by two years
in command of the *Furious* and *Vindictive*, attached to
Vernon, during which time he delivered a series of lectures
to the Naval War College. In 1913 he became Assistant
Director of Operations at the Admiralty. After a short
spell in 1915 as liaison officer with the Italian fleet he
commanded the *Commonwealth*, Third Battle Squadron, from
1915 to 1917, and the *Conqueror*, Grand Fleet, 1917 to 1918.
In 1918 he was appointed Director of Training and Staff
Duties at the Admiralty but in 1919 returned to sea in the
Erin. He was promoted to rear-admiral in 1920 and appointed
first to revive the War Course and later to be President
of the Royal Naval College, Greenwich. From 1923 to 1925
he was Commander-in-Chief, East Indies, and was promoted
to vice-admiral in 1925. He set up and headed the Imperial
Defence College between 1926 and 1931, being promoted to
admiral in 1929. He retired in 1931 and in 1934 was
appointed to the Vere Harmsworth Chair of Imperial and Naval
History. He subsequently became Master of Downing College,
Cambridge. Richmond's active interest in naval history, in
which he came to specialize, began while he was still a
serving officer. He also had strong views on contemporary
naval policy which were not always acceptable to the Admiralty.
He was the author of numerous books, lectures and articles on
the Navy in history and in the present day. His most
famous work is *The navy in the war of 1739 to 1748* (3 vols,
Cambridge, 1920).

See A.J. Marder, *Portrait of an Admiral; the life and papers
of Sir Herbert Richmond* (London, 1952) and D.M. Schurman,
Education of a Navy (London, 1965).

The papers were presented to the Museum by the family in 1948 and 1966 and additional material was presented by Captain S. W. Roskill in 1962. They consist of logs, 1887 to 1891 and 1894; diaries, 1886 to 1920; diaries of Lady Richmond, 1914 to 1915; commonplace books on service topics; lectures and lecture drafts; press cuttings; photographs and a large amount of official, semi-official and private correspondence. There are letters written home by Richmond, 1879 to 1900, and 1904 to 1906, and his letters to and from Admiral W.H. Henderson (*q.v.*), 1912 to 1933. In addition there are some papers of Sir Julian Corbett (1854-1922) the naval historian, which were given to Richmond by Lady Corbett. (15ft; 465cm)

247 RIOU, Edward, *Captain*, 1762-1801

Riou entered the Navy in 1774, first joining the *Barfleur* at Portsmouth. He served in the *Romney* on the Newfoundland Station, 1775 to 1776, when he sailed in the *Discovery* on Cook's third voyage. On his return home in 1780 he was promoted to lieutenant and appointed to the *Scourge* in the West Indies, where he stayed until 1782. He then served in the *Mediator* in the Channel from 1782 to 1783 and in the *Ganges*, guardship, from 1783 to 1784. Riou was then on half-pay for two years. In 1786 he travelled on the continent. Later in the year he was appointed to the *Salisbury*, Newfoundland, serving there until 1788. In 1789 he was appointed to command the *Guardian*, carrying convicts and stores to Australia. The ship struck an iceberg and was badly damaged but Riou managed to sail her back to the Cape of Good Hope. He returned home in the *Sphinx* in 1791 and was promoted to commander and to captain within the year. From 1793 to 1795 he commanded the *Rose* and *Beaulieu* in the West Indies but was invalided home in 1795 and appointed to command the *Princess Augusta*, Royal Yacht. He served on the courts martial following the mutiny of 1797. In 1799 he commissioned the *Amazon* and in 1801 went with the Baltic Fleet where he was killed at the battle of Copenhagen.

The papers form part of the Royal United Service Institution collection transferred to the Museum in 1968. There are logs, 1776 to 1778, 1782 to 1784, 1786 to 1790, 1793 to 1795 and 1799 to 1801; a diary for 1786; mathematical work books and a sketch book. The loose papers include a biographical memoir, letters by Riou to his family, his own correspondence, papers relating to his voyage in the *Guardian* and notes on the trials of the mutineers of 1797. (2ft; 61cm)

248 ROBERTS, John Charles Gawen, *Admiral*, 1787-1874

Roberts' name was entered in ships' books from 1794 onwards but he apparently served first in the *Dreadnought* in the Mediterranean from 1801 to 1804. He was promoted to lieutenant in 1805 and served in several ships before being appointed to command the *Merope* on the east coast of Spain in 1812. From 1814 to 1815 he was in the *Pylades* on the North American Station. He was promoted to captain in 1815 but had no further service. He retired in 1846 and rose to admiral on the retired list. Roberts took the surname of Gawen in 1851 for family reasons.

The papers were presented by Miss E.H. Borough in 1952. They consist of logs, 1801 to 1804, 1812 to 1815; letter and order books and ship's general orders, 1812 to 1815. (1ft; 31cm)

249 RODDAM, Robert, *Admiral*, 1719-1808

Roddam entered the Navy in 1735 and after serving in the West Indies was promoted to lieutenant in 1741. His first command was the *Viper* in the Channel in 1746 and he was promoted to captain in 1747, afterwards commanding the *Greyhound* in the North Sea and in North America. In 1753 Roddam commanded the *Bristol* guardship at Plymouth and in 1755 was appointed to the *Greenwich* in the West Indies where, in 1757, she was captured by superior French forces. At his court martial he was honourably acquitted. He commanded the *Colchester* in the Channel in 1759 and in 1760 went to St. Helena to escort the homecoming East India convoy. Between 1770 and 1773 Roddam commanded the *Lenox*, for most of the time as guardship at Plymouth. After a period on half-pay he was appointed to the *Cornwall* at Portsmouth in 1777 but in 1778 he was promoted to rear-admiral and served as Commander-in-Chief at the Nore for the remainder of the war, being promoted to vice-admiral in 1779. Roddam flew his flag in the *Royal William* during the Spanish mobilization, 1790, but was not employed again. He became an admiral in 1793.

The papers were deposited on permanent loan by the Holderness-Roddam family in 1967 and 1973, apart from one volume purchased in 1938. They consist of an almost complete service record from 1746, including a log, 1759 to 1778, together with letter and order books, 1746 to 1783, 1789 to 1792, and two signal books. There is a very full administrative correspondence during the American War of Independence and the 1790

crisis. There are no personal papers in the collection.
(4½ft; 139cm)

Estate and family papers are in the Northumberland Record
Office.

250 ROWLEY, *Sir* Charles, 1st Bt., *Admiral*, 1770-1845

Rowley entered the Navy in 1785, serving first on the North
American Station. He was promoted to lieutenant in 1789 and
to captain in 1795. After several commands he was appointed
to the *Ruby* in 1804 and to the *Eagle* in 1806. Between 1806
and 1814 he commanded the *Eagle* in the Mediterranean, at
Walcheren, off Cadiz and, from 1811 to 1813, was in charge of
a squadron in the Adriatic. He was promoted to rear-admiral
in 1814 and knighted in 1815. From 1815 to 1818 he commanded
at the Nore and from 1820 to 1823 was Commander-in-Chief,
Jamaica. He was promoted to vice-admiral in 1825, served at
the Admiralty from 1834 to 1835 and, following his promotion
to admiral in 1841, was Commander-in-Chief, Portsmouth, from
1842 to 1845. He was created a baronet in 1836.

The papers were acquired through the Royal United Service
Institution in 1936. They consist of letter and order books
1806 to 1814 and 1820 to 1823 (1ft; 31cm) and standing
orders and memoranda to ships in Cawsand Bay, Plymouth, 1804
to 1809 and at Spithead, 1809 to 1810. (1ft; 30cm)

251 SAXTON, *Sir* Charles, 1st Bt., *Captain*, 1732-1808

Saxton entered the Navy in 1745 and was made a lieutenant in
1753. After service off Africa and in the East Indies, he
became a captain in 1762. He was then on the Newfoundland
Station in the *Pearl* until 1766. In 1779 he commissioned
the *Invincible* in the Channel and in her, in 1780, went out
to the West Indies under Sir Samuel (later Viscount) Hood
(*q.v.*). After a period of ill-health, during which time Sir
Richard Bickerton (1727-1792) commanded the *Invincible*, he
served at the Chesapeake and at St. Kitts. He returned to
England in 1783. In 1790 he was appointed Resident Commissioner at Portsmouth Dockyard. He was created a baronet
in 1794 and retired in 1806.

The papers, part of the Grey collection, were presented in
1945 by Captain Sir Cecil Graves. They consist of a report

and notes on settlements in Nova Scotia, 1762, an order book, 1780 to 1783, a book of 'remarks made in the presence of the French' in the *Invincible*, 1781 to 1782, accounts of Portsmouth Dockyard produced for the 1792 Visitation and general rules for courts martial using the precedents of 1746, 1763 and 1773. (5 vols)

252 SCOTT, *Reverend Doctor* Alexander John (Chaplain, Royal Navy), 1768-1840

Scott was ordained in 1792 and from 1793 served as a chaplain in the Navy. His competence in French, Spanish and Italian was of special use in the Mediterranean. In 1803 Nelson persuaded Scott to go with him to the Mediterranean. Although he was officially chaplain of the *Victory*, he was also able to render efficient service as a private secretary and interpreter. He continued with Nelson on this footing until Trafalgar. Scott afterwards was Vicar of Southampton and in 1816 was presented to the Crown living of Catterick.

See Alfred and Margaret Gatty, *Recollections of the Life of the Rev. A.J. Scott, DD, Lord Nelson's chaplain* (London, 1842).

The papers were deposited in 1953 on permanent loan by the City Library, Birmingham. They consist of drafts of Nelson's letters in French and intercepted papers and intelligence, 1803 to 1804. (1 file)

253 SCOTT, *Sir* James, *Admiral*, *ca.*1790-1872

Scott entered the Navy in 1803, was made a lieutenant in 1809 and after service in the Channel, off the African coast and in North America, was promoted to captain in 1828. He commanded the *President*, flagship, West Indies, 1834 to 1836, and when she was flagship, Pacific, 1836 to 1839. Scott saw no further service after 1841 and was promoted to rear-admiral in 1854, vice-admiral in 1861 and admiral in 1865.

He published *Recollections of a naval life* (London, 1834).

The papers were presented in 1932. They consist of logs, 1834 to 1839, a night order book, pay book, sick book and other documents relating to the running of the *President*. (10 vols)

254 SCOTT, William Dundas (shipbuilder), 1846-1924

In 1868 Scott began a venture, financed initially by his
father, that resulted in the shipbuilding partnership of
Messrs Scott and Linton of Dumbarton. The company failed
the following year, Linton blaming the creditors for
preventing the completion of ships under construction,
which included the *Cutty Sark*.

The papers were presented in 1959 by Scott's daughter, Mrs
M. McCall, and consist of thirty-five documents; these are
mainly letters received by Scott between 1868 and 1870 and
there is a letter from Hercules Linton, 1877. (1 file)

255 SERGISON, Charles (Clerk of the Acts), 1654-1732

Sergison began his career as a dockyard clerk in 1671 and
in 1675 was appointed an extra clerk to the Comptroller of
Victualling Accounts in the Navy Office. In 1677 he was
made Chief Clerk to the Clerk of the Acts in which office
he remained until 1686. For two years he was secretary of
the new commission for conducting current business and
continued with the title of Secretary when the Navy Board
was re-consituted in 1688. In the following year he was
made Assistant Clerk of the Acts and in 1690 became Clerk
of the Acts, a post which he held until 1719.

Documents from the collection form the basis of Commander
R.D. Merriman's *The Sergison papers* (Navy Records Society,
1950) and of *Queen Anne's Navy* (Navy Records Society, 1961).

The papers were purchased in 1914 by Dr R.C. Anderson, who
in 1937 presented them to the Museum. When he resigned
office Sergison, as was common practice at the time, took
with him a number of official and semi-official volumes
relating to Navy Office business. Many were later dispersed
by his descendants and this collection constitutes the
residue of Sergison's papers. It consists of Navy Board
Minutes, 1673 to 1718 (seventy-six volumes), and copies of
Admiralty orders to the Navy Board, 1603 to 1717 (thirteen
volumes), mostly after 1674. There are also a large number
of miscellaneous documents, including lists of ships in Sea
Pay, 1660 to 1685 and 1684 to 1718, lists of officers, 1688
to 1716, Instructions for Ordnance, 1660 to 1688, Instructions for the Navy, 1686 to 1688, an abstract of Navy
Board Warrants, 1660 to 1717, an abstract of numbers of
dockyard workmen, 1686 to 1718, the Ordinary Estimate, 1692,

papers relating to a victualling enquiry, 1710 to 1713, and an account of the Select Committee to Examine and State the Debt of the Navy, 1714. Finally there are copies of Hollond's 'Discourse on the Navy' and 'Survey of the South Coast' by Edmund Dummer, Surveyor of the Navy between 1692 and 1699. (21ft; 646cm)

256 SHARPE, Philip Ruffle, *Vice-Admiral*, 1831-1892

Sharpe went to sea in the *Blazer*, Captain Owen Stanley (1811-1849), in 1845. He entered the Navy in 1846 and sailed with Stanley in the *Rattlesnake* on her surveying voyage to Australia, 1846 to 1850. Two years later he was again appointed to the *Rattlesnake*, as mate, and sailed in her to the Arctic to relieve the expedition searching for Sir John Franklin (*q.v.*). In 1854 he was promoted to lieutenant. From 1857 to 1859 he was in the *Magicienne* and served during the Second Chinese War. He was promoted to commander in 1863 and in 1867 was appointed to command the *Waterwitch*, hydraulic gun boat, during tests on her performance. In 1868 he was appointed to the *Lapwing* on the west coast of Ireland and then escorted the ships towing the new floating dock to Bermuda, continuing to the West Indies. He was promoted to captain in 1870 and from 1875 to 1878 commanded the Indian troopship *Crocodile*. He retired in 1886, became a rear-admiral in 1887 and a vice-admiral in 1892.

The papers were deposited on loan by Sharpe's grand-daughter, Mrs. Corran, in 1960. There are diaries, 1857 to 1859, and letterbooks, 1867 to 1870 and 1875 to 1877, together with official service documents and a few letters and photographs, Sharpe's own copy of *The Voyage of the Rattlesnake*, by John MacGillivray (London, 1852, 2 vols), and typed extracts from an autobiography up to 1849. The letters include one from Sharpe's brother-in-law, William R. Hobson, a lieutenant in the *Fox*, under Captain F.L. McClintock (*q.v.*), describing the finding of relics of the expedition led by Sir John Franklin (*q.v.*). There are service papers, three logs and a notebook kept by Commander Philip William Carwithen Sharpe (1884-1957), Sharpe's son, as a midshipman in the *Majestic*, Channel, 1900 to 1901, *Diana*, Mediterranean, 1901 to 1902, and *Ariadne*, West Indies, 1902 to 1903. There are also a few service papers of Second Officer Mary Gertrude Sharpe, W.R.N.S. (Mrs. M.G. Corran). (1ft; 31cm)

257 SHIRREFF, William Henry, *Rear-Admiral*, 1785-1847

Shirreff entered the Navy in 1796, was promoted to lieutenant
in 1804 and to captain in 1809. Between 1817 and 1821 he
commanded the *Andromache* in the Pacific, at the time of the
Chilean War of Independence. He also despatched Edward
Bransfield (*ca*.1783-1852), Master of the *Andromache*, in the
hired ship *Williams of Blyth* to claim the South Shetland
Islands, 1819 to 1820, for Britain. Between 1830 and 1837
Shirreff was Captain of the Port of Gilbraltar under the
Colonial Service. In 1838 he was appointed to Captain-
Superintendent of Deptford Victualling Yard. He was promoted
to rear-admiral in 1846.

The papers were presented by Mr. L.G. Carr Laughton in 1940.
There are three letterbooks for the years 1818 to 1820, one
for 1830 to 1837 at Gibraltar, another for 1838 to 1841 and
a report on dockyards made to the Admiralty in 1846. (6 vols)

258 SILVESTER, *Sir* Philip Carteret, 1st Bt., *Captain*, 1777-1828

Carteret was the son of Rear-Admiral Philip Carteret (*q.v.*)
and adopted the name of Silvester in 1822. He entered the
Navy in 1792 and joined the *Lion* under Captain Sir Erasmus
Gower (*q.v.*) on Lord Macartney's Embassy to China. He
continued to serve under Gower in the *Triumph* in 1795 in the
Channel and was promoted to lieutenant in that year. He then
served in the *Impérieuse*, Channel and North Sea, 1795 to
1796, in the *Greyhound*, 1796 to 1798 in the Channel and the
Cambrian, 1801, to St. Helena. His first command was the
Bonne Citoyenne in the West Indies in 1802. In 1804 he was
appointed to the *Scorpion*, North Sea, until 1806, after
which she went to the West Indies until 1807. In 1809
Carteret commanded the gun boats in the Walcheren Expedition.
Carteret was given command of the *Naiad* for a year in 1811
and then the *Pomone*, 1813 to 1814, both on the Lisbon Station.
After the war he commanded the *Active* on the Jamaica Station
but saw no further service after 1817.

The papers, part of the Carteret collection, were purchased
from Maggs Bros. in 1933. They consist of logs, 1792 to
1798, 1801 and 1815 to 1817, letterbooks, 1806 to 1807 and 1811
to 1814, and correspondence, 1792 to 1815, including a series
from Sir Erasmus Gower (*q.v.*), 1792 to 1814. Finally there
are papers relating to the family and records of several tours
made during his retirement. (4ft; 122cm)

259 SISSON, James Joseph Lawson, *Commander*, 1846-1883

When he was a boy Sisson's family moved to Switzerland where
he went to school. He entered the Navy in 1860 as a cadet in
the *Britannia* and was promoted to midshipman in 1862. After
serving in the *Neptune*, 1861 to 1863, in the Mediterranean,
the *Edgar* in home waters, 1863 to 1866 and the *Doris* in North
America and the West Indies from 1866 to 1869, he was
promoted to lieutenant in 1869. From 1872 to 1875 Sisson was
in the *Peterel* on the Pacific Station. After a spell in the
Malabar in 1878 he commanded the *Firebrand* at the Cape of
Good Hope from 1879 to 1882. He retired as a commander in
1882 and in 1883 was appointed Port Captain of Natal but died
the same year.

The papers were presented in 1952 by Sisson's son, Mr. J.J.L.
Sisson. They consist of a diary, 1859 to 1860, logs, 1865 to
1869 and 1872 to 1876, family letters received and Sisson's
own letters to his father, 1860 to 1883. There is also
some biographical material, a pocket book and sketch book.
(1ft; 31cm)

260 SMITH, *Sir* William Sidney, *Admiral*, 1764-1840

Smith entered the Navy in 1777 and served in North America
and the West Indies, where in 1780 he was promoted to
lieutenant. After the American War of Independence, he
travelled in France, North Africa and the Baltic as a
government agent and at the outbreak of the Revolutionary
War he was in Smyrna. He joined Hood at Toulon and took
part in its evacuation and burning. In 1794 he was employed
in the North Sea and in 1796 off Le Havre, where he was
captured during a cutting-out expedition. For two years he
was a prisoner but escaped in 1798, when he was given
command of *Tigre* as senior officer in the Levant. In 1799
his success at the defence of Acre halted the advance of
the French army. He was elected Member of Parliament for
Rochester in 1802. On the resumption of the war Smith
commanded a squadron off Holland. In 1805 he was promoted
to rear-admiral and went to the Mediterranean where he was
active off the coast of South Italy. He took part in the
expedition to the Dardanelles in 1807 and in the following
year went briefly to the South American Station. In 1810
he was promoted to vice-admiral and went in 1812 to be
second-in-command of the Mediterranean Station, returning
in bad health in 1814. He saw no further active service
and retired to Paris after 1815. He was made an admiral in
1821.

Among the biographies are Sir John Barrow, *Life and corre-
spondence of Admiral Sir William Sidney Smith, G.C.B.*
(London, 1848) and Edward Russell, 2nd Baron of Liverpool,
*Knight of the sword; the life and letters of Admiral Sir
William Sidney Smith, G.C.B.* (London, 1964).

The papers were acquired in two sections. The first is part
of the Phillipps collection, purchased in 1946 by Sir James
Caird, and the second was purchased at Sotheby's in 1975.
They consist of loose letters and notes written between 1790
and 1840 by many of the important naval figures of the day.
There are notes on his experiences as a prisoner of the
French, a number of letters relating to the Mediterranean,
1799 and some to his brother John Spencer Smith, who was
Minister Plenipotentiary at Constantinople, 1798 to 1801.
Finally there are many letters received by Smith during his
retirement abroad. (3 boxes)

261 SMITH-DORRIEN, Arthur Hale, *Rear-Admiral*, 1856-1933

Smith-Dorrien entered the *Britannia* in 1870 and then went to
the *Trafalgar*, which was the cadet training ship at that time.
His first service was in the *Endymion* between 1872 and 1873,
after which he joined the *Volage* during an expedition, 1874
to 1875, to observe the transit of Venus at Kerguelen Island,
Indian Ocean. He then served in the *Sultan*, Channel Squadron,
before taking his gunnery and Greenwich courses. In 1876 he
was appointed to the *Shah* on her commission as flagship in the
Pacific and was present at the action with the Peruvian
turret-ship *Huascar*. During the Zulu war of 1879 he was in
the Naval Brigade and was also promoted to lieutenant. From
1880 he was in the *Eclipse*, East Indies Station, operating
against the slave trade; he ended the commission by service
in the Naval Brigade in Egypt, 1882. On his return home he
was appointed Flag-Lieutenant to the Commander-in-Chief,
Devonport. From 1884 to 1885 he served in the Mediterranean
and then in China in the *Invincible*; from 1886 to 1887 he was
in the Red Sea in the *Condor*; from 1887 to 1889 he was in the
Espiègle, in the Pacific and then from 1889 to 1893 was in
the *Phaeton* on the Mediterranean Station. He was appointed
commander in 1893, going to the *Britannia* and in 1897 to the
Alacrity, Admiral's despatch vessel on the China Station.
Having become a captain in 1900, in 1901 he commanded the
Rainbow. He retired in 1904 and was promoted to rear-admiral
on the retired list in 1909.

The papers were presented by Rear-Admiral Smith-Dorrien's
nephew, Mr D. Smith-Dorrien, in 1952. They are composed of

four volumes of watercolours, photographs, newscuttings and documents covering his career from his schooldays in 1865 until the end of his naval service, together with three volumes of caricatures and sketches. (1½ft; 46cm)

262 SMITHETT, *Sir* Luke (Master, Packet Service), *ca*.1800-1871

Smithett joined the packet service in 1814 and was on the Dover Station from 1821 to 1825, when he went to the Portpatrick service. He returned to Dover in 1831 and was still there in 1837 when the operation of the mail steam vessels was transferred from the control of the Post-Master General to that of the Admiralty; he continued to serve at Dover until 1855, when another change in policy led to the substitution of contract packets; the naval connection was formally ended in 1860. Smithett subsequently held occasional employment as a pilot for the Royal Yacht but no record can be found of any further service after 1857. He was knighted in 1862.

The papers were purchased through the Caird Fund in 1954 from Messrs Elkin Matthews and are principally orders, appointments and testimonials, 1825 to 1854. (1 vol)

263 SPRATT, Thomas Abel Brimage, *Vice-Admiral*, 1811-1888

Spratt entered the Navy in 1827, was made a lieutenant in 1841 and a commander in 1849, his ship then being the *Spitfire*, a survey vessel in the Mediterranean; he continued in command of her until the end of the Crimean War, becoming a captain in 1855. In 1856 he was appointed to the *Medina* and remained surveying in the Mediterranean until 1863. He was a Commissioner of Fisheries from 1866 to 1873 and was promoted to rear-admiral in 1872. In 1878 he became a vice-admiral and from 1879 was Acting Conservator of the Mersey Conservancy Board. Spratt published books and articles on the Mediterranean, chiefly on the history and antiquities of Crete.

The papers were presented in 1951 in two sections, the first by Miss Borosins and the second by Brigadier C.C. Phipps. They consist of various reports, 1850 to 1884, which include surveys (particularly of the Black Sea area); remarks on Crete and the Cretans; on the coal trade of the Black Sea; on a new harbour at Malta; on an electric cable between Malta and Alexandria; reports submitted to the Teignmouth Harbour

Commission and Fishery Commission reports for England and
Ireland. Spratt's correspondence consists of a few letters
received and some draft replies, 1853 to 1860. The
memorandum of his service, 1837 to 1862, contains an account
of his part in the Crimean War. His publications are also
listed. (2 boxes)

264 STEEVENS, Charles, *Rear-Admiral*, 1705-1761

Charles Steevens entered the Navy in about 1720, was promoted
to lieutenant in 1729, to commander in 1744 and to captain
in 1748. During the early part of the Seven Years War he
served in the Channel but in 1757 was sent out to the East
Indies as Commodore of a small squadron in the *Elizabeth*; he
was also promoted to rear-admiral in that year. In 1760 he
was appointed Commander-in-Chief of the station, moved to the
Norfolk and undertook the blockade of Pondicherry, which
surrendered in 1761.

See Nathaniel Steevens, *The naval career of Rear-Admiral
Charles Steevens from 1720 to 1761* (published privately, 1874).

The papers were presented by a descendant, Miss P.N. Steevens,
in 1965. They consist of a letter to Steevens from the
Nabob of Arcot, 1760, and the draft and printed copy of his
life written by his grand-nephew, Nathaniel Steevens. Also
in the collection is the plan of learning of the Naval
Academy, Portsmouth, 1753, of Charles Stevens, midshipman
(1735-1756), nephew of Rear-Admiral Steevens, and a book of
jokes, morals and proverbs. (4 vols, 1 file)

265 STEPHENSON, *Sir* Henry Frederick, *Admiral*, 1842-1919

Stephenson entered the Navy in 1855. He served in the Crimea,
India and Canada, being promoted to lieutenant in 1861 and to
commander in 1868. He was in command of the *Rattler* when she
was lost in La Pérouse Strait in 1868. He became a captain
in 1875. From 1875 to 1876 Stephenson commanded the *Discovery*
in the British Arctic Expedition led by Captain G.S. Nares
(*q.v.*). He commanded the *Carysfort*, Mediterranean, 1880 to
1883, and took part in operations in Egypt in 1882. During
the 1890s he was Commander-in-Chief both in the Pacific and
the Channel, being appointed rear-admiral in 1890, vice-
admiral in 1896 and admiral in 1901.

The papers were presented by Stephenson's nephew, Captain P.K. Stephenson, in 1953. There are letterbooks for 1868 and 1880 to 1883, and a printed account of the court martial following the loss of the *Rattler*. Most of the collection relates to the Arctic expedition, 1875 to 1876. It includes Stephenson's diary in three volumes, a letter-book, a book of general proceedings of the *Discovery*, a rough survey book and a scrapbook, with letters and orders from Nares and some other loose papers. There are also printed volumes of the official reports of the expedition and of earlier arctic expeditions. (2ft; 62cm)

266 STEPHENSON, Thomas, *Captain*, 1741-1809

Stephenson entered the Navy as a first class volunteer and was promoted to lieutenant in 1778. He left the Navy in 1785 and became a 'free mariner' in India. He commanded, among other ships, the *Mary*, her last voyage being from Bengal to England, 1795 to 1796. Stephenson then returned to the Navy after an absence of twelve years. He was promoted to commander and to captain in 1798, when he went to the *Defence* in the Channel. In 1800 he was given command of the *Princess Charlotte*, but appears to have had no further command after 1802.

The papers were presented by a descendant, Mr C.R. Bury, in 1952. They consist of order books, 1795 to 1801; a log, 1798 to 1799; a signal log, 1799, and sailing directions of the Channel, North America and the West Indies. There are also two logs of the *Columbia*, 1814 to 1815, kept by Midshipman F. Thompson, a signal notebook by Thomas Michel, and the personal papers of Lieutenant John Houghton, (1787-1820), 1813 to 1815, a nephew of Stephenson's also on board the *Columbia*. (4 vols, 1 box)

267 STEWART, Archibald Thomas, *Commander*, 1876-1968

Stewart entered the Navy in 1890 and joined the *Boadicea*, flagship of the East Indies Station, in 1892. He transferred to the *Bonaventure* in 1894 and in the following year to the *Active*, training squadron. For the remainder of his career he served mainly in the Mediterranean, retiring with the rank of commander in 1920.

171

The papers were presented in 1963 by Commander Stewart. They
consist of two logs, 1892 to 1896, as well as documents
collected by Stewart. These include some letters received
by Lord Charles Beresford, 1886 to 1889, and a small
manuscript booklet entitled, 'Reasons by the officers of the
Brunswick for leaving the fleet, 1st June 1794'. (2 vols,
4 files)

268 STEWART, *Sir* William Houston, *Admiral*, 1822-1901

William Stewart, eldest son of Admiral of the Fleet Sir
Houston Stewart (1791-1875), entered the Navy in 1835. He
became a lieutenant in 1842, a commander in 1848 and a captain
in 1854. In 1860 he joined the *Marlborough* as Flag-Captain
to Sir William Fanshawe Martin (1801-1895), in the Mediterranean,
where he remained for three years. The rest of his service
was in administrative appointments. He was promoted to rear-
admiral in 1870 and from July of that year was Admiral
Superintendent of Devonport Dockyard until the end of 1871,
when he was appointed in the same capacity to Portsmouth.
From 1872 to 1881 he was Controller of the Navy, although
without a seat on the Board of Admiralty. He became a vice-
admiral in 1876 and admiral in 1881, when he was appointed
Commander-in-Chief, Devonport. Here he remained for the
full period of three years and retired in 1885.

The papers were presented by Miss Grace Stewart, the Admiral's
granddaughter, in 1968. They consist of letters to Sir
William, 1879 to 1884, including those from the First Lord,
William Henry Smith (1825-1891) and other private correspondents. His period in the *Marlborough* is represented by
letters as well as a book of remarks on the discipline of
the ship. There is a book entitled the 'Dimensions, cost
etc. of H.M. Ships built under contract and in the Dockyards',
1860 to 1873. The collection also contains the proceedings
of the Naval Brigade attached to the expeditionary force for
the relief of Tokar in 1884 when Lieutenant Houston Stewart,
Sir William's son, in command of the Right Half-Battery, was
killed at the action of El Teb. A midshipman's log for the
Ariadne, Portsmouth, 1871, *Minotaur*, Channel Squadron, 1872,
and *Narcissus*, West Indies, October 1872 to 1873, belonged
to Lieutenant Houston Stewart. Finally there are a few letters
written to Sir William's father, Sir Houston Stewart, between
1853 and 1854 when Sir Houston was Superintendent of Malta
Dockyard. (1 box)

269 STOKES, John Lort, *Admiral*, 1812-1885

Stokes entered the Navy in 1824 and joined the *Beagle* the following year. He served in her for eighteen years, surveying first in South American and then in Australian waters. He was Assistant Surveyor under Robert Fitzroy (1805-1865) during the voyage of 1831 to 1836 and was promoted to lieutenant in 1837. When, in 1841, John Clements Wickham (1798-1864) was invalided during the Australian survey, Stokes took command of the *Beagle* and completed the commission, returning to England in 1843. He was promoted to captain in 1846. From 1847 to 1851 he commanded the *Acheron* on the survey of New Zealand. His last employment was in the English Channel survey, 1859 to 1863. He was promoted to rear-admiral in 1864, vice-admiral in 1871 and admiral in 1877.

The papers were purchased from the family at Scotchwell House, near Haverfordwest, in 1960. They include logs, 1837 to 1843, 1848 to 1849, 1851 and 1859 to 1863, letter-books, 1841 to 1843, 1848 to 1851 and 1860 to 1862, and correspondence, 1844 to 1858. There are no papers for the first voyage of the *Beagle*. For the second and more famous voyage, 1831 to 1836, on which Charles Darwin sailed, there are some official service documents of Stokes, some orders, notes on surveying, rough notes on navigation in South American waters and a few rough sketches. For the third voyage, 1837 to 1843, there are survey note-books, some letters and orders, a night order book, a game book, a list of the crew, some accounts, an album of sketches and some loose sketches. The bulk of the collection relates to the voyage of the *Acheron*. There is a draft narrative of the first part of the voyage, together with survey notebooks, an abstract of the ship's positions, miscellaneous letters and papers and views, sketches and rough charts. This last group comprises about 150 single items, mostly coastal views. Some of the more finished sketches can be identified as the work of William Swainson (1789-1855), Frederick John Owen Evans (1815-1885), later Hydrographer to the Admiralty, and W.J.W. Hamilton, an artist who accompanied the expedition. His sketchbook is also in the collection. Finally there are survey notebooks and a calculations book for the English Channel survey. (4 ft; 122cm)

270 STOPFORD, *Sir* Montagu, *Vice-Admiral*, 1798-1864

Montagu Stopford, nephew of Admiral the Hon. Sir Robert
Stopford (*q.v.*), entered the Navy in 1810. He was
promoted to lieutenant in 1819 and to captain in 1825.
After intermittent service on various stations he was
promoted to rear-admiral in 1853. He was Captain of the
Fleet during the Crimean War and between 1855 and 1858 was
Superintendent of Malta Dockyard. He became a vice-
admiral in 1858.

The papers were presented in 1966 by Captain L.M.P.
Stopford. They consist of memoranda issued to the fleet
in the Crimea, 1854, records of arrivals and sailings of
ships at Malta, 1855 to 1856, and the commission appointing
Stopford Superintendent of Malta Dockyard. (3 files)

271 STOPFORD, *the Hon. Sir* Robert, *Admiral*, 1768-1847

Stopford entered the Navy in 1780, passed as lieutenant in
1784 and was promoted to captain in 1790. He served in the
Channel and the West Indies until 1802 but on the resumption
of hostilities was appointed to the *Spencer* in the Channel
Fleet until 1805. Between 1806 and 1807 he was Member of
Parliament for Ipswich. After further service in the West
Indies, he was promoted to rear-admiral in 1808 and went to
the East Indies as Commander-in-Chief until 1813. He was
promoted to vice-admiral in 1812 and admiral in 1825. In
1827 Stopford was appointed Commander-in-Chief, Portsmouth,
and after holding office for the usual term of three years,
was on half-pay until 1837 when he was appointed Commander-
in-Chief, Mediterranean. His period of command included the
Syrian campaign and the bombardment of Acre, 1840. In 1841
he was appointed Governor of Greenwich Hospital.

The papers were bequeathed to the Museum in 1950 by Commander
R.N. Stopford. They consist of an order book, 1803 to 1805,
official service documents and private and semi-official
letters from many important officers of the time. Among
them is one from Nelson (*q.v.*), 1805, from the Duke of
Wellington, 1811, and a series of thirty-five from
William, Duke of Clarence, 1827 to 1828, when Lord High
Admiral. For the Mediterranean command there are letters
from the 2nd Earl of Minto (*q.v.*) and Lord Ponsonby (1770-
1855), ambassador at Constantinople. Finally, there is a
volume of letters from well-known literary and social figures

received by Stopford and Field-Marshal Thomas Grosvenor (1764-1851) between 1791 and 1850, including one from Sir Walter Scott (1771-1832). Stopford and Grosvenor both lived at Richmond, Surrey. (7 vols)

272 STOPFORD, Robert Fanshawe, *Admiral*, 1811-1891

Robert Stopford, son of the Hon. Sir Robert Stopford (*q.v.*), entered the Navy in 1825 and was promoted lieutenant in 1831. He was present at the siege of Acre, 1840, and was sent home with his father's despatches after the action. In 1841 he was promoted to captain and commanded the *Talbot* in the Mediterranean for one year, employed for some of the time in surveying the Skerki Channel off Sardinia. He commanded the *Asia*, 1848 to 1851, in the Pacific Squadron under Rear-Admiral (later Admiral) Sir Phipps Hornby (*q.v.*). He was promoted to rear-admiral in 1860, vice-admiral in 1866 and admiral in 1871.

The papers were bequeathed to the Museum in 1950 by Commander R.N. Stopford. They consist of loose papers mounted in a volume, relating mainly to the *Talbot* and *Asia* periods, with official service documents. (1 vol, 2 charts)

273 STUART, *Lord* William, *Captain*, 1778-1814

Stuart was a lieutenant in 1797, was promoted to commander in 1798 and to captain in 1799. As Senior Officer he served at Gibraltar in *Le Grenier*, 1800, and then successively in the *Champion*, Adriatic, 1801 to 1803, and off Flushing in the *Crescent*, 1804 to 1806. He was in the *Lavinia* from 1806 to 1810, during which time the frigate squadron under his command during the Walcheren expedition contributed to the surrender of Flushing, 1809. Stuart was Member of Parliament for Cardiff from 1802 to 1814. His last service was in the *Conquistador*, in home waters from 1811 until 1814.

The papers were presented by the British Records Association in 1936. They consist of order books, 1799 to 1810 and 1811 to 1814; logs, 1811 and 1813 to 1814; in and out-letterbooks, 1809 to 1814, and loose papers, which are mainly orders received from the Admiralty, Ordnance, Navy and Victualling Offices and various senior officers, 1811 to 1814. There are also requests for surveys, returns and other administrative ships' papers, 1811 to 1814. (2½ft; 76cm)

274 TAIT, *Sir* William Eric Campbell, *Admiral*, 1886-1946

Tait entered the Navy in 1902 and served in the Pacific from
1903 to February, 1905, in the *Grafton*, and then in the
Mediterranean, in the *Drake*. He went to the *Flora*, China, in
1908 and became a lieutenant in 1909. In 1910 he joined the
Home Fleet, serving in a number of ships, including the
Hindustan and the *Collingwood* until 1912. He was promoted
to lieutenant-commander in 1917, commander in 1921 and captain
in 1926. After a course at Greenwich, Tait returned to sea
in 1928 and took command of four cruisers; these included the
Capetown in 1929 and the *Delhi* in 1930, on the America and
West Indies Station. He was appointed Deputy Director of
Naval Intelligence in 1932 and in 1933 went out to the Far
East to report on the possibility of an outbreak of hos-
tilities with Japan. In 1938 he became a rear-admiral and in
1941 was appointed vice-admiral and Commander-in-Chief,
African Station. On his appointment as Governor of Southern
Rhodesia in 1944, he retired and was promoted to admiral in
1945.

The papers were deposited on loan by Tait's daughter, Mrs S.
L. Ashton, in 1962. They contain two logs, 1903 to 1905, a
photograph album, 1908 to 1914, and loose papers; these
include letters of proceedings, 1929 to 1930, remarks on the
officers and men of the Argentine Navy, on Brazilian and
American naval personnel, and intelligence reports, 1932 to
1933. (3 vols, 1 box)

275 TENNANT, *Sir* William George, *Admiral*, 1890-1963

Tennant joined the *Britannia* in 1905, from 1906 to 1909 was
in the Channel in the *Prince of Wales*, *Venerable*, *Implacable*
and *Queen* and was promoted to lieutenant in 1912. After
specializing in navigation he served from 1914 to 1916 in
the *Lizard* and *Ferret*, Harwich Force, and in the Grand Fleet
in the *Chatham* and *Nottingham*. Still in 1916, he returned to
the Harwich Force in the *Concord* and remained in her as
navigator until 1919. He was navigator during the two royal
tours around the world in the *Renown*, 1921 and the *Repulse*,
1925, the year he was promoted to commander. He was made
captain in 1932. From 1935 to 1937 he was on the
Mediterranean Station in the *Arethusa* followed by two years,
1937 to 1939, as naval instructor at Imperial Defence College.
At the beginning of the Second World War, Tennant organized
the embarkation of the allied armies at Dunkirk. He next
commanded the *Repulse* and survived her sinking by air attack

at the end of 1941. In 1942 he was promoted to rear-admiral and commanded a cruiser squadron of the Eastern Fleet. He joined the staff for 'Overlord' in 1943 and was responsible for the 'Mulberry' harbours. In 1945 he went as Flag-Officer, Levant and Eastern Mediterranean, was promoted to vice-admiral in that year and to admiral in 1949 at the end of his term as Commander-in-Chief, America and West Indies, 1946 to 1949.

The papers were presented by Lady Tennant in 1967. They include official service documents; midshipman's logs, 1905 to 1909; diaries of war service, written up in 1919, and one for the cruises of 1925; a work book, 1927; papers on the loss of the *Repulse* , 1941; tactical and secret papers on the 'Mulberry' operations, 1944, and engagement diaries, visitors' books, notes for speeches and lectures, 1946 to 1949, as well as many general papers and notebooks relating to Tennant's historical interests and the role of the three services in defence strategy. (5ft; 182cm)

276 THESIGER, *Sir* Bertram Sackville, *Admiral*, 1875-1966

Thesiger entered the Navy in 1887 and served on the Cape Station in the *Narcissus* in 1892. In 1893 he joined the *Active* , Training Squadron, and was promoted to lieutenant in 1895. He served subsequently in the *Pique*, 1895 to 1897, and *Cressy*, 1902 to 1903, both on the China Station, until his promotion to commander in 1905. After a period, 1905 to 1907, in the *Cornwallis*, Channel Fleet, he was at the Gunnery School at Sheerness until his appointment to the *Scylla* on the North American Station, 1909 to 1911. Here he became involved in the Nicaragua and Honduras troubles, 1909 to 1910. In 1912 he was promoted to captain and from 1914 to 1916 commanded the *Inconstant* and briefly the *Inflexible*, Grand Fleet. Between 1917 and 1919 he was in the *Calypso* in the North Sea and the Baltic and from 1920 to 1922, when he attained flag-rank, he commanded the *King George V* in the Mediterranean. He was appointed Admiral Superintendent of Portsmouth Dockyard, 1925 to 1927, and then Commander-in-Chief, East Indies, 1927 to 1929, retiring as an admiral in 1932. During the Second World War her served as Commodore of Convoys and later as Flag-Officer, Falmouth.

He was the author of *Queries in seamanship* (Portsmouth, 1928).

The papers were deposited on loan in 1972 by Lady Thesiger. They consist of a diary, a typescript autobiography and

photograph albums, which cover most of Admiral Thesiger's
service; there are also official service documents and groups
of papers, arranged by subject, for Estonia, Smyrna,
Portsmouth Dockyard, East Indies, the Marine Society and
Convoys. (3ft; 92cm)

277 THOMPSON, *Sir* Charles, 1st Bt., *Vice-Admiral*, *ca.*1740-1799

Thompson entered the Navy in 1755 and became a lieutenant in
1760. During the Seven Years War he served on the Channel,
Mediterranean and North American Stations. He was promoted
to captain in 1772 and appointed to the *Chatham* and then to
the *Crescent*, which he brought home from the West Indies in
1774. After further service in the West Indies, he was moved in
1780, into the *Alcide*. Between 1787 and 1790 he commanded
the *Edgar*, guardship at Portsmouth. His next appointments were
to the *Elephant* during the mobilization of 1790 and in 1793
to the *Vengeance*, which he took to the West Indies. Thompson
was promoted to rear-admiral in April 1795 and to vice-
admiral in June 1795. In 1796, with his flag in the *London*,
he commanded a detached squadron in the Channel. He was
second-in-command at the battle of Cape St. Vincent, 1797,
for which he was made a baronet, remaining with the fleet
until removed at the insistence of St. Vincent, because of his
censure of the execution of four mutineers on a Sunday. He
commanded the fleet off Brest during 1798 but his health
failed and he died shortly after striking his flag early in
1799. Thompson was Member of Parliament for Monmouth, 1796
to 1799.

The papers were presented in 1957 by a descendant, Admiral
Sir William Andrewes. They consist of loose orders received,
1772 to 1780, 1795 to 1798, and letter and order books, 1795
to 1798. There are also official service documents and a
number of miscellaneous papers and notes collected by
Thompson, 1746 to 1799. These include extracts of logs of
the ships under his command, including the *Ulysses*, 1794,
Captain, 1798, *Triton*, 1799, *Alalanti*, 1799, *Dragon*, 1799,
and *Seahorse*, 1799; notes on the wreck of the *Ipswich*, 1746,
and drafts of letters to Earl St. Vincent (*q.v.*). (2½ft;
76cm)

278 THURSFIELD, Henry George, *Rear-Admiral*, 1882-1963

H.G. Thursfield, son of Sir James Richard Thursfield (*q.v.*),
joined the *Britannia* in 1896. As a midshipman he went to

North American and the West Indies in the *Renown*, 1898 to 1899, was then in the Channel in 1900, in the *Majestic*, until he went to the Mediterranean, serving in the *Venus*, 1900, and the *Andromeda*, 1901. He became a lieutenant in 1902 and after serving as a torpedo officer in various ships was selected to join the first War Staff Course to be held in the Royal Navy, 1912. In 1914 he was promoted to commander and after a short period of service at the Admiralty was sent to the East Indies. He was commander of the *Dreadnought*, Grand Fleet, in 1916 but returned to staff duties in 1917 under Vice-Admiral Sir William Pakenham (1861-1933) in the *Lion*. Promoted to captain in 1920 he was sent, in 1925, on a naval mission to Greece. On Thursfield's return to England he held appointments at the Staff College, Greenwich, and at the Admiralty, retiring with flag rank in 1932. From 1936 he was editor of *Brassey's Naval Annual* and was naval correspondent of the *Times*; although he retired from the *Times* in 1952, he remained editor of *Brassey's* until his death. Between 1948 and 1951 he was a trustee of the National Maritime Museum.

A volume of *Naval Journals, 1789-1817* (Navy Records Society, 1951) was edited by him.

The papers were presented in 1958 and 1962 by Rear-Admiral Thursfield. They consist of correspondence with his family, 1896 to 1918; logs, 1898 to 1902; notes for torpedo courses at *Vernon*, 1905, and for the course at the Royal Naval College, 1906; watch, station and fire bills, 1913; lecture notes, 1921 to 1922, and standing orders for the *Concord*, 1922 to 1923. (2½ft; 76cm)

279 THURSFIELD, *Sir* James Richard (journalist) 1840-1923

Thursfield joined the *Times* as a leader writer in 1877 and by about 1880 he had begun to specialize in naval affairs. He represented the *Times* in the naval manoeuvres of 1887 and in every subsequent year when correspondents were admitted. When Mahan's book *The influence of sea power upon history* appeared in 1890, Thursfield's review was the first that adequately recognized its importance. He lectured at the invitation of the Staff College, Camberley, in 1902 on the 'Higher policy of defence' and at this time became closely associated with Sir John (later Lord) Fisher (1841-1920). After the war he wrote the four naval volumes of *The Times documentary history of the war*. Thursfield was knighted in 1920.

The papers were presented in 1947 by Sir James Thursfield's son, Rear-Admiral H.G. Thursfield. They contain correspondence

with Sir John Fisher, 1900 to 1908, articles and pamphlets
by Thursfield, 1906 to 1910, reports on naval manoeuvres,
1894 to 1901, and a long series of confidential Admiralty
and official memoranda sent to him by Fisher. (2ft; 61cm)

280 TIDDEMAN, Richard, *Captain*, *ca*.1702-1762

Tiddeman was promoted to lieutenant in 1732. He served
successively in the *Wolf*, West Indies, 1732, the *Rupert*,
West Indies and Channel, 1733 to 1734, the *Princess Amelia*,
1734 to 1735, and *Buckingham*, 1735 to 1736, both at Portugal,
going then to North America, 1737 to 1742, in the *Phoenix*.
He commanded the *Deal Castle* and the *Fame* in the West Indies
from 1744 until 1745 when he was promoted to captain, In
1745 he went to the *Eltham*, taking her out to the East Indies
in 1747. On his return to England in 1750 he became Captain
of the *Harwich*, and was sent yet again to the East Indies in
1758 in the *Grafton* to reinforce Sir George Pocock's (*q.v.*)
squadron. He transferred to the *Elizabeth* in 1759 and
became second-in-command of the Station in 1761. He was
commodore of the expedition against Manila in 1762 but was
drowned the morning after the surrender when his barge over-
turned.

The papers were presented by Tiddeman's great-granddaughter,
Miss G. Spenser Tiddeman, in 1937 and consist of logs, 1729
to 1762, account books, 1745 to 1762, and ships' muster rolls,
1743 to 1749. There is also an account book of an unidentified
merchant in Bristol, 1698 to 1724. (2½ft; 76cm)

281 TIZARD, Thomas Henry, *Captain*, 1839-1924

Tizard was educated at the Royal Hospital School, Greenwich,
and entered the Navy as a master's assistant in 1854. He
served in the *Dragon* with the Baltic Fleet during the Crimean
War and then in the Mediterranean. In 1857 he was appointed
to the *Indus* on the North American and West Indies Station.
On his return home in 1860 he was promoted to second master
and served for just over a year in a cadets' training ship.
In 1861 he was appointed to the surveying ship *Rifleman* on the
China Station. Following his promotion in 1864 to master, he
commanded the *Rifleman*'s tender *Saracen* on surveys in the
South China Sea. Between 1868 and 1879 he was first employed
in survey ships in the Mediterranean and then on the
oceanographic voyage of the *Challenger*. He was promoted to

staff commander in 1874. In 1880 he was appointed to command
the *Knight Errant* on the survey of the west coast of Britain.
In 1882 he commissioned the *Triton* for work on the east
coast survey also both in 1880 and 1882 he took scientific
expeditions to the Faeroe-Shetland Channel. In 1889 he was
promoted to staff captain and in 1891 he was appointed
Assistant Hydrographer of the Navy and elected a Fellow of the
Royal Society. He continued to serve at the Admiralty until
1907 but was placed on the retired list, with the rank of
captain in 1896.

Some details about Tizard are contained in the biography of
his son, Sir Henry Tizard, *Tizard* by Ronald W. Clark (London,
1965).

The papers were presented in 1959 by Sir Henry Tizard. They
consist of logs, 1854 to 1867, and diaries, 1880 to 1890.
(7 vols)

282 TUPPER, Charles George de Beauvoir, *Lieutenant*, 1872-1893

Tupper joined the *Raleigh*, flagship at the Cape of Good Hope,
as a midshipman in 1888 and remained in her until 1891. He
became a lieutenant in 1892. In 1893 he was on the South
American Station in the *Racer* and died when a powder magazine
exploded at Rio de Janeiro.

The papers were presented by Major J.C. Wilder in 1956. They
include two journals, 1889 to 1891, official service documents,
a collection of Admiralty charts, 1867 to 1881, and the
official letters received by Tupper's mother reporting his
death. (5 vols)

283 TYLER, *Sir* Charles, *Admiral*, 1760-1835

Tyler entered the Navy in 1771 and was promoted to lieutenant
in 1779. During the American War he served chiefly in the
Channel and the Mediterranean and in the early part of the
Revolutionary war in the Mediterranean. In 1799 he was
appointed to the *Warrior*, at first in the Channel and after
1802 in the West Indies, and in 1805 to the *Tonnant*, with the
Mediterranean fleet. He was severely wounded at Trafalgar.
He was promoted to rear-admiral in 1808 and hoisted his flag
as second-in-command at Portsmouth. Between 1812 and 1816
he was Commander-in-Chief at the Cape of Good Hope, after which

he had no further service. He was promoted to vice-admiral in 1813 and to admiral in 1825.

See W.H. Wyndham-Quin, *Sir Charles Tyler, G.C.B. Admiral of the White* (London, 1912).

The papers were bequeathed in 1952 by Mrs I.M. Bond, a descendant. They consist of service documents and letters received, including those from Nelson (*q.v.*), 1805, Lord Mulgrave (1755-1831), 1807 to 1808, and Admiral Collingwood (*q.v.*), 1808 to 1809. There is also one letter from Lady Hamilton, 1808, and letters to Lady Tyler, 1800 to 1815. (1 file)

284 UPTON, Henry, *Commander* (H.E.I.C.), b. 1769

Upton entered the East India Company's service as a midshipman in 1788 and served in the *Rockingham* during two voyages to China. He was in the *General Goddard* as Fourth Officer on a voyage to Madras and Bengal from 1793 to 1794 and remained in her as part of the Cape Expedition of 1795. Nine Dutch Indiamen were captured during this cruise and Upton was detached in one of them as prize master. He went to China in the *True Briton* in 1804 and to Bengal in the *Windham* in 1809, from which ship he was captured. However, after the taking of the Île de France (Mauritius), Upton joined the *Ceylon*, 1810, and brought her home. His next voyage was to China, 1814, in the *Glatton*; upon her arrival at St Helena her captain died and Upton was sworn in to command. Nothing further is known about his career.

The papers were purchased in 1963 from Mr S.H.F. Upton and include logs, 1791 to 1794 and 1804 to 1815, signal books, undated memoranda, accounts, rules, port regulations and service documents. (1ft; 30cm)

285 VERNON, Edward, *Admiral*, 1684-1757

Vernon, popularly referred to as 'Old Grog', became a lieuten-ant in 1702, a captain in 1706 and saw service in the Mediterranean, West Indies and the Baltic. At the outbreak of war with Spain in 1739 he was appointed Commander-in-Chief, West Indies, and was successful in capturing Portobello and at the bombardment of Cartagena, although unsuccessful in attempts to land at Cartagena and at Santiago de Cuba. Vernon returned to England in 1742. In 1745, at the threat of a

French invasion, he was appointed Commander-in-Chief at the Downs but fell foul of the Admiralty, was superseded and later struck off the list. He was Member of Parliament for Penryn, 1722 to 1734, Portsmouth, 1741, and Ipswich, 1741 to 1757.

Among the biographies is G.H. Hartmann, *The angry Admiral, the later career of Edward Vernon, Admiral of the White* (London, 1953). Many of the papers have been published by B. McL. Ranft, *The Vernon papers* (Navy Records Society, 1958).

The papers were purchased at Sotheby's by Sir James Caird in 1934. There are a few letters, 1714 to 1716, from Vernon's father and brother but the main part of the collection consists of correspondence received and draft replies, 1739 to 1742 and 1745, as well as Vernon's own order books, 1739 to 1741, and his out-letterbook to the Admiralty. Also included in the collection are a few papers of other members of the Vernon family, 1632 to 1837. (2ft; 61cm)

286 VERNON, *Sir* Edward, *Admiral*, 1723-1794

Edward Vernon, a distant relation of Admiral Edward Vernon (*q.v.*), saw much of his early service in the Mediterranean and was promoted to lieutenant in 1743. At the beginning of the Seven Years War he was again in the Mediterranean and then in command of the *Revenge*, Channel Fleet, between 1760 and 1763. After guardship duty during the peace, he was appointed, in 1776, Commander-in-Chief, East Indies. Vernon was promoted to rear-admiral in 1779, returned to England in 1781 and saw no further service. He became a vice-admiral in 1787 and admiral in 1794.

The papers were purchased by Sir James Caird at Sotheby's in 1934. They consist of official service documents, 1743 to 1794, and orders and letters relating to the East Indies command, 1776 to 1779. (1 box, 2 vols)

287 VIVIAN, Gerald William, *Captain*, 1869-1921

Vivian entered the Navy in 1882 and was promoted to lieuten-ant in 1892. He went to the China Station in 1902, becoming acting commander of the *Rosario* in 1904 and was also promoted to the rank of commander in that year. Between

1905 and 1906 he was commander of the Royal Naval College, Greenwich, and then served in the Mediterranean and at Chatham. From 1911 to 1912 he was on the west coast of America in the *Shearwater*, was promoted to captain in 1912 and in 1913 qualified in flying; he then commanded the *Hermes*, employed on special duties attached to the Royal Flying Corp (Naval Wing). During the First World War he served in the *Sirius*, 1914, the *Patia*, 1914 to 1915, the *Liverpool*, 1916 to 1917, and the *Roxburgh* on convoy duties, 1918. Vivian was Commodore of Chatham Barracks from 1920 to 1921.

The papers came to the Museum in the 1940s; their provenance is uncertain. They cover the period from 1904 to 1921 and include memoranda, appointments, sailing orders and Admiralty letters, 1904 to 1918; correspondence, 1913 to 1921; reports on the dockyard at Esquimalt and on the landing party for the protection of British subjects at San Quentin, Mexico, 1911, and reports and papers relating to the Air Department, 1915 to 1918. (1ft; 30cm)

288 WALKER, *Sir* Baldwin Wake, 1st Bt., *Admiral*, 1802-1876

Walker entered the Navy in 1812, became a lieutenant in 1820, a commander in 1834 and a captain in 1838. With Admiralty permission he entered the Turkish navy in 1838, returning to England in 1845. He was appointed Surveyor of the Navy in 1848 and held this office for twelve years, during which time the change from sail to steam was largely effected. He had become a rear-admiral in 1858 and on leaving the Admiralty was appointed, in 1861, Commander-in-Chief at the Cape of Good Hope. In 1865 he was promoted to vice-admiral but had no further employment and became an admiral in 1870.

The papers were presented in 1939 by Miss H.M. Walker, Sir Baldwin's granddaughter. They are part of the family collection and relate only to his period as Surveyor of the Navy. This includes private correspondence, 1848 to 1860, and draft replies; returns and reports from various dock-yards, 1852 to 1859; memoranda and other papers about the problems of ship construction, 1851 to 1860, and printed papers on parliamentary and naval affairs, 1847 to 1859. (1ft; 30cm)

289 WATERS, George Alexander, *Captain*, 1820-1903

Waters, a master's assistant in 1842, served on the East
Indies Station first in the *Vixen* and then in 1843 in the
Jupiter. He was made second master in 1845 and master in
1848. Between 1852 and 1856 he served in the Black Sea in
the *Simoom* and in the *Shannon* until 1861. During the Indian
Mutiny, 1857, Waters was left in command of the *Shannon* while
her captain, Sir William Peel (1824-1858), led the Naval
Brigade. He later served as master, and staff commander when
the rank was redesignated, in several ships. His active
career ended as staff captain with two appointments as Queen's
Harbour Master, first at Malta and then at Sheerness. He
retired in 1876.

The papers were presented in 1950 by Captain Water's daughter-
in-law, Mrs Jessie Waters. They consist of logs, 1842 to 1843,
and 1852 to 1861. There are loose letters, 1857 to 1858,
including those from Captain Peel and the officers of the
Naval Brigade concerning the Indian Mutiny and a book in
Chinese endorsed 'taken from the house three or four miles
below Nanking, 26 Aug. 1842', which is a coal-merchant's
receipt book. (5 vols, 1 file)

290 WEBLEY-PARRY, William Henry, *Rear-Admiral*, 1764-1837

Webley, who later assumed the surname of Webley-Parry,
entered the Navy in 1779 and became a lieutenant in 1790.
He was in the *Juno* at the defence of Toulon, 1794, and was
in *L'Aigle*, also in the Mediterranean, from 1795 to 1796,
being present at the siege of Bastia and the attack on
Tenerife. During the battle of the Nile, 1797, he was first
lieutenant of the *Zealous* and became a commander in 1798. He
was promoted to captain in 1802, serving later at Copenhagen,
1807, in the *Centaur* and was then with Admiral James
Saumarez (1757-1836) in the Baltic. In 1810 he was in the
Mediterranean under Sir Samuel Hood (*q.v.*). He sailed in
1811 for the East Indies and brought home a convoy of East
Indiamen in 1813. After 1815 he held no further appointment
but was promoted to rear-admiral in 1837.

The papers were presented in 1955 by Webley-Parry's great
grandson, Admiral Herbert W.W. Hope. They consist of a
collection of certificates and commissions, 1780 to 1837;
Admiralty and admiral's orders, 1797 to 1813; miscellaneous
papers, including a list of Webley's midshipman's outfit in
1780; private letters, among which are fifteen addressed to

his mother, 1794 to 1798, and a log of the *Centaur*, 1807,
which was presented to the Museum separately in 1936.
(1 file, 1 box)

291 WEMYSS, Edward William Elphinstone, *Vice-Admiral*, 1866-1938

Wemyss entered the Navy in 1879. He served in the Mediterranean
from 1881 firstly in the *Superb* and then in the *Monarch*, being
present at the bombardment of Alexandria, 1882, and during
the subsequent Egyptian campaign. In 1887 he was promoted to
lieutenant and in 1888 joined the Training Squadron in the
Volage. He went to the *Polyphemus*, Mediterranean Station, in
1889, becoming a commander at the end of that year. In 1891
he was appointed to the *Raleigh*, flagship at the Cape of Good
Hope, and was involved in the suppression of slavery off the
east coast of Africa. Wemyss became a captain in 1906, serving
from 1909 to 1911 on the Australian Station in the *Cambrian*.
He was promoted to rear-admiral in 1917 and retired,
becoming a vice-admiral in 1922.

The papers were presented by Vice-Admiral Wemyss' widow,
Mrs M.A. Wemyss, in 1955. They contain logs, 1881 to 1884;
photograph albums, 1882 to 1911; newspaper cuttings, 1900
to 1911, and printed material, including a booklet on the
Mosquito Reservation at Bluefield, Nicaragua. (1ft; 30cm)

292 WHITE, Arnold (journalist), 1848-1925

By the end of the nineteenth century, White was well-known as
an upholder of anti-German policies and an advocate of a
strong navy, exerting his influence through articles in the
Daily Express and a column in the *Referee* under his pseudonym
'Vanoc'. He thus became involved in the naval policies of the
day and was an active member of the British Navy League, For
Herbrand Arthur, eleventh Duke of Bedford (1858-1940), he also
acted as supplier of information and political agent.

The papers were deposited on permanent loan by the Bedford
Estate Office in 1972. They consist of two hundred and two
files arranged alphabetically, as White left them, by
subject. The topics covered by the collection include
gunnery, 1903 to 1905 and naval policy and strategy, on which
White exchanged letters with Lord Fisher (1841-1920), Lord
Charles Beresford (1848-1930) and Sir Percy Scott (1853-1924).
On lower deck conditions the correspondence is largely with

Lionel Yexley (1861-1933) and there are notes and letters on Ireland, emigration and eugenics. A number of original letters were removed by White but it was his practice to leave typed copies in their place; those of Lord Fisher come into this category. (7ft; 214cm)

293 WHITSHED, *Sir* James Hawkins, *Admiral of the Fleet*, 1762-1849

Whitshed, who until 1791 had the name Hawkins, entered the Navy in 1773 and was promoted to lieutenant in 1778. Becoming both commander and captain in 1780, he was appointed to the *Rose* in home waters from 1784 to 1786. In 1799, having been promoted to rear-admiral, he was sent to join Earl St. Vincent (*q.v.*) in the Mediterranean, serving subsequently in the Channel from 1800 to 1801. Whitshed became a vice-admiral in 1804, was Commander-in-Chief at Cork between 1807 and 1810, when he was promoted to admiral, and was later Commander-in-Chief, Portsmouth, 1821 to 1824. He became Admiral of the Fleet in 1844.

The papers, part of the Pollard-Whitshed collection, were presented by Mr H.H.W. Pollard in 1946. They include a letterbook of the *Rose*, 1784 to 1785; sailing directions and orders of battle, 1800 to 1801, and three letters concerning the possibility of mutiny in the Channel Fleet, 1800. (1 vol, 2 files)

294 WIGRAM, *Sir* Robert, 1st Bt., (shipbuilder), 1744-1830

Wigram began his career with the East India Company as a surgeon. He contracted an illness, however, which affected his eyesight so that he could no longer practise as a surgeon nor could he go to sea again. He then set himself up as a drug merchant. In 1788 he bought the *General Goddard* and then the *True Briton*, which was built in Wells' Yard, Deptford in 1790. Wigram built up the business and acquired a large interest in the Blackwall Yard and in 1810 became Chairman of the new East India Dock Company. He retired in 1819 and sold the yard to two of his sons, Money and Henry Loftus Wigram, and to George Green.

The papers were presented in 1961 by the Reverend Sir Clifford Wigram and consist of two business ledgers, 1810 to

1865, and family legal documents, 1765 to 1826. (1 box, 2 vols)

There are further papers relating to Wigram in the Green collection of documents concerning Blackwall Yard (See Volume 2).

295 WILKINSON, William, *Commander*, 1777-1857

Wilkinson was master of the *Minotaur*, 1807 to 1808, and took part in the attack on Copenhagen. After cruising in the Channel and the Atlantic between 1808 and 1810 in the *Christian VII*, he was discharged from active service because of ill-health but was given shore appointment as Superintendent of the Wharf at the Victualling Yard, Deptford. From 1832 this post became known as Master Attendant and King's Harbour Master. Wilkinson retired in 1833 and was promoted to commander in 1846.

The papers were purchased from Mr Sidney Raine in 1960 and comprise fifty-six letters, written mainly by Wilkinson to his wife, 1807 to 1833. (1 folder)

296 WOODRIFF, Allan Robert, *Lieutenant*, 1846-1876

A.R. Woodriff, son of Commander John Robert Woodriff (*q.v.*) and grandson of Captain Daniel Woodriff (*q.v.*), served on the North America and West Indies Station from 1868 to 1871, when he became a lieutenant. After a period in China, 1873 to 1874, he returned to England and was drowned in 1876.

The papers were presented by Miss O.M. Brodie in 1973. They consist of service documents, 1868 to 1874, an undated letter, from Woodriff while a sub-lieutenant to his mother and letters of condolence after his death. (1 file)

297 WOODRIFF, Daniel, *Captain*, 1756-1842

Woodriff became a lieutenant in 1782. In 1789 he commanded the troopship *Endymion*, which was wrecked in 1790 at Jamaica; he was honourably acquitted at the subsequent court-martial. On his return to England in 1794 he was appointed Principal Agent for Transports, and was involved in the

evacuation of troops from the Low Countries. He became a
commander in 1795. He was promoted to captain in 1802, the
year he took command of the *Calcutta*. After survey work in
the Bass Straits, the ship returned to Spithead, 1804, was
converted into a warship for convoy duties and went to St.
Helena. On the return journey the *Calcutta* was attacked by
the French and captured. In 1808, a year after his release,
Woodriff became Superintendent of Prisoners of War at Forton,
near Gosport, until in 1814 he went to Jamaica as Resident
Commissioner at Port Royal. Returning to England in 1822,
he was offered, in 1837, either flag-rank or an appointment
to Greenwich Hospital; he chose the latter.

The papers were presented in 1973 by Miss O.M. Brodie,
Woodriff's great-granddaughter. They include a log, 1790;
extracts from Woodriff's journal, 1794; copies and drafts
of letters and memorials, 1805 to 1815; Woodriff's will,
1828, and that of his wife Sarah, 1846. (1 box)

298 WOODRIFF, John Robert, *Commander*, 1790-1868

J.R. Woodriff, second son of Daniel Woodriff (*q.v.*), entered
the Navy in 1802, became a lieutenant in 1811 and served on
the Channel and Cape Stations between 1812 and 1814. From
1836 until 1848, when he was promoted to commander, he was
attached to the Weymouth District of the Coast Guard.

The papers were presented in 1973 by Miss O.M. Brodie. They
consist of personal and service documents, 1802 to 1867,
including a letter of 1842 from John Robert's brother,
Commander Daniel Woodriff (1789-1860), whose papers are in
the National Library of Australia at Canberra. (1 box)

299 WREY, William Bourchier Sherard, *Captain*, 1865-1926

Wrey entered the Navy in 1878. As a midshipman in the *Superb*,
he was present at the bombardment of Alexandria, 1882, and
was in the *Carysfort* in 1884 during the attack on Suakim.
Still on the Mediterranean Station, he served in the *Téméraire*,
1884 to 1885. He was promoted to lieutenant in 1888, spent
eight years on the China Station and became a commander in
1900. In 1909 he was made Divisional Officer of the Coast
Guard, Southern District, with the rank of captain. At the
outbreak of war he was recalled to service as Principal

Naval Transport Officer at Southampton and remained there
until 1918.

The papers were presented in 1954 through Commander W.M.
Phipps Hornby (*q.v.*), the executor of Captain Wrey's widow.
They include logs, 1882 to 1885; photographs, 1882 to 1918;
office diaries, 1918 to 1919, and secret sailings, reports,
statistics of troops embarked and disembarked at Southampton
and other official papers, 1914 to 1918. There are also
papers of the following relatives: General John Tatton
Brown, R.M., notes and memoranda, 1823 to 1826 and 1849;
Commander John Bathurst (d.1866), commissions, 1838 to 1860;
Captain Lord Francis Granvill Godolphin Osborne (1864-1924), a
log, 1888 to 1889, and notebooks, 1887 to 1889. (2ft; 61cm)

300 YORKE, Charles Philip (First Lord of the Admiralty), 1764-
1834

Charles Yorke entered Parliament in 1790 and was appointed
First Lord of the Admiralty in 1810, holding office until
his resignation through ill-health in 1812.

The papers were purchased from Messrs Robinson in 1939.
They are mainly private letters received between 1810 and
1812 from many correspondents, including Admirals G.C.
Berkeley (1753-1818), Sir Charles Cotton (1753-1812),
Samuel, Viscount Hood (*q.v.*), Sir Richard Keats (*q.v.*),
Sir Charles Penrose (1759-1830), Sir James Saumarez (1757-
1836) and Sir William Young (1751-1821), while a number
are addressed to Yorke's brother, Admiral Sir Joseph Yorke
(1768-1834). (1ft; 30cm)

Indexes

CHRONOLOGICAL INDEX

This chronology has been split into periods which relate to the history of the Royal Navy, since the greater part of the volume contains records of naval officers. Non-naval material has, however, been included. For individual actions see the General Index. References are to the numbers of the biographical entries rather than to pages.

The bracketed dates represent specific references in the text and the unbracketed numbers refer to the full biographical entries rather than to pages.

*References are to the serial numbers of the biographical
entries rather than to pages. Ships belong to the Royal
Navy unless otherwise stated. Prizes are indicated only
when they have not been incorporated into the Navy. It
should be noted that at any one time there is only one
ship serving under any one name.*

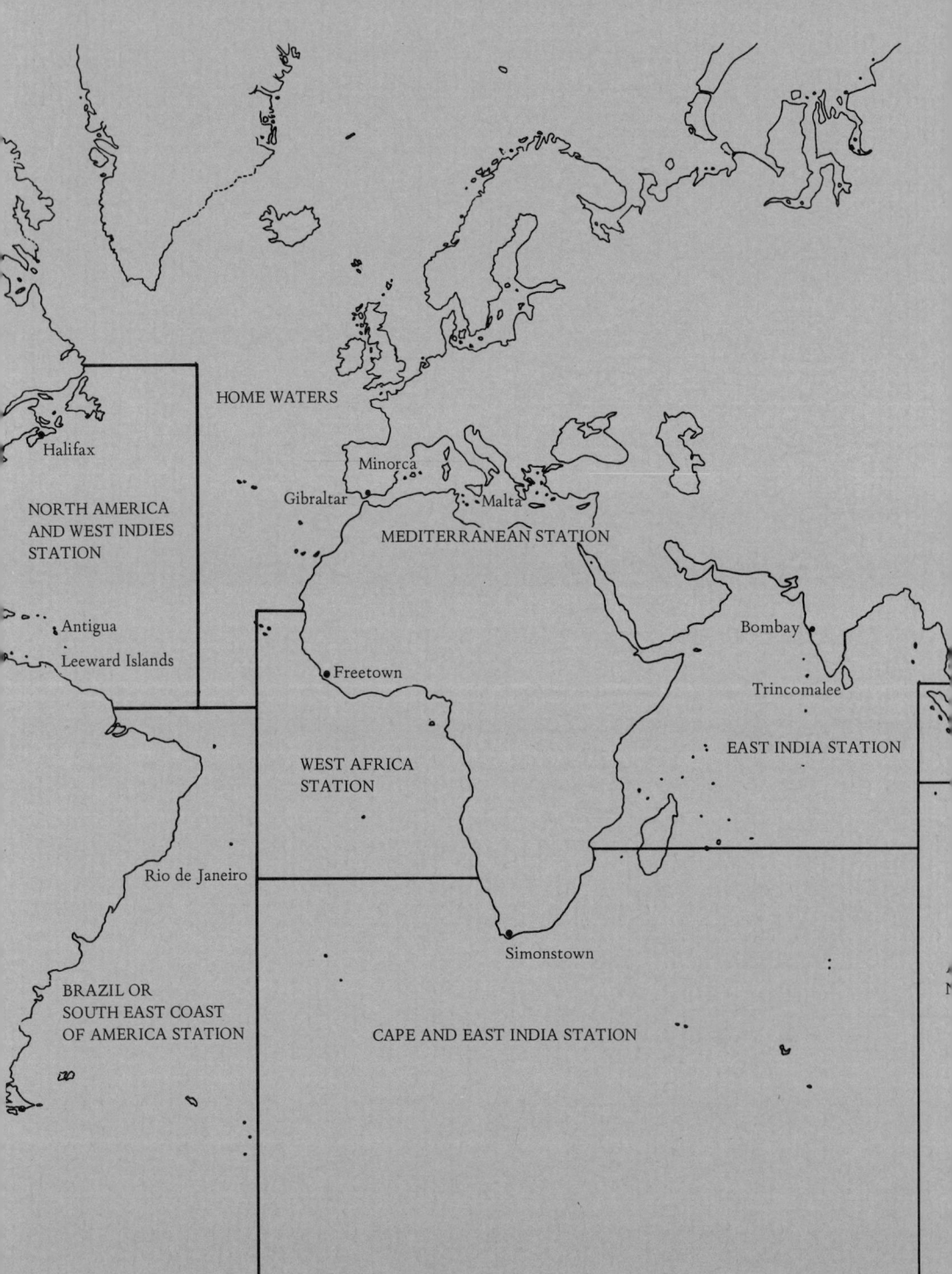

HOME WATERS

Halifax

NORTH AMERICA
AND WEST INDIES
STATION

Antigua
Leeward Islands

Minorca

Gibraltar

Malta

MEDITERRANEAN STATION

Bombay

Trincomalee

Freetown

WEST AFRICA
STATION

EAST INDIA STATION

Rio de Janeiro

Simonstown

BRAZIL OR
SOUTH EAST COAST
OF AMERICA STATION

CAPE AND EAST INDIA STATION